Bonneville & TR6
Motorcycle Restoration Guide
1956-1983

David Gaylin

OCTANE
PRESS

To my daughter Charlotte who taught me
how to use a keyboard, a cabernet and
care when sorting life's priorities.
No father has ever been a prouder pupil.

Originally published by Motorbooks, Feb. 1997
Octane Press, Edition 1.3, December 2019
Copyright © 2011 by David Gaylin

ISBN 978-0-9821733-8-1

Library of Congress Cataloging-in-Publication Data

Gaylin, David.
Triumph motorcycle restoration guide: Bonneville & TR6, 1956-1983 David Gaylin.
Includes index.
1. Triumph motorcycle — Conservation and restoration.

Book design by Tom Heffron
Copyedited by Joseph Holschuh

On the front cover: A 1969 TR6C owned by Fred Broadway of Fredericksburg, Virginia
and restored by Deer Park Cycle of Eldersburg, Maryland. *Lightner Photography*

On the back cover: The back cover art is a modified 1967 advertisement.
Modifications by Tom Heffron. *Author's Collection*

Printed in the United States of America

www.octanepress.com

Octane Press is based in Austin, Texas

Contents

Acknowledgments 4

Preface 5

Introduction 7

Chapter 1 **Historical Perspective** 10

Chapter 2 **1956–1959 TR6 Trophy** 21

Chapter 3 **1959 Bonneville** 38

Chapter 4 **Duplex Twins 1960–1962** 52

Chapter 5 **Unit-Construction Twins 1963–1965** 70

Chapter 6 **Unit-Construction Twins 1966–1970** 97

Chapter 7 **TT Specials 1963–1967** 143

Chapter 8 **Umberslade Twins 1971–1975** 167

Chapter 9 **Meriden Co-op 750 Twins 1976–1979** 196

Chapter 10 **Final 750 Twins 1980–1983** 218

Appendix A **Specifications and Technical Data** 241

Appendix B **Triumph Resource Directory** 264

Index 269

Acknowledgments

As anyone who has ever written a book knows, it can't be done alone! It is necessary to give credit and thanks to those who assisted in the creation of this work. Individuals who unselfishly contributed motorcycles, photographs, as well as precious time include Mike Benolken, Fred Broadway, Dick Brown, Marge Coates, Frank Diehl, Laura Ergle, Bill Ferriell, Mary Frances, Jack Geoghegan, Wayne Hamilton, George Joyce, Gene Knapp, Phil Lankford, Lightner Photography, Motorcyclist's Post, Gary Nixon, Doug Peterson, Greg Pound, Regester Photo Service, Tim Savin, Chuck Spilman, Jaye Strait, Bob Sullivan, Les Sumner, Jerry Wheeler, Harry Woolridge, and Bob Worden.

I would also like to thank John Healy for pointing out errors in the text. Michael Lock, CEO of Triumph Motorcycles (America) Ltd., kindly allowed use of the Triumph trademark. Lee Klancher and Tom Heffron at Octane Press provided expertise and MUCH patience. And a special thanks to Lindsay Brooke, without whose photographs, guidance, and editorial skills the finished product would have been a great deal poorer.

Preface

No single publication or person should be used as the solitary source of information for a motorcycle restoration project. Although an attempt has been made here to include as much relevant material as possible, there are many other resources that should be consulted. In doing so, you may find some details conveyed here that directly conflict with those offered elsewhere. This is to be expected, and indicates only differing origins of information found during research.

The bottom line is this: The more reference sources a restorer consults, the closer he or she is likely to find accurate information.

Rather than a reference manual for restoration procedures and techniques, *Triumph Bonneville & TR6 Motorcycle Restoration Guide* is a guide to authenticity that will assist the restorer with model recognition points. This book has been compiled chronologically, to allow users to focus on sections that pertain to their machine without having to toil through voluminous text and details of peripheral Triumph models. The description of each yearly range builds on the season (or seasons) preceding it, and usually it is only the evolutionary modifications that are related within a given year.

For this reason, readers may find it necessary to examine the sections a year or two ahead of their motorcycle to locate needed details. Each model year has been divided into two sections — Engine and Drivetrain, and Frame and Cycle Parts — with the text focusing on discernible features vital for a restoration. Several of Triumph's production years incorporated so many modifications that they limit a complete description of each. For these, the restorer should consult the specifications appendix.

Readers should also keep in mind that details related here for any given model year inevitably may not be the only form in which a machine was offered. All descriptions of machine features are supported by documentation, but there always remains the possibility of other variations. Ultimately, Bonneville and Trophy details that could not be authenticated by period or original factory data were omitted.

The restored motorcycles used to illustrate this book, as accurate as they may be, were not used as text references. They are after all "restored" and have erased forever all evidence of original manufacture. Wherever possible, the nature of each machine pictured in this book has been identified as: restored, unrestored, or a sales literature image.

The information contained herein is based solely on factory and period literature such as photographs, bulletins, technical manuals, correspondence, and only as a last resort, advertising literature. In addition, many important points of recognition were found in original magazine road test and feature articles, many containing unshakable period photography of the motorcycles described.

—*David Gaylin*

Introduction

Over the 30-plus years I have been involved in the Triumph restoration hobby, one of the most common mistakes made by restorers and enthusiasts is to acquire a single piece of factory literature, then use it as a sole reference point for a project. Often those fortunate enough to locate a factory parts book take it as the gospel and are unwilling to deviate from its specifications. But even with factory revision sheets, almost all of these parts manuals exhibit some disparity from what Meriden actually produced. These discrepancies were sometimes temporary, sometimes by design, and sometimes beyond the control of Triumph. Factory literature is not infallible. Nowhere is this more evident than in sales and advertising material. After obtaining a sales brochure, many restorers make the mistake of rebuilding their motorcycle to replicate the image pictured in the art. Some even go as far as to match a machine's paint finish from a brochure — a very reckless pursuit, as printed ink colors almost always differ from reality.

Moreover, catalog images were often creatures of company propaganda. They were subject to embellishments and retouching by the ad department, always depicting the most advantageous view, with control cables and other unsightliness minimized or completely obliterated. Inevitably, the brochures represented only what the factory had hoped to manufacture. Of course, mostly they got it right, but many times they didn't.

When using a brochure, parts book, or any other document, it is a good idea to make certain it relates to the country or market in which your machine was originally sold. This is important because motorcycle specifications and finishes varied between markets during the same model year.

Of course, there is nothing wrong with an American restorer rebuilding his machine to European specs, if that is the desired outcome. But many times a restorer will obtain a foreign market brochure and unwittingly rebuild his machine to match, only to find out later that the motorcycle is finished in a foreign market color! This is just another reason not to base a project on a single point of reference.

Any source of information whether from print or person, should be part of a library of reference material gathered. These should include as many factory publications as can be found, such as a parts catalogs, sales literature, magazine ads, and of course, workshop and owners manuals.

Clearly, the best source for the visual points of a restoration are magazine road tests. Most were accompanied by photographs of the machine, and although often in black and white, the images are from the period and free of factory or designer interpretation. But once again, just because a machine's details are clearly pictured does not mean this was the only way a model was offered, and that all other versions should be discounted. To help the restorer find a period road test covering his or her Bonneville, TR6 or TR7, a listing of British and American magazines appears in the Appendix.

Another commonly made error is the misjudgment of what is and is not original. For example, a 1956 Trophy 650 that was restored in 1967 will be wearing a 40-year-old paint job today. Add to this an uncertain (undocumented) history and possibly a high price paid for the machine, and a new owner will become convinced he has found an untouched example! Even after confronted with a mountain of documentation to show otherwise, they will not be swayed. This is unfortunate, and if friendship is to be maintained, it's sometimes best not to be too insistent — after all, they just might be right!

But if you are satisfied that you've indeed found an original unrenewed machine, the next question should be whether or not a restoration ought to be undertaken at all. This really is a matter of the owner's priorities and how much the machine has suffered. But many owners place a high value on shiny finishes and showroom appearances. They'll rush into a motorcycle restoration, giving no thought to the historical artifact they're about to destroy. There are no shortages of restored Triumphs, even accurate ones, at bike rallies and concours. But even the examples properly completed are nothing more than someone's interpretation of how they originally appeared.

Untouched machines, sometimes with tired paint and partially rubbed-off pinstriping, have a special place in the Triumph hobby because their correctness cannot be questioned. It is these machines that reveal the truths of factory decal placement, cable routing, original fastener plating, etc. These motorcycles also offer the advantage of continued use without fouling a fresh paint job, and allow a fuller enjoyment than do those that are "too good to ride!"

Concours Advice

It is natural that after a comprehensive and exhaustive restoration, a proud owner can't wait to show his work to others. So after transporting his pride and joy to the event and waiting all day in anticipation, how does it happen that the owner finds his motorcycle taking second place to one that is inferior, inaccurate, or over-restored?

Yes, it happens to everyone, and there are as many reasons for it as there are motorcycle shows.

Perhaps the most common explanation is that those making the evaluations may not be qualified to do so. An old saying goes that those most competent to assess restored machinery are also the most unwilling to do so! Show organizers are often more concerned with a person's availability and willingness to judge, rather than their qualifications. Those who are unlucky enough to be conscripted for judging duty, usually forfeit their time and enjoyment of a show without any recompense.

And when these volunteers are finally rewarded for their service — with arguments and verbal abuse from restorers — it's no wonder that they bolt whenever the word 'judge" is heard again! A concours entrant should always try to keep these things in mind when waiting for the awards ceremony.

Assuming that in some cases your motorcycle may be evaluated by individuals completely unfamiliar with Triumphs, it's always sound policy to make as accurate as possible general features that the judge will probably spot, such as paint finishes, plating, and so on.

For instance, many restorers opt for stainless steel wheel spokes and fasteners. An owner may also want the superiority of powder coating, or perhaps Imron paint for the sheet metal, both materials being clearly superior to the finishes used by the Triumph factory. However, most show judges tend to focus on what they know, and although he or she may not know what the correct carburetor or decal looks like, they may zoom right in on those stainless spokes and make that the focal point of their decision.

Beyond the accuracy of a restoration, owners can increase their advantage in concours competition by equipping their machine with factory or period accessories. In case of a tie, these add-ons can spell the difference between a first- or second-place trophy. These can include items such as saddle bags; tank bags; windshields originally sold by TriCor, Motoplas, Britax, and so on, as well as performance goodies. But it is always wise to bring documentation and ads to enlighten the uninformed judge. As with the original factory specifications of a machine, it's up to the entrant, not the judge, to provide the proof. A few final words of advice to contestants in any motorcycle concours: Don't take it too seriously, and DON'T FORGET TO HAVE FUN! I've seen grown men in tears and others ready to inflict bodily harm all because their motorcycles failed to fetch the anticipated recognition. A restorer should never lose sight of the fact that the machines themselves are the awards. Whether someone else on any given day appreciates your efforts is really irrelevant, if you (the owner) are pleased with the result.

Chapter One

Historical Perspective

The history of Triumph motorcycles and the companies that manufactured them is well documented. While it is not the objective of this book to recount this tale once again, a brief retrospective will help the reader and user of this guide, especially when models and features are mentioned that are outside the realm of the Bonneville and TR6.

It's not hard to look back at the beginning of Triumph and find irony in its origins. That such a famous British marque began as a bicycle firm by an expatriate German in the city of London, far away from the industrial Midlands, is no small paradox. But Siegfried Bettmann began what would later become Triumph by exporting British-made bicycles in 1885. This was a time when popularity for the new transportation fad was at an all-time high and English cycles were the most sought after in the world.

In the following year, Bettmann changed the brand name of his product from the Bettmann bicycle to Triumph, a word that exuded strength and was the same in many of his export markets. When he was satisfied that bicycles were more than a fad, Bettmann decided to manufacture his own product and took on as a junior partner Mauritz Shulte, another Nuremburger and a capable engineer. They moved their fledgling concern to Coventry, where foundries, machine shops, and raw materials were more readily available. Soon afterward they were making their own bike and selling more of them at home than abroad.

The arrival of the pneumatic rubber tire brought the Triumph Cycle Company, Ltd., as it was now known, into contact with Irish financier Harvey du Cros and the Dunlop Tire Company. Du Cros had been impressed with the two Germans and the direction they were taking, so much so that he invested a significant amount of his money in Triumph. Bettmann, Shulte, and a few other investors they had gathered along the way now had the capital to be major players in the growing industry.

Motor-assisted bicycles were a phenomenon and seemed a logical diversification for Triumph. After attempts to arrange marketing licenses from two established motorcycle makers, Triumph's own motorized cycle was offered to the public in late 1902. Basically, it was a Belgian-made Minerva motor clipped to the front downtube of a Triumph bicycle. The company continued this practice of using proprietary motors until 1905.

The Trusty Triumph-an early Model H. Thirty thousand of this reliable mount were built for the Allied armies during World War I. *Author collection*

Finally Triumph was able to offer a machine powered by its own engine. Designed completely in-house by Mauritz Shulte and Charles Hathaway, the unit was a 3 horsepower side-valve single, fastened within a sturdier, purpose-built chassis, which also supported a combination fuel/oil tank from the top rail. The front forks were strengthened, the spokes thickened, and tire sections increased, to make a true motorcycle.

Through these early Triumph years, bicycle manufacture still took priority. But Shulte's interests were clearly with the internal combustion engine. Steady improvements to the powerplant saw Triumph's first 3 1/2-horsepower single and a carburetor of its own design in 1907. Progress was also made on the running gear, including a rocking front fork suspension that was remarkably effective. The 1911 Triumph motorcycles featured a free engine clutch in the hub of the rear wheel and magneto ignition. Above all, Triumph had gained a name for utter reliability at a time when motorcycles were famous for the opposite. Its reputation is credited by many for rescuing the British

motorcycle industry, securing for the Coventry maker a predominant position within it.

By 1913, Triumph was the premier maker of British single-cylinder motorcycles. During this time Mauritz Shulte experimented with a prototype engine design that later became the brand's hallmark — a vertical twin. This design had its crankshaft throws set at 180 degrees, which meant the pistons rose and fell alternately. The iron cylinder and head were of one casting and the side-mounted valves were deployed in front and back of the cylinders. An aluminum crankcase, split horizontally, supported an external flywheel on the right and the primary drive sprocket on the left. The engine was designed to fit into Triumph's existing frame.

The prototype twin was amazingly modern in its overall design, yet it did not see production. Two-strokes had become very popular, and Shulte decided to postpone the twin in favor of a two-stroke design of his own.

The introduction of the 550cc Model H four-stroke single in 1914 added to Triumph's momentum. Although it still had a belt final drive and the dated back-and-forth suspension,

Triumph's 1934 500cc single eventually became the Tiger-90.

gone were all vestiges of Triumph's bicycle beginnings. If there was a single model that solidified Triumph's fortunes in its early years, it was the Model H. Almost 30,000 of them were supplied to the British and Allied armies during World War I. The factory called them "Trusty Triumphs" as a marketing slogan, but it really was the truth. Both owners and army dispatch riders actually used this term when referring to the brand name.

By 1920, Triumph's output approached 10,000 machines a year, and the factory was now a sprawling multistoried complex in the center of Coventry.

The product range was supplemented with improved versions of the Model H, including an overhead, four-valve variant (Model R) for 1922, designed under contract by the engineering firm of Harry Ricardo. The following year they began manufacturing automobiles. Through the decade came more single-cylinder designs, including the even sportier 500cc model TT, the 350cc model LS with unit construction, and the very affordable price-leading Model P.

Triumph produced more than 30,000 motorcycles in 1929, an achievement not seen

again until the 1960s. But more and more of the company's attention and resources were being devoted to the automobile side of the business.

The Great Depression took a little longer to reach England, but when it arrived, the Coventry bike builder was hit very hard. Triumph's answer was to offer more models, not less, in an effort to find buyers — wherever they might be. By 1933 the marque's range consisted of 18 models — from 125cc two-strokes all the way to 500cc racers. Triumph's new chief designer, Val Page, who had joined the company a year earlier from Ariel, created a new generation of side- and overhead-valve singles. His flagship model was a 650cc overhead-valve vertical twin that was amazingly modern in its specification. The rigid one-piece crankshaft had three bob weights, a separate lateral flywheel, and throws set at 360 degrees. Its single overhung camshaft was positioned just behind the cylinders, actuating both sets of inclined pushrods — the exhaust pushrods falling between the cylinders as in later BSA and Norton twins. The four-speed gearbox bolted directly to the back of the motor, making the overall design of semi-unit construction, and the 650's primary drive transferred directly through helical gears without an intermediate pinion, which meant the engine spun in a reverse rotation.

Other innovations included a linked front/ rear braking system and a quickly detachable rear wheel. But Page's 650 engine also had a few significant drawbacks. Its wet-sump lubrication made the engine very tall. Initially the bike came equipped only with a handshift gearbox, at a time when foot-operated boxes were commonplace on most sport models. And overall, the motorcycle was very heavy which relegated it to a sidecar horse. Although very reliable, the new 650 did not sell well. But the economic times had worsened, and with Triumph's motorcycle and car divisions competing for a shrinking amount of development and marketing capital, something had to give. In 1932 the bicycle business was sold off and the following year a group of Triumph shareholders wanted to discontinue motorcycle production altogether and expand the automobile division. On April 18, 1933, Siegfried Bettmann retired from Triumph at age 70. The way was now clear to dispose of the motorcycle business.

The Turner Era

The company most familiar to Triumph enthusiasts came into existence in 1936, when the motorcycle division of the Triumph Company, Ltd., was sold to Ariel owner Jack Sangster. In his agreement, Sangster acquired all inventories, tooling, and the right to continue manufacture under the Triumph name.

To lower the initial expenditure, Sangster persuaded the Triumph (car) company to lease, rather than sell to him, the factories where the two-wheelers were made. The Triumph Engineering Company, Ltd., was a little-used Triumph entity, and it was also purchased by Sangster for purposes of incorporation. The transfer was executed on January 22, 1936.

Immediately Sangster installed his chief designer from Ariel, Edward Turner, as managing director. Turner had created the Square Four motorcycle and restyled Val Page's singles into what became the Red Hunter series. Turner's designs had rescued Ariel from receivership and Jack Sangster wanted to perform the same trick again with Triumph. Different this time, however, was Turner's complete autonomy — not only would he determine design, he would also make the financial decisions as well. Turner convinced Sangster to give him full reign in everything but ownership!

His first moves were swift and forceful. Overnight he restyled the Val Page range of singles and threw out his 650 twin. The 650 was expensive to make (and purchase) and it wasn't a big revenue producer.

Turner rationalized the remaining range into two types of frames and front forks and eventually a single gearbox of new design. He resculpted the fuel tanks into a more pleasing teardrop shape and finished the OHV models in a new color scheme of silver trimmed in dark blue. More chrome-plating was also applied to

Granddaddy of the Bonneville and TR6, the classic 1938 500cc Speed Twin. Its timeless design paved the way for virtually all other vertical twins after World War II. *Gaylin*

The engine of a restored 1938 Speed Twin. Motor's resemblance to the last Triumphs produced in 1983 is obvious. *Gaylin*

the tanks as well as the headlights, wheel rims, and the new upswept exhaust pipes.

Finally, the 250, 350, and 500 Mark 5 models were rechristened the Tiger 70, 80, and 90, respectively. They were an instant hit and put the new company on a firm financial footing.

Edward Turner's next move impacted the entire motorcycle world, when he announced for 1938 the 500cc Speed Twin. Designated the 5T, Turner's vertical twin shared very little

with the earlier 650. For starters he made it a 500, in order to use the existing 63-millimeter pistons of the Tiger 70. The stroke was a short 80 millimeters, which gave an actual capacity of 498.76cc.

A three-piece, bolt-up crankshaft spun in two large ball bearings and had a central flywheel. This design allowed a twin-cylinder engine with the width of a single. The Speed Twin engine was so narrow, in fact, that it

The Tiger-100's designation was to signify an honest top speed of 100 miles per hour. It was introduced in 1939 as a sport version of the Speed Twin.

shared the exact same primary and final drive chain lines of Triumph's existing models.

The 360-degree crank's even firing intervals gave the balancing characteristics of a single. It had two overhung camshafts positioned front and rear that were driven directly by the crankshaft through pinions on the right side. The interchangeable camshafts ran in bronze bushings and actuated the overhead valves via long pushrods that were enclosed in chrome-plated tubes. These nestled in the hollows between the cylinders, fore and aft. Over the valves, two rocker arms enclosed in separate polished alloy boxes shared a common spindle. Adjustment of the valve clearances was through two large screw caps in each enclosure.

The one-piece cylinder barrel was cast-iron and finned completely around the bores. It was secured to the vertically split, alloy crankcase by six studs and nuts. The iron cylinder head followed the same contour as the top of the barrels and was attached with eight bolts. It

had parallel intake tracts but splayed (spread) exhaust ports and with its narrow engine — the appearance resembled a twin-port single to a conservative British market. Only the pushrod tubes gave away that this was a twin.

The power and acceleration characteristics of the 5T engine were of course superior to a single, but the design was remarkable in that it made use of the existing Tiger 90 frame and four-speed gearbox. At 365 pounds, the machine's overall weight was 5 pounds lighter than the 500 single.

The engine was really the only new component and the rest of the Speed Twin's running gear was identical to that used on the big Tiger model. It had the larger of the two rigid frames Triumph was using, as well as the heavyweight Webb front forks. As found on the sport models, the 5T came with a 20-inch front wheel and 19-inch rim at the rear. The 4.0-gallon (U.S.) chrome-plated fuel tank was also a Triumph item that housed a diamond-shaped instrument

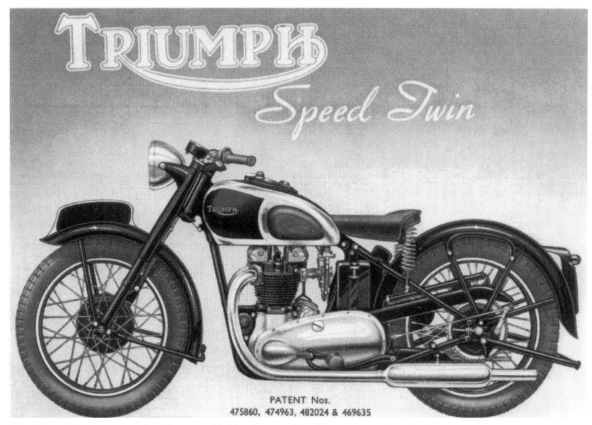

PATENT Nos.
475860, 474963, 482024 & 469635

The Speed Twin, pictured in the rare 1946 sales catalog. America preferred the Tiger-100.

panel on the top, in easy view of the rider. The Bakelite dash panel included an ammeter, oil gauge, lighting switch, and detachable inspection lamp that also lit the instruments from beneath when left in position. The saddle was a solo bicycle type, hinged at the nose and sprung at the rear and for passengers, a pillion pad was available that fastened to the rear fender.

Perhaps the most sensational feature of the new Speed Twin model was its finish. Just prior to production, Turner decided to deviate from the Silver Sheen and black scheme of the Tiger singles and paint the complete motorcycle in a deep maroon. The color was called Amaranth Red and was applied to the frame, forks, fenders, oil tank, toolbox, and all brackets and mounting hardware. The decorative fuel tank panels and wheel rims were also trimmed in red and handlined in gold. Contrasting accents were provided by chrome-plating on the headlight, exhaust pipes and mufflers, fuel tank, wheel

rims, seat springs, handlebars, and all control levers. A dramatic look was completed with highly polished alloy side covers on the engine and front brake plate.

The Speed Twin's snappy acceleration and pleasing exhaust note were welcomed by motorcyclists accustomed to the "chuff and chugging" of single-cylinder engines. In the trusty Triumph tradition it was stone reliable, had an honest top speed around the 90 miles per hour mark and cost only £5 more than the Tiger 90. Turner's gamble paid off, perhaps in bigger returns than he had anticipated.

Demand for the new Speed Twin overwhelmed the factory and set the rest of the motorcycle trade on its ear. Just two years earlier Triumph was at death's door; now the marque was again the industry leader, due to Turner and his revolutionary twin. And because of the intervention of World War II, it would be 10 years before any of the other major marques could answer with a vertical twin of their own. All of the classic Triumph twins derived from the original Speed Twin layout. From 1938 on, the Triumph marque would be forever linked with vertical twin design.

In 1939, a sport version of the 5T was announced. The Tiger-100 (T100) was really just a tuned Speed Twin with a slightly larger carburetor, polished internals, and higher compression. The engine modifications added eight more horses and allowed a top speed very close to the "ton" (100 miles per hour). It was fitted with a new, larger fuel tank and finished in the Tiger scheme of Silver Sheen with black, but the fenders were changed to the lighter color. Demand for the T100 soon outpaced that of the Speed Twin, and solidified Triumph's industry leadership. The trend of announcing a new model followed later by a sporting edition was a policy that Turner practiced many times in the years to come.

World War II interrupted Turner's plans for an all-twin range and a great deal more. Like other British motorcycle makers, Triumph's energies were consumed by the war effort. In November 1940, the original Coventry factory was destroyed by the German Luftwaffe, but through major government assistance Triumph built a new modern facility outside the city, in the greenbelt area of Meriden. The new works was completed in only 18 months. So when the hostilities ended, Triumph, with its new factory and superior range of twins, was in the best position to dominate an industry limping back to life.

Looking at British industry in 1946, it was hard to tell who had actually won the war. Any company that survived the destruction had to fight for allotments of raw materials to make their product. The fact that Triumph had anything to offer in 1946 was only possible again through government intervention. The company was able to get aluminum and steel only by guaranteeing that a major portion of their goods would be exported to America, in an effort to pay down England's war debt and to inject U.S. dollars to Britain's reconstruction. It was the British government's post-war policy

It was the policy of Triumph's managing director Edward Turner to spend no factory funds on (road) racing. But after Irishman Ernie Lyon's victory in the 1947 Manx Grand Prix on this specially prepared Tiger-100, Turner allowed replicas to be built in small batches. Production "Grand Prix" models received a different tank, seat, and fender color. *Author collection*

Many of Triumph's U.S. road racing wins were due to TriCor tuner Cliff Guild. His careful assembly and preparation of 500 twins put many in the winners circle including Gary Nixon and Don Burnett. Pictured is Cliff aboard a brand-new 1954 Tiger-100 at the eastern-U.S. distributorship. Small sport fuel tank and high bars were fitted to many U.S. models.
Author collection

that mandated Triumph sell large numbers of motorcycles in the United States.

The lack of raw materials made Turner's decision to offer only twin-cylinder models an easy one. The official 1946 range consisted of only the Speed Twin, Tiger-100, and a "hoped for" new 350 (3T) twin that did not appear until 1947. The 5T and Tiger were unchanged from the 1940 versions except for telescopic front forks and relocation of the generator to a position within the front mounting plates of the engine. The Lucas dynamo stuck through into an extended timing chest and the drive was taken from the exhaust cam gear, while the magneto remained in its original spot behind the motor.

The new fork design was clean and narrow, and complemented the original looks of the machine. Besides a smaller 19-inch front wheel, the 500 twins did not change from their prewar specifications.

A new rear wheel hub with internal springing was finally made available in 1947. The axle was suspended between compressed springs and when fitted to the frame, permitted an inch or so of vertical wheel travel. This "sprung hub" was a clever device that could be retro-fitted to existing machines back to 1938. Unfairly, it gained a bad reputation as being prone to oscillations, but only under racing conditions. For everyday street use, it was faultless.

With minor detail variations, the Triumph range continued basically unchanged until 1950, with the significant addition of the Grand Prix road racer and Trophy (TR5) models in 1948-49. Both were derivatives of the Tiger-100 and featured the aluminum "square" cylinder head and barrel, first used on a World War II generator set made by Triumph for the RAF. Triumph's next real step forward was the introduction of the 650cc Thunderbird (designated 6T) in 1950. Although outwardly no different than the Speed Twin, the engine's stroke was slightly lengthened to 82 millimeters and the bore was opened up to 71 millimeters. With compression at 8.5:1, the engine made 34 horsepower, a great deal more midrange torque and an honest top speed over 100 miles per hour. The bottom end was strengthened slightly by the switch to a roller main bearing on the timing side only.

The Thunderbird's cycle parts were identical to the 5T and Tiger, which by this time had lost its tank top instrument panel and gained the sheet metal headlight/instrument enclosure. In addition, 1950 was also the first year to see an all-painted (no chrome) fuel tank, the glitter instead provided by four horizontal chrome bars on each side that ran from the front of the kneepads to the forward edge of the tank. The cast Triumph emblem did not change and remained in the same location.

It was again decided to finish the entire machine in a single color, and for this first year it

For 1955 the Trophy-500 received a new swing arm frame with center stand. Most were fitted with a twinseat but solo saddles were still made available in the western US. Movie actor James Dean lounges on his new TR5 purchased from California dealer Ted Evans (his decal can be seen on the oil tank). *Author collection*

was a somber slate blue. The following year the paint was changed to a lighter and much more attractive metallic blue. Curiously, the finish in both years was described by the factory as Polychromatic Blue. A new one-piece twinseat available for all but the TR5 Trophy made the machines appear more modern, but they were still fitted with the same basic frames developed for the 1936 Val Page singles!

By late 1953, Turner and Triumph were the rulers of the motorcycle world, but they didn't stop to rest on their accomplishments. They continued to improve the existing range and

add new models, including the 150cc Terrier single and the long-awaited sport version of the 650 Thunderbird. Christened the Tiger-110 (T110), it was the first Triumph model fitted with a swinging-arm rear suspension. The front section of the frame followed the standard Triumph practice of a single down tube giving way to a duplex cradle beneath the motor. The swinging fork pivoted from cast lugs at the base of the single seat post and was controlled by a pair of hydraulically damped Girling shock/ spring units. The rear sub-frame fastened at the top to the seat post and to the lower cradle

The new showroom of the U.S. Triumph Corporation in 1955, shortly after completion. Machine in the window is a 650cc Thunderbird while bike closest to camera is a 500cc TR5. Trophy features easily noticed are the sport fenders and low competition handlebars. More difficult to spot is the painted front rim, Lucas reflectors on the base of the back number plate, and "Triumph twin seat" imprint on the rear of the saddle. *Author collection*

at the bottom. A deeply valanced rear fender was supported by a strap that crossed the subframe at the top of the shocks and by tubular lifting handles that extended rearward from the same area.

A new stepped twinseat was designed that was broader and slightly longer than the unit fitted to the rigid frame models. The T110's oil tank was reshaped to correspond with an enclosure on the opposite side of the bike that incorporated the battery and toolbox. The overall look was that of a single compartment and very tidy. The rest of the T110's running gear and styling was much the same as before.

The engine was basically the 650 Thunderbird, tuned to give more ponies. It was fitted with higher compression pistons, ruder camshafts, and a larger carburetor, which together boosted horsepower to 42. A bigger, 8-inch scooped front brake handled the increased muscle and a quickly detachable rear wheel was made available. The engine mods made the 650 a firebreather capable of speeds in excess of 110 miles per hour. Understandably, it was very popular, especially in the United States.

Edward Turner's practice of ongoing improvements of the model range kept Triumph at the head of the industry until the late 1960s, long after his retirement. From this policy of evolution during 1955 sprang one of Triumph's most coveted models, the Trophy 650.

Chapter Two

1956–1959 TR6 Trophy

It might be an oversimplification to say that Triumph created the 1956 TR6 by plugging a Tiger-110 engine into a TR5 frame, but that's basically what the factory did. This is demonstrated in the parts book for that year, where the same likeness is used to depict both TR5 and TR6 models — only the engines' cylinder fins differ for each view. So when describing the Trophy's running gear, we can also look to the TR5 for assistance.

The cradle-type swing arm frame (#F3904 front/F3635 rear) was the same unit across the range and can be readily identified through the serial number stamped on the left side of the steering head. The chassis was equipped with both center and prop stands, and was modified from the previous year in having a sidecar lug added at the base of the seat post and adjustable steering lock stops at the head casting.

The enclosed-spring Girling suspension units (#S/MDA4/104) were also the same shocks fitted to all Triumph's sport models. Their 110-pound spring rate was standard, but heavier-rate springs were available as optional equipment.

Up front, the machine was supported by TR5 telescopic forks fitted with (#H384) main springs. The hydraulically damped units differed from the street models in that the seals on the lower legs were further protected by corrugated rubber bellows (gaiters) rather than steel shrouds.

No headlamp cowling or nacelle was fitted to the TR6. Instead, a separate chrome-plated 700series Lucas instrument was used that wore a small panel on the rear shell. This panel incorporated an ammeter and lighting switch as well as a receptacle for a plug-in wiring harness. The plug allowed quick removal of the 7-inch headlight for sporting purposes while a provision for a pilot, or parking light, was made within the reflector for road applications. The part number for the complete unit was given as 51892A. To protect against chafing, the wiring harness was encased in a 1-millimeter plastic sheath from the seat to the headlight.

The Trophy 650 rolled on steel rims, a 20-inch WM-1 in front, and an 18-inch WM-2 at the rear. These were originally shod with Dunlop Trials Universal tires. Later in the production run, models intended for the eastern United States were fitted with a 19-inch WM-2 rim up front. This change also included a switch to the ventilated 8-inch front brake as fitted to the Tiger-110.

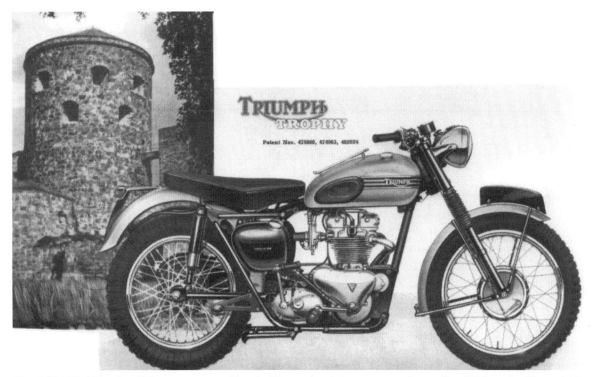

The 1956 TR6 Trophy 650, as envisioned by the Triumph ad department. Basically a TR5 with a Tiger-110 motor, its cast-iron cylinder was painted silver to preserve the alloy appearance of the 500. Off-road tires and high-level pipes made it a favorite in California.

Although officially listed as an option, most TR6s came equipped at this time with a quick detachable (QD) rear wheel. As its name implied, this wheel could be quickly removed without disturbing the drive chain, sprocket, and brake unit. The QD wheel was mated to the drive assembly via a splined ring, and by withdrawing the axle (and spacer) the wheel could be quickly slipped free. Cadmium-plated spokes were laced to all-chrome rims that did not have their raised center ribs painted.

The Smiths 120-mile per hour chronometric speedometer (#S433/3) was the lone instrument fitted and its drive was taken from the gearbox. Controls on the low handlebars (#H1003) were arranged in the same layout as the TR5, with the throttle, choke lever, and kill button clamped on the right, and spark advance lever (when equipped), and newly combined horn/dipper switch on the left. For handgrips, Triumph was still fitting the long, thin rubber cover (#H0230)

that was embossed with the Triumph trademark in opposite directions to allow its use on either end of the bar. The chrome-plated clutch and brake levers were the ball-ended type.

It should be pointed out here that the machines were always shipped from Coventry in a partially knocked-down state and had to be reassembled by the dealer prior to delivery. Although the factory set guidelines on this procedure, execution often depended on the assembler's preference or experience. Normally the handlebars would be stowed in the shipping crate with the controls and cables attached, but the switch to higher U.S. pattern bars (#H1014) sometimes took place when the bike was uncrated at the dealership. Under these conditions it wasn't unusual to see a new machine delivered with the less used kill/dipper switches up next to the grip, and the more important air/magneto controls located further in on the bars.

In this photo taken in February 1956 we can clearly see many details of a brand new TR6 including the routing of the HT leads and rocker supply line, rubber boot on the clutch arm and the combined horn/ dipper switch mounted on the clutch lever base. Kill button appears to be clamped on the right side of the handlebars. *Author collection*

As found on the TR5, the Trophy 650 came outfitted with the smaller sport saddle (#F3785). This seat, covered in solid black "Vynide" with white piping around the perimeter, used the same base pan as fitted to the Tiger Cubs and earlier rigid framed twins. By simply moving the attachment brackets and bending the contour to suit different frames, Triumph was able to use this same seat on all sport models until the duplex frames appeared for 1960.

A restorer looking for one of these rarer seats might be able to pilfer one from a plunger-frame T20 if a donor machine can be found. The larger touring seat (#F3647) as fitted to the Tiger-110 was available on special order. This is borne out by the road test of a factory-fresh 1956 TR6 in *Cycle* magazine, so equipped.

The fuel tank fitted to U.S. models was the smaller 3 1/4-gallon (U.S.) vessel, compared to the standard 4 1/4-gallon unit used on the Trophy in other markets. The smaller tank came with

clip-on knee pads, as compared to the recessed, screwed-on grips found on the larger version. The rear tank mounting bracket was now completely rubber insulated. Two lever-type fuel taps were supplied and clear plastic hoses with crimped metal ferrules reached to all fittings.

Like the steel rear and alloy front fenders, the tank was finished in Shell-blue Sheen (Dupont Dulux 202-57095). Center stripes on the guards were black, bordered by white pinstriping and applied right to the very edge of the fender.

Black lining was also applied between the chromed styling bands on the tank. Although silver-gray is given as the paint finish for both 500 and 650 Trophy models in the home market, most TR6s were sent abroad and how many were finished in this somber color is unclear. All Trophies came with the tank-top package rack that proved useful in enduro competition but was easily (and often) removed elsewhere. For this the factory made available plugs (#F3026) for the mounting holes.

The remaining cycle parts were in black stoved enamel which included the frame, number and engine plates, skid plate, chain guard, battery box, oil tank, and fender stays.

1956 Engine and Drivetrain

The TR6 motor was internally identical to the unit found in the 1956 Tiger-110. Its most obvious difference was the all-alloy appearance of the engine's top end, aimed at complementing (or mimicking) the 650's little brother, the TR5. The look was accomplished by switching the cylinder finish from black to silver, to match the new diecast aluminum head fitted to the 650s for the first time.

Designated the "Delta" head because of its shape, the part number of the new component was listed as E3608. However, from engine number 75026, a revised cylinder head (#E3644) was fitted that had a slightly different shaped combustion chamber. New pistons with different valve cutouts were also listed but the compression ratio remained unchanged.

Iron valve guides were integrally cast, and the rocker boxes and pushrod tubes redesigned for the new head. Gone were the external oil return pipes. Instead, the head's redesign allowed the exhaust and intake valves to share a common well, fore and aft, for drainage directly over each pushrod tube. These tubes now extended from the crankcase directly to the cylinder head and not, as previously, to the rocker boxes.

Internally, sport cams (#E3325) were installed which allowed a compression ratio of 8.5:1. In the bottom of the power unit, shell-type big end bearings replaced the plain white metal type used until then — the new ones being of thin walled, steel Babbitt construction and key coded for rebuilding. Larger openings in the big end of the RR56 alloy connecting rods were necessary to allow the change, and the balance factor on the crankshaft was altered to suit. The rest of the engine was built to Tiger-110 specifications except for the "Trophy" designated patent plate on the timing cover.

The TR6 breathed through a 1 1/16-inch Amal Monobloc carburetor (#376/40) insulated, via a fibrous gasket at the intake manifold, from the higher temperature transmitted by the new head. This instrument was connected to a Vokes D-type air cleaner that nestled between the battery box and oil tank — the latter having to be removed in order to change the filter. A low-speed cough was also another failing of the early Monobloc setup.

All first-year Trophy 650s were fitted with a high-level two-into-one Siamese exhaust system that dumped out on the left side of the machine and fed a single silencer. The pipe diameter was 1 1/2 inches. Amazingly, no heat shields for the pipes or silencer were offered by the factory, but many period aftermarket guards can still be found on unrestored machines.

The 1956 TR6 was magneto ignited and a Lucas K2FC wader-type unit (#42298) with a vented cap was used. The parts book for that year states that only manual advance magnetos were fitted, but a great number came with an auto advance instead, especially to the eastern United States. The fore-mounted 6-volt Lucas E3L generator or dynamo (#20009) made 60 watts of power and its polarity was positive ground. For this year only a small rubber boot (#200830) was fitted to protect the connection of the wire leads at the exposed end of the generator body.

The gearbox was the same unit used across the twin-cylinder range, except for different ratios obviated by the 650 engine. The redesigned clutch received a new cork material that was impregnated with neoprene and bonded to a solid plate, as opposed to the cork-filled window arrangement of previous years. Externally, the generator-type primary chaincase was unchanged from the others and used the same identification number (#T1190) as in 1955.

1957 TR6 Trophy Models

In America, three distinct variations of the Trophy were offered in 1957. One variant, the TR6C, was virtually the same model offered in the United Kingdom and markets other than the United States. It will be easier to describe and understand these models if first taken one at a time.

TR6A

Perhaps the most desirable of all the pre-unit Trophy 650s, this model was Triumph's "hot rod" for 1957. The engine specifications of the TR6A were generally unchanged from the previous season. But the switch to a more traditional (appearance-wise) twin downswept exhaust system found more favor with those who preferred this bike for street use. The exhaust setup was not the same as fitted to the Tiger-110. Its pipes (#E3628/32) were 1 1/2 inches wide and the straight-through mufflers (#E3816/17) were much less restrictive than the T110 components. With this easier breathing came a little more power and a much throatier sound.

Another welcome addition to the TR6A was the Smiths tachometer (#RC109) joining

A 1957 U.S.-spec Trophy 650, restored by Triumph expert Mike Benolken. By the second year of production, American variants were assuming their identities with distinctive colors and sport seats. Tiger-110 tanks and touring saddles were also an option. Period TriCor tank bag might look out of place on the off-road version, but is right at home on this TR6A street model. *Gaylin*

the other instrument on the front. The tach drive was taken from the exhaust pinion on the timing chest and a new cover (#E3677) was fitted to permit a gearbox and drive cable. The brass "Trophy" patent plate was relocated over the new bulge in the Triumph's "pants." The TR6A came with standard gear ratios and the tires were also changed to ones more suited for road use — a 4.00x18-inch standard universal replaced the trials pattern at the rear and a ribbed 3.25x19-inch in the front.

TR6B

This model was basically the same specification as the standard 1956 TR6 with Siamesed two-into-one exhaust. The only change came in tire and wheel sizes — a burly 4.00x18-inch knobby at the rear and the front trials universal was now reduced in diameter to

a 3.25x19-inch skin. No tachometer was fitted as standard, although special orders or dealer conversions were not uncommon.

TR6C

This designation was created to identify a model that for all purposes was a "leftover" from the prior season. Still finished in Shell-blue and wearing the horizontal tank band emblem, most if not all of these models had 1956 engine and frame serial numbers. The compression ratio on the TR6C was 8:1 for most machines. Changes from 1956 specifications included the road tires from the A model and downswept exhaust from the Tiger-110. Price was the TR6C's strongest feature, so no rev meter was fitted and the gear ratios were standard.

Besides the differences among the three new variants, there were many changes intro-

This drive side view of Benolken's restored 1957 Trophy Bird shows fuel line routing and the factory's silly horn location. Optional straight-through mufflers give an indescribable sound at any rpm! If you're looking for one to copy. *Gaylin*

Exploded view of the Trophy front fork.

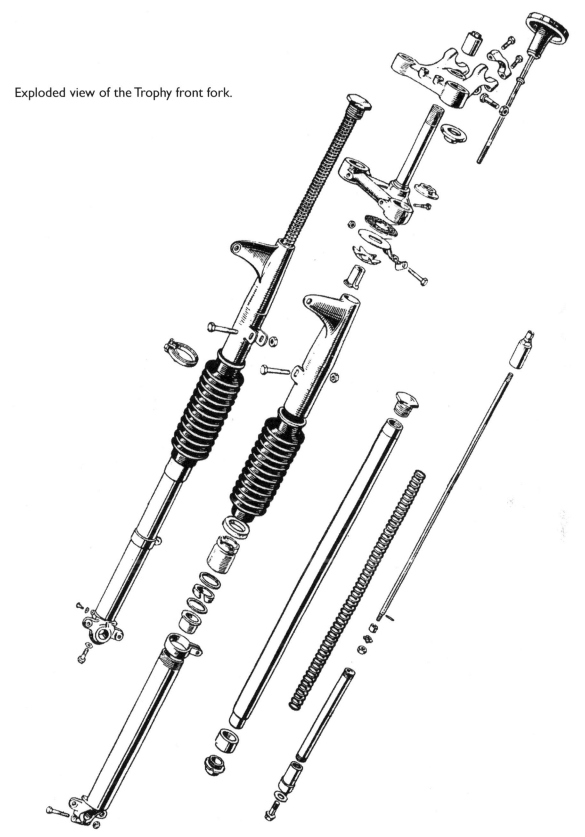

The engine of a restored 1957 TR6A. Details of the special timing cover with integral tachometer drive and original patent plate can be seen. To keep the HT leads out of trouble, the Triumph factory corralled them at the carburetor manifold with a small clip. Rubber boot over the clutch arm is also accurate. *Gaylin*

duced across the range of 1957 Trophy 650s. Beginning again with the most noticeable, the paint finish was switched to a more vibrant combination of Aztec-red (Dupont #1633H) and Ivory. Both colors were applied to the fuel tank by separating them horizontally using the cast emblem, knee pad, and trim motifs as a partition. Behind the rubber grip, the division was tapered off to the comer of the tank, divided only by gold pin striping.

The tank emblem was also completely new. A zinc-based alloy diecasting, it was comprised of two streamlined bullets with a grille between them and a superimposed Triumph "sweeping R" logo set in the center. The entire emblem was chrome-plated, but the hollows of the grille were finished in a semi-flat black and the letter centers in white. Extending from the emblem in both directions were thin motif strips which hooked over the

Quality reproductions of most Triumph decals are available to today's restorer from various sources, including the Vintage Motor Cycle Club of Great Britain. As Mylar pressure-sensitive stickers were still at least ten years away (in 1956), all transfers used during the period of manufacture were either varnish-based or the water slide type, with varnish applied over afterwards.

Transfers are frequently treated as an afterthought by the restorer. They are often applied in the wrong location or an incorrect style is used. The "Minimum Oil Level" (#A3) decal was placed on the tank centrally from front to back and approximately three-fifths of the way from the bottom. It was never fixed toward the very top or bottom as is repeatedly seen on many restorations. The oil tank also wore a pair of boxed lubrication instructions always hidden as far under the seat as possible.

The "Drain Oil Every 1500 Miles" (#A40) and "Use Only BP, Energol," etc. (#A44) transfers were applied to the Trophy's oil tank valance near the filler neck, to be noticed only by the owner. However, it is not uncommon today to see a renewed machine parading these stickers halfway down the tank as though the restorer wanted all to see that he had them.

Perhaps the most common mistake is the overuse of the scripted "Made in England" (#D3361) sticker. This was actually a BSA decal and wasn't used on Triumphs until the parent company began integrating the two marques in the late 1960s. Even then, it did not appear on twins until the 1971 model year. To see this BSA sticker unknowingly applied to earlier Triumphs is very distressing.

In 1956, the "Made in England" transfer (#A61) was a larger version of the graphics then being used on the Triumph headlight nacelle. The 1 3/4-inch-long design used block-style, capital letters and was surrounded by a thin line, all in gold. It was positioned at the top of the fuel tank directly opposite the filler neck, sometimes in dead center, other times occupying the balancing location for the fuel cap.

Another transfer stating valve clearances (#A53) was placed on the tin cover over the forward engine mounting plates. Ramped cams required different valve settings and machines equipped with these sported a different decal (#A51), giving the clearances as 0.01 inches for both exhaust and inlet valves. Again this transfer was intended by the factory to be noticed only by those servicing the motorcycle and this location was thought to be obscure. So indistinct was this sticker that many rebuilders today omit it either unintentionally or because of a lack of availability.

tank's (tunnel) edge at the front and fastened in behind the knee pad toward the rear. The inspiration for this new design was said to have come from the massive radiator grilles then in vogue on American automobiles. The new graphics were perhaps not Triumph's most attractive, but they were successful in capturing the era's image.

The two-tone color scheme was carried over to the fenders with the main color in ivory and a center stripe in the orangish Aztec-red. The border pinstriping was in gold. On models destined for Britain and other markets, the single color finish was still listed as silver-gray.

1957 Frame and Cycle Parts

The fuel tank (#F4116) retained the same shape, contour, and capacity as in the previous model year, but the base mounting plates on the underside were extended to the very edges to improve support and rigidity. The larger Tiger-110 tank (#F4115) was also made available for the United Kingdom/general export market.

The chassis remained unchanged but the centerstand was modified by extending and strengthening the foot lever, to give less trouble when hoisting the machine to rest. The new part number was given as F4304.

Changes in suspension for 1957 included new Girling shock units (#SB4/259) at the rear, which were adjustable for three load settings and initially had a lighter mainspring rate of 100 pounds. But subsequent to engine number 08563, the spring rate was changed to 110 pounds. And the rubber attachment points of the unit were metal reinforced. The front forks also underwent revision in the area of the front axle. On the previous fork, the spindle had to pass through the right slider and was secured by a clamping arrangement at the base of its left-side counterpart. The new forks had detachable caps at the base of both legs that were secured by two screws on each side.

A lug was also brazed directly on the fork to anchor the brake backing plate in place of the body clamps of the earlier setup. The new fixing point also served to connect and support the fender stays. This stronger, lower fork arrangement was intended to serve the 8-inch diameter, air-scooped front brake of the 500cc Tigers which were now fitted as standard on all the TR6s.

Drive chain protection was improved by deepening the inside valance of the chain guard, giving a greater degree of enclosure around the wheel sprocket. The replacement part number for the new chain guard was F4138. Also at the rear, heavier butted wheel spokes were standard after engine number

This photo of a 1957 TR6B model was taken when the bike was still fairly new. Siamese exhaust system and larger, touring seat are original items but the handlebars and front fender have deviated from factory specs. *Author collection*

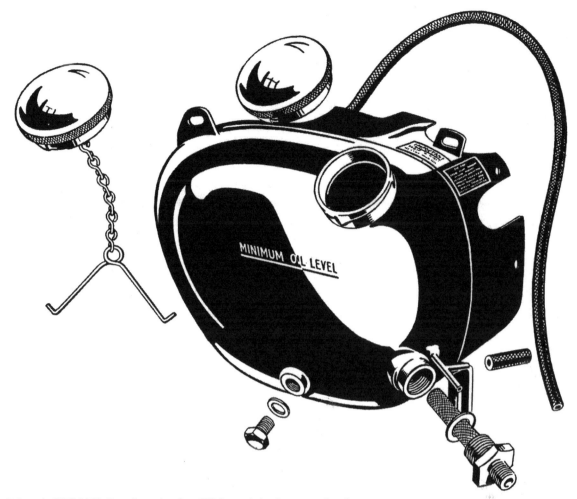

Oil tank (#F3219) fitted to the first TR6 models showing decal positions.

05000. Sadly, this was also the year that saw Triumph quit offering tire pumps as standard equipment in the United States.

All 1957 Trophies received a new style Lucas generator (dynamo) that had a one-piece metal end cover instead of the earlier Bakelite cap and band assembly. The unit's output was still rated at 60 watts, but a new part number (20035A) was assigned.

Two new transfers made their appearance in 1957. One was applied on the assembly line at Meriden, the other available only in America. Triumph's success at the Bonneville Salt Flats in Utah was heralded with a new "World Motorcycle Speed Record Holder" (#A56) that incorporated the now well-known winged Thunderbird. The decal was

placed on the fuel tank above the "Made in England" sticker, opposite the fuel filler cap. The location eventually changed to the headlight ears by the time of the Duplex frame models. Because no headlight nacelle was fitted to these sport models, the location of this decal would alternate back and forth between the two spots until 1970, when it made its final appearance.

The "Trophy Bird" (#AD7) transfer was offered only in the United States for application on each side of the redundant front number plate that was still being fitted to American machines. In blue and white, the image carried the model name under the winged Thunderbird emblem and was sometimes applied by the dealer prior to delivery. Other times it was available only upon customer request, for additional charge.

Close-up view of the 60-watt Lucas generator (#20035A) with solid end cap. Subtle valve clearance transfer (#A53) can also be seen on sheet metal cover above. These would eventually be relocated to the underside of the hinged twinseats. (Restored) *Gaylin*

1958 TR6 Trophy Models

Just two variants of the Trophy 650 were offered in 1958, as stocks of the leftover economy (TR6C) models in the United States were finally exhausted. Only the roadster (TR6A) and scrambler (TR6B) versions remained. A quick look at the 1958 models suggests no changes from the previous year. But there were many subtle technical and detail improvements.

The most conspicuous difference was the appearance of the "Slick Shift" gearbox. It was developed in an attempt to make gear changes

possible without use of the handlebar clutch lever. The new shift lever assembly was simply redesigned to act directly against the clutch thrust rod within the cover of the gearbox. Pressure on the foot lever in either direction disengaged the clutch until the pedal was returned to its rest position. But the gearbox could still be shifted in the traditional fashion for those wishing to do so.

The Slick Shift undoubtedly was easier to understand by those new riders with no experience with manual transmissions, but

Only under the seat would the Lucas (#70048A) horn be more ineffective and Triumph would eventually move it there! Battery box and oil tank were always black on the U.S. Trophy models but not so on the Bonnevilles. (Restored) *Gaylin*

most seasoned motorcyclists didn't have the patience to relearn the delicate touch needed to operate the new auto-clutch as intended. Many gear cover cam rollers were removed to ensure operation in the normal manner.

So what at first appeared to be a completely new transmission was only a redesign of the outer and inner covers. The new arrangement meant a clutch arm that now laid over horizontally and a new chrome-plated metal access cover. A rubber grommet was still used to cover the cable-to-clutch arm connection. On some U.S. models, a

silver sticker (to match the cover of the gearbox) advertising the new feature was placed just above the redesigned access cover. This decal was generated by the American distributors and was not seen on machines in the United Kingdom.

Other 1958 gearbox upgrades included a better garter-type oil seal of the mainshaft, at the driveside of the case. And in an attempt to halt the pesky leaks around the kickstart shaft, Triumph fitted a rubber collar, held under light compression between the starter lever and transmission cover.

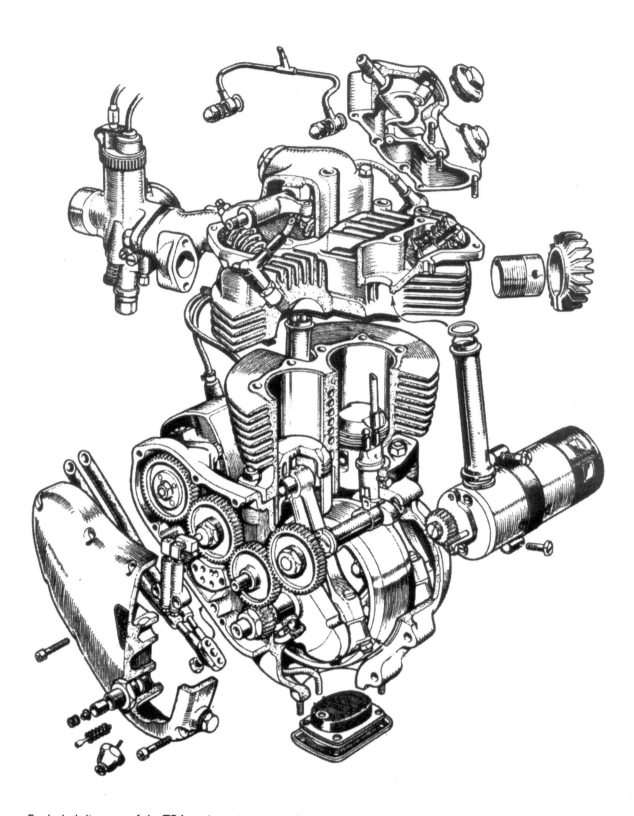

Exploded diagram of the TR6 engine.

1957 was the first year the Triumph ad department used color photography in its catalog. But still, retouching was thought necessary. This image of a 1957 U.S.-spec Trophy 650 shows a machine finished in the home market color of Silver Sheen. TR6s sent state-side were in Aztec-red and ivory.

The motor received yet another cylinder head redesign. The new component (#E3924) was given a slightly smaller combustion chamber which permitted more "meat" between the exhaust valves and mounting holes — an area in which earlier heads were prone to crack. Smaller chambers and smaller valves meant less power, and sound examples of the earlier head are much sought after today.

Also for the first time a twin carb, splayed-port head (#E3938) was offered as a performance accessory. A complete kit (#CD110) with an extra carburetor (#376/40) was also made available, but conversions were made only at the dealer level or by the customer. Any twin-carb TR6s offered by Triumph would have been experimental in nature and few in number.

1958 Frame and Cycle Parts
The biggest news for the TR6's running gear that year was an all new single-leading shoe (SLS) front brake. The 8-inch full width hub was similar in aspect to the 7-inch version fitted to the Model Twenty-One 350cc twin. The brake's aluminum backing plate slotted into a boss on the lower fork leg giving a much cleaner look than the anchor brace used before. The end cover (#W1332) for the left side was a chrome-plated metal stamping with a radial flute design. These ribs strengthened the cover and gave the suggestion of a cooling vane for the front brake unit. Like those fitted to the rear wheel, straight butted spokes were now used at the front as well, but wheel and tire sizes remained the same as before.

The two-tone paint scheme of the export models also remained as before in Aztec-red and Ivory, and silver-gray was still the standard finish for Britain, although the two-color finish was available for more money. A new alloy fender (#H1216) and stays were fitted to the front wheel, but the rear guard continued unchanged.

WORLD MOTORCYCLE
SPEED RECORD HOLDER

Decal #A56 was assigned to all Triumphs from 1957 to 1970.

The control cable adjusters were moved to the handlebar levers where access was improved and the lever's base provided a solid anchor for the adjusters to act against. The clutch and brake levers were changed to a bigger ball-ended type, and new high-rise handlebars (#H1179) were catalogued for the United States and Canadian markets.

A new front frame section (#F4414) was listed that included a provision for an antitheft lock at the right hand side of the steering head. This feature amounted to a small protruding boss which accepted a removable lock body that could be inserted to secure the fork, or withdrawn for riding. A thin metal dust cap was provided to protect the cylinder when in use.

The wider touring twin-seat (#F3647) was sporadically substituted with the sport saddle to Trophies leaving the factory for all markets. Seats with safety straps were fitted to machines bound for California where they were mandated, but ultimately some of these motorcycles found their way to the eastern states as well.

1959 TR6 Trophy Models

The Trophy 650 models reflected little change for the new year, as attention was directed elsewhere in the range. But the TR6 was the beneficiary of improvements developed for other new models. The crankshaft (#E3894) was a stiffer one-piece forging, with a separate flywheel. The centrally-mounted wheel was pressed in place and secured by three 7/16 bolts that stabbed in from the outer periphery. After engine number 027610, new bolts (#E3907) were used as the earlier ones weren't up to the job. The Trophy also profited from the new pistons (#CP157) fitted to the T120

1959 official factory photo of the home-market Trophy-650 now with full width front hubs. It was the ad department's practice to retouch the original photographs and minimize (or in this case eliminate) all cables and wires. *Author collection*

Bonneville, which had thicker crowns and modified skirts. The latter change was claimed to reduce engine noise.

An oil level plug was added to the underside of the gearbox outer cover, and at engine number 023111, an additional transmission adjuster was fitted. The front brake cam lever was redesigned for greater leverage during long periods of use, although the parts book reflected no variation in ID number. Otherwise the TR6 drivetrain went unchanged for the new model year.

On the scrambler models, the exhaust system was changed to a set of twin (one for each side) 1 3/8-inch upswept pipes (#E4026/28) and mufflers. Heat shields (#E4032/3) that clamped around each exhaust pipe to protect the rider's legs also became available for the TR6B, while the antitheft lock at the steering head was not.

1959 Frame and Cycle Parts

Most of the new season's upgrades for the TR6 were in the area of cycle parts. The Aztec-red and Ivory paint scheme was reversed on the fuel tank — red was now on the bottom. Finish on the mud-guards remained as they were with Ivory as the main color. The silver-gray scheme was no longer listed for the home market and the two-tone finish became standard. The Tiger's bigger twinseat was now also listed as standard on all Trophies, but the smaller, sport saddle would still fit and was available on order.

All TR6s received a new 1-gallon oil tank (#F4329) equipped with a breather tower and drain tube. The froth tower, as it was called, was partially obscured by the seat but was still outboard of the frame rails. Oil tanks of the factory racers had this feature as standard dating back to the Grand Prix model and it was now deemed necessary because of the high-performance potential of the Trophy's new twin-carb brother. The container was also interchangeable with the Tiger-110 and remained in black enamel with gold transfers. Additional engine and cycle part developments for that year were synchronous with the 1959 Bonneville and will be examined in the next chapter.

Chapter Three

1959 Bonneville

The first year Bonneville was a milestone machine for Triumph and motorcycling in general. Without question, it remains one of the most desirable Triumph motorcycles made by the Coventry factory. Naturally the more accurate the restoration of one of these models can be, the more value and general appeal it will have.

Ostensibly the 1959 T120 was nothing more than a twin-carburetor Tiger-110 with a few slight differences. There are many details, however, that were unique to the Bonneville that might easily be overlooked by a restorer, but not by a savvy concours judge.

Within the past decade much has been put forth about this model and some of it has been misleading. For example, the 1959 factory spares catalog indicates that production began with engine number 020076 and some have taken this as the Bonneville's starting number. However, the parts book addresses all "B" range (non-unit) twins including the Trophy and Tiger models. Bonneville production actually began with engine number 020377 on September 4, 1958. Any T120s bearing lower serial numbers are probably counterfeited examples. So we will describe the motorcycle with the restorer in mind and try to flag a few of the known inconsistencies along the way.

Engine and Drivetrain

The Bonneville's principal badge of identity was its splayed-port diecast alloy cylinder head (#F4019). Externally it can be easily recognized by the casting characteristics around the intake pathways, which still contained the raw, unmachined bosses of the parallel inlet tracts as used on the Trophy and Tiger 650s. The machining of the new widened induction tract had been tooled in right on top of them. Further identification is provided in the oil drain well below the intake rocker box, where the earlier number E3548 can be found as a casting mark.

The splayed intake ports were threaded and the flanged stubs that screwed into them were secured by large jam nuts. From these flanges hung two 1 1/16-inch Amal "chopped" Monobloc carburetors (#376/204), so nicknamed because they lacked integral float bowls. A single GP fuel reservoir (#14/617) was used instead and was fixed separately to a position directly behind the carburetors. In an attempt to isolate the bowl from engine vibration, it was suspended from the seat post

In Britain, the hot-rod of Triumph's 1958 range was the Tiger-110. When the twin-carb 650 was introduced, it came only in this package. Aside from paint finish and the engine's top end, the T110 and early T120 are the same. 1959 Bonneville restorers can (and often do) cannibalize the Tiger models. Factory photo. *Author collection*

by a stiff rubber block fastened at each end via ring clamps. To allow this, the valances of the oil tank and battery box were modified around the now redundant air filter connector opening.

Two gas taps at the tank fed the top of the bowl through a Siamese banjo fitting, while a joint on the underside supplied gasoline to the carburetors through a "T" fitting in the plumbing.

In hindsight, the float bowl's original mounting arrangement seemed very much a jury-rig, especially considering how much trouble the system gave during hard stops. In an attempt to alleviate the "loading" problem, late in the season Triumph offered a kit consisting of a metal extension plate that attached to the existing rubber block. It moved the bowl 3 inches further forward between the carburetors. But even this "quick-fix" design wasn't as trouble free as two complete (#376/40) Monobloc instruments, a route taken by many Bonneville owners. A 240 main jet in each mixer was listed,

although the U.S. distributors suggested a 300 jet during the break-in period. The spark plug recommendations were KLG FE100s or Lodge RL47s.

Another detail resulting from the factory's concern about vibration was the safety wiring of the three screws that held the "dummy" float bowl covers in place. These screws (#376/151) had taller heads that protruded past the cover's surface and were drilled for the wire. Probably because of the time factor, Triumph did not design an air filter arrangement to accompany the new carbs, instead fitting only chromed bell-mouth rings at the carburetor's opening. The restorer must take care to find the correct carburetor tops (#376/107), as there is not much clearance between them and the fuel taps hanging down off the tank. Incorrect Amal components or fuel tank hardware will result in the segments fouling each other.

The rest of the engine shared specifications with the TR6 Trophy and Tiger-110. The pistons

Factory publicity photo of the first-year Bonneville in U.K. trim with low bars and large fuel tank. Some T120s there would also get black oil tanks and battery boxes while US models had these in Pearl-gray. Sport and touring twinseats were alternated in all markets. *Author collection*

(#CP157) were the new improved items that gave a compression ratio of 8.5:1 and had thicker crowns and modified skirts designed to clear the crankshaft weights at high rpm. The crankshaft was a one-piece forging with straight-sided cheeks and a detachable flywheel. The Bonneville was a B range model and as such saw new flywheel securing bolts after engine number 027610. The camshafts were also the same components — E3134 intake and E3325 exhaust.

The engine exhaled through what was basically a T110 exhaust system with 1 1/2-inch pipes (not 1 5/16-inch, as per TR6), but with straight-through mufflers. The silencers were changed to the standard Tiger (#E3651/2) components after engine number 024337.

Another widely held myth is that all first-year Bonnevilles wore Tiger-110 patent plates on the timing chest. Although it's true that a small number of early production machines left the factory this way, the bulk of 1959 T120s were fitted with a badge that read "650 Twin." To understand all this, realize that by 1959, Meriden was producing a 650 twin with four distinct model names, each requiring a different patent plate. So the decision was taken to rationalize these items by adopting the "650 Twin" tag as employed on the Thunderbird. This reduced the amount of ID plates and listed part numbers. So restorers intending to use a Tiger-110 tag should check their engine number before attaching what can only be considered in most cases incorrect.

The T120 drivetrain was identical to that found on the other sport 650s, except for the gearbox. A transmission with a Slick Shift gearbox cover was fitted as standard to all T120 models, but fearing runaway engine rpm between shifts, the factory disabled the feature by removing the mechanism's pin and roller. Although appearing to have a Slick Shift gearbox, the motorcycle had to be clutch-shifted in the traditional manner. The final drive sprockets were as per Tiger-110 and a QD rear wheel was available.

The electrical components were not dissimilar from the Tiger 650. Lucas "red label" K2FC magnetos were fitted with red, flange-

Drive side of Dick Brown's impeccably restored 1959 Bonneville. Low pattern handlebars give a more appropriate appearance when paired with the headlight nacelle, but most Bonnevilles exported to America arrived with high-rise bars instead. *Gaylin*

mounted pickups and manually operated spark advances. Automatic advance units could, of course, be installed but were not listed as available until later in the model year.

Subsequent to engine number 024137 a more effective voltage regulator was provided as standard equipment to monitor the Lucas E3L dynamo. This 60-watt generator was the updated version with a one-piece metal end cover. It threw the juice to an all-black Lucas (#PU7E-9) storage battery that was still being secured by a trunnion and strap arrangement within the left-hand compartment, which also shared the tool kit. The 6-volt system was positive-grounded.

Frame and Cycle Parts

Like the Trophy 650, the bulk of Bonneville production was earmarked for America. These machines were fitted with the smaller

3 1/4-gallon (U.S.) sport tank (#F4116) with clip-on kneepads.

As a rule, the larger 4 1/2-gallon (U.S.) container (#F4115) went with the U.K. and general export models, but either version was available in all markets, although sport-tanked home market bikes were more common than the reverse.

Handlebars fitted to all U.S. Bonnevilles were a high-rise type (#H1010) with special bends to agree with the nacelle enclosure, while machines for home and general export received the lower swept-backs (#H1009) that were preferred there. The factory also listed an optional racing-type dropped handlebar (#H1082) especially suited to the nacelle. These were 7/8 inches in diameter, which necessitated adaptor shims under the mounting clamps and an entirely different set of controls (and grips) for the smaller bars.

Another factory photo of the 1959 Bonneville. Seen from this perspective we have a better view of the exhaust system, foot controls and black painted front hub. *Author collection*

The standard controls were laid out as per Tiger-110. The clutch lever, combined horn button/dipper switch, and separate manual spark advance was placed on the left, with the throttle and front brake on the right. By using a two-into-one junction box within the throttle cable, the standard twist grip was retained. The brake and clutch levers were the chrome-plated, big ball-ended type. One difference from the T110 controls was the absence of an air control lever on the right-hand side. The 1959 Bonnevilles had no choke assemblies.

The Bonneville's headlight nacelle was the same as fitted to the other generator-type B range machines. Lucas components included a 7-inch glass/reflector unit, bulb holder, ammeter, kill button, and lighting switch. With the parking (or pilot) lamp now relocated within the light unit, a chromed grille was fitted to the previous spot on the nacelle over the Lucas horn (#70048A). No provision was made for a tachometer, so the lone Smiths instrument was a 120-mile-per-hour chronometric speedometer (#S467/107/L). The clutch and brake cables were now routed through separate rubber-trimmed holes in the nacelle top, but the thinner throttle and magneto wires still entered the enclosure through the handlebar grommets.

The front wheel and fork clip was identical to that used on the Tiger 650 models, including an 8inch full width hub and integral brake drum. A single-leading shoe brake was backed by a polished, diecast aluminum plate that slotted directly into the lower right fork slider. Early examples were still fitted with the radially fluted, chrome-plated cover (#W1332) on the left side of

In the beginning, Meriden treated the T120 as a high-performance model expecting many examples to be used as racers. But the factory-installed safety wire on the fuel tank bolts and Monobloc cover screws was used more to combat vibration than meet the rigors of competition. Wire wrap should form a closed triangle and is incomplete on this restored example. *Gaylin*

the wheel. This was changed to a simpler pressing (#W1334) without the grooves on later models.

The black-enameled hub was laced to an all-chrome WM2-19 steel rim (#W1230) with dull cadmium-plated spokes. With this type of plating becoming increasingly difficult to obtain today, many restorers are turning to stainless steel spokes.

The Triumph factory most assuredly would have used stainless spokes had the process been less costly then, but modern concours judges are inclined to focus their attention on finishes, and stainless steel even when unpolished is easy to spot!

It might be appropriate to point out here that the fork slider nuts (#H0390) were

This now famous factory photograph shows 1959 U.S.-spec Bonnevilles being assembled at Meriden. Of note is the small sport tank and Pearl-gray toolbox. These examples are being fitted with touring saddles, but narrow TR6-type seats were also specified for America. Under magnification, safety wire can be seen on the fuel tank mounting bolts as well as the carburetors. *Author collection*

chrome, not cadmium-plated. As a rule when restoring Triumph motorcycles with early telescopic front forks, the slider nuts were usually cadmium-plated on machines with rear stands such as rigid-framed models. The front suspensions on these motorcycles were always compressed, even when at rest, obscuring these nuts and negating the need for a polished finish. With the introduction of swinging arm frames and centerstands taking more of the weight from the front end, the fork slider caps were now exposed and thus required a chromed finish.

The front tire fitted to 1959 Bonnevilles was a 3.25x19-inch Dunlop highway rib. The 3.50x19 rear skin was a Dunlop Universal and covered a WM2-19 (#W79A) steel rim. The same chromed wheel rim was used on the

quickly detachable wheel, which was also listed as available for the T120.

The part number for the rear Girling suspension units was SB4/279. The spring rate for the standard unit was 100 pounds, but other components were available from 150-pound sidecar springs to 90-pound roadracing items.

Many documents and period photographs have survived to substantiate that the factory did indeed fit both the sport seat and the broader touring saddle to 1959 T120s. Unfortunately (or fortunately, depending on your view) no records were kept as to how many or where they went. Under these circumstances a restorer is safe using any bench that was available to a pre-unit Triumph twin during that season.

The first wave of Bonnevilles sent to the United States were equipped with the wider

Another close-up of a restored Bonneville's engine compartment. Among the nonstandard details seen here are the beveled carburetor tops and uncompleted safety wire wrap between the Monobloc side cover screws. Lodge, Champion, and KLG spark plugs were all fitted as OEM in 1959. KLG plug caps add an authentic touch. *Gaylin*

and heavier Tiger-110 (#F3647) twinseat. These were covered in solid black "Vynide" with thin white piping at the upper edge. When America's dissatisfaction with this styling reached the factory, the specification was changed to the sport seats.

The sport saddle (#F3785) fitted to the Trophy was desired by those wanting weight reduction and a more athletic look. They were also covered in solid black vinyl with white piping, but trimmed along the bottom with a gray strip approximately 3/4 inch wide. A great number of these seats were also solid black, without the gray trim at the bottom. All machines sent to California required passenger safety straps as mandated by the state's DOT. The straps and

This close-up image of the 1959 Bonneville engine shows the model's plumbing and Tiger-110 patent plate fitted to early machines. *Author collection*

mounting hardware were made available in kit form to be installed at the point of delivery. This minimized assembly line complexity for U.S. East and West Coast machines.

The narrower seat is preferred today by Bonneville and TR6 restorers, and sound examples are difficult to find. As related in Chapter 2, the base pan of this saddle is the same as fitted to rigid-framed twins and plunger-framed Tiger Cubs. By moving the attachment points and reshaping the contour, these stand-ins can be made indistinguishable from originals.

Except for the main machine colors, the running gear of the 1959 Bonneville was the same as that found on the Tiger-110 models. Beginning with the fuel tank, colorations were Tangerine on the bottom and Pearl-gray on top. No Dupont numbers have surfaced to

The first group of 1959 Bonnevilles were sent out with the fluted front wheel cover (#W1332) of the previous year. Subsequent machines came wearing with the simpler Thunderbird (#W1334) lid. Triumph fitted 19-inch Dunlop tires to the front and back of the new model. (Restored) *Gaylin*

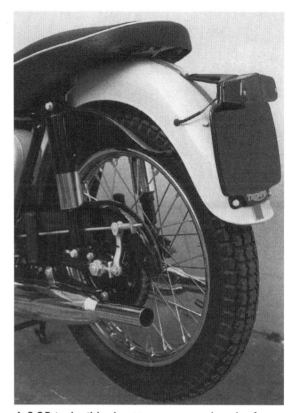

A 3.25-inch ribbed pattern was used at the front and a 3.50-inch tire with universal tread on the rear. The fender's painted center stripe correctly stops short of the edge on this restored example. Triumph trademark transfer (#D68) in gold and white graced the bottom of every T120 and TR6 rear number plate leaving the factory. *Gaylin*

correspond with these colors, but there is plenty of surviving sheet metal in original paint to provide an unshakable color match.

The gas tank's colors were divided horizontally by the "mouth organ" tank badge and trim strips as detailed in the previous chapter. For whatever reason, there were a small batch of Bonnevilles finished in Azure-blue and Pearl-gray (blue on the bottom) toward the end of the 1959 production run. However there is no documentary or photographic evidence to support that any of these were exported to the United States, and given the circumstances and bloated inventories of the U.S. distributors at the time, it is very unlikely that this happened. The small

numbers of these blue T120s would have gone to satisfy the neglected U.K. and general export markets, including Canada.

The front and rear mudguards of the Bonneville were the one-piece deep valanced items as on the Tiger and Thunderbird, but in Pearl-gray. The raised center ribs were painted in Tangerine and pinstriped in gold. The front fender was susceptible to cracking in the area of the center brace, and beginning with engine number 021941, machines had their stays welded directly to the sheet metal. Both mudguard tips had a rolled edge and the painted center stripes stopped short of the edge and were squared off by the gold lining.

Details of the 1959 Bonneville's plumbing. Smooth black rubber hoses connect all fittings between tank, float bowl, and carburetors, while rubber lines with a herringbone pattern are used between the oil tank and pump manifold. Early production machines had their fuel bowl suspended from the seat post by a 3-inch rubber block. Later models came with the reservoir moved another 3-inches forward to combat fuel starvation and loading during launches and abrupt stops. (Restored) *Gaylin*

The oil tank and battery box were for the most part also finished in gray, not black. This was done to distinguish the model from the Tiger, although there is evidence that some home market bikes (only) were fitted with black-enameled compartments. The remaining cycle parts were finished in black enamel including the frame, fender stays, nacelle and fork, chain guard, engine plates, number plates, and wheel hubs.

Transfers marking the new model's name were applied in two places. The "Bonneville 120" decal (#A57) was fashioned in a stylish gold script and its 2-inch length was the appropriate size for its nacelle location just above the black-enameled steering damper knob. The decal was

Another restored 1959 Bonneville with all-black sport seat and battery box. On this Canadian example both features are correct. A very desirable motorcycle! *Lindsay Brooke*

U.S.-spec 1959 Bonnevilles were fitted with the smaller 3 1/4-gallon sport fuel tank (#F4116) of the TR6. The rubber kneegrips were not the type that screwed directly to the tank but were instead fitted over a detachable metal plate. It is unlikely that any of the later-made machines finished in Azure-blue and Pearl-gray found their way into the United States. (Restored) *Gaylin*

The instrument panel on a restored Bonneville shows the correct gauges and switches. Rubber handlebar ties were not used by the factory but decal placement is accurate. The scripted "Bonneville 120" (#A57) is positioned below the damper knob on the nacelle with the "World Speed Record Holder" (#A56) appearing between the knob and kill button above. Made in England (#A61) sticker is applied opposite the filler cap on the fuel tank but sometimes appeared with the "Speed Record Holder" transfer on the nacelle. *Gaylin*

also applied centrally to the battery box lid, but its small dimension in such a big area made it appear very lonely. Some restorers employ larger versions of this scripted sticker on the lid and although inaccurate, it does look healthier!

The remaining motorcycle transfers were as found on others in the range. The "World Motorcycle Speed Record Holder"(#A56) was positioned between the damper knob and kill button on the headlight nacelle while the "Made in England" box sometimes accompanied it or was placed down on the fuel tank opposite the

filler cap. The oil reservoir wore the usual lube instructions and recommendations as well as a "Minimum Oil Level" (#A3) sticker. And a transfer stating valve clearances (#A53) at 0.002 inches for the inlet and 0.004 inches for the exhaust was fixed to the sheet metal cover over the front engine plates.

1960 Leftover U.S. Bonnevilles

These models are mentioned here because they were simply unsold 1959 machines with updated titles, a practice that was still permitted at the time. Identical to the previous year's specification, with headlight nacelle and deep valanced fenders, all would still have 1959 engine serial numbers even though a current registration document might indicate otherwise.

Most of these bikes were among the last produced in 1959 and were fitted with auto-advance magnetos and no spark control lever on the left side of the handlebar. The position of the carburetor's remote float bowl had been modified (moved 3 inches forward) on all these T120s prior to delivery.

Restorer's Tip: Paint Matching

When duplicating a finish, restorers should always take into account the amount of oxidation or solar bleaching on the sample used. Original factory paint chips can be found, but these too will also have suffered from years of exposure to oxygen, the sun, or both, something most paint specialists are reluctant to accept.

Without question, the best way to match any factory color is to locate a piece of sheet metal (tank, fender, side cover, and so on) in its original finish. Rubbing away the top surface in an area that hasn't deteriorated too severely in the elements will bring the most accurate and satisfactory results.

The "Bonneville 120" transfer was also applied centrally to the battery box cover. Originally available only in gold, black decals were made available the following year. (Restored) *Gaylin*

Tangerine and Pearl-gray was the only color scheme cataloged for these bikes (in 1960), reinforcing the probability that no blue 1959 Bonnevilles came to the United States. The presence of these unsold motorcycles in large numbers was the impetus to create a separate designation for the genuinely new machines that were being introduced for the following year. It is these motorcycles that will be described in the next chapter.

Chapter Four

Duplex Twins (1960–62)

Triumph's entire range of non-unit 650 twins were radically changed for 1960, with the introduction of a completely new frame (#F4608) designed to improve handling and overall stability. The handling characteristics were affected most noticeably by a steeper (by 2.5 degrees) steering angle. With the revised fork position, the wheelbase was shortened to 54.5 inches.

But the most conspicuous change in the new machines was the twin front down-tubes. The previous arrangement saw a single tube in front that split into a twin cradle beneath the drive unit and continued back to the seat post. The new chassis began the "duplex" framework right from the steering head.

The top rail of the new frame swept back to the seat post to form a right angle under the seat, as before. However, there was no lower bracing rail to hang fuel tank mounting brackets or aid in steadying the top of the motor. A pair of front fuel tank supports were now brazed part way down on the front tubes and a rear single attachment point was incorporated into the rear of the top tube.

The new design clearly made the machine easier to assemble at the factory, but proved too fragile in its original form — especially under the harsh American applications of dirt and desert racing. Meriden finally realized this, and lower tank rails became part of the design after engine number D1563. Dealers later were offered complete front frame clips (#F4846) to replace the weaker chassis, the retrofit often taking place after a machine had been in the owner's hands. Because of this practice, some surviving 1960 models with early numbers might bear an updated frame.

Another mid-season change involved the (#F4712) propstand. Whether the culprit was the steeper fork angle or stiffer springs, it was soon learned that the kickstand was too short for the new frame. Later machines were fitted with a longer (#F3723) replacement.

As indicated above, the fuel tank securing arrangement was also completely new. Instead of being bolted directly to the frame, the container rested in three small rubber cups, two on the front down tubes and one on the rear spine of the top tube. The seamless tank was held in place by a chrome-plated steel strap, itself isolated from metal-to-metal contact by a rubber belt beneath it. The strap was pinned directly to the frame at the rear, and adjustable

TRIUMPH

the best motorcycle in the world

. . . with a range of high quality,
high performance models from 200 cc to 650 cc.

TRIUMPH ENGINEERING CO. LTD., COVENTRY, ENGLAND

Triumph racer and TriCor salesman Walt Fulton straddles a 1960 TR6A Trophy 650, equipped with a TriCor windshield and saddlebags. To demonstrate how sales literature can fib, this same image was used for the cover of the 1961 color catalog but with a bathtub Tiger-110 model drawn in beneath Fulton. *Author collection*

for tension at the front through a yoke and draw bolt arrangement. The bolt passed through the steering head casting and tightened from below.

Restorers should take care not to over tighten the draw bolt, as tank fractures could result. A service bulletin from January 1960 instructs that the tank should "float free" in the rubber mounts. Lateral stability is ensured by fitting rubber padding around the top frame tube within the tank's tunnel. The factory

supplied these rubber blocks (#F4770) on all machines, after engine number D104.

Fresh mounting plates for the engine were designed to address the new frame, especially at the front were the motor had to catch two tubes instead of just one. This mounting was a one-piece unit, with the joining section positioned to the top. On the TR6B and TR7B models which were sporadically equipped with skid plates (#F4695), no frontal sheet metal covers

This advertisement art from 1960 shows an American TR6B with high-level siamese pipes and black midsection enclosures. Sales literature images usually started out as a photograph and were then retouched beyond the point of credibility — sort of like restoring a motorcycle that has survived in original condition!

(as found on the Tiger and Thunderbird) were fitted. While on the road-going Bonnevilles and Trophies, the absence of the bash guards exposed the front of the crankcase to constant spatter from the front wheel.

On the T120s, the new top engine stay (#E4164) was a single flat strap that fastened to the motor at the intake rocker boxes, then extended rearward to catch the underside of the top frame tube. This solid plate was also used to suspend the remote fuel bowl, detailed later in this chapter. The TR6 torque stay arrangement consisted of two separate straps that attached to the same frame casting, but were twisted 90 degrees at the other end to adapt the through bolts on the intake valve covers.

This support design was satisfactory to arrest the back-and-forth engine shakes, but like the previous form that saw the exhaust rocker box fixed to the front down tube, it did nothing to absorb the up-and-down pulses inherent in the parallel twin. Until the very end in 1983, Triumph engineers never adequately

buttressed the vertical vibrations generated by this engine design.

The rear subframe (#F4684) followed the similar practice of the previous design, but was simplified in its construction. At the top it was fastened to the front section in the usual manner but the bottom rails now attached to the lug at the base of the seat post and no longer reached to the front down tube. Substantial top tubes extended past the new Girling shocks (#64054164) to support the far end of the rear fender, obsoleting the old lift-handle arrangement. And the mounting plates for the mufflers and passenger footrests were replaced with tubular supports welded directly to the subframe itself. All these modifications, of course, helped speed assembly of the machine while also significantly strengthening it in the rear.

New front forks were shared by both 650s and were similar to those on the unit 350-500 twins, but with external rubber boots and detachable end caps at the slider's bottom. The

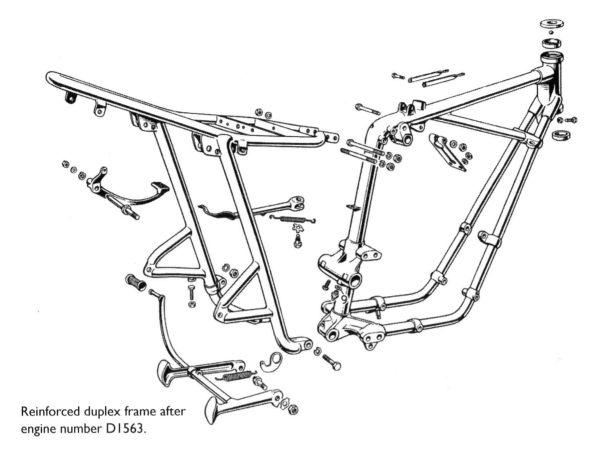

Reinforced duplex frame after engine number D1563.

Sales literature image of a British market Bonneville from 1960. Features of note are the large-capacity fuel tank with screw-on kneegrips, Pearl-gray oil tank, and low slung handlebars. Tachometers were also withheld from U.K. T120s requiring no timing cover drive. Dark shadow behind the carburetor is the centrally mounted fuel bowl.

This factory photograph of a 1960 U.S.-spec Bonneville (TR7A) divulges the differences from the U.K. version. Smaller sport tank, high-rise handlebars, and tachometer arrangement are the most conspicuous. The hawk-eyed will also spot the plug beneath the QD headlight and kill button toward the center of the handlebar. *Gaylin*

sliders were also incorporated with bosses that directly secured the brake backing plate and central fender brace. The black elastic gaiters were molded in a glossy rubber and clamped only at the bottom. A Trophy-type fork crown with integrally cast handlebar clamps was fitted to both, and a new steering damper backing plate which anchored to the frame without a bolt was also fitted.

Trophy wheel and tire specifications were now adapted by the Bonneville. The road models were equipped with 3.25x19-inch ribbed tires at the front and 4.00x18-inch universals at the rear. The scrambler models came with a

Line drawing of a 1961 British-market Bonneville.

blocked-tread trials pattern, otherwise the dimensions were identical. The WM2-19 front rim (#W1230) was chrome-plated and lashed to a black enameled center hub with cadmium covered spokes. At the rear, a wider WM3-18 rim (#W1007) served the thicker tire. Bonnevilles supplied to markets other than North America were sometimes equipped with a 3.25x19inch rear tire and WM2-19 rim. A black enameled QD rear hub was fitted to most American bikes; machines with the standard, less expensive hub had to be specially ordered.

A new quickly-detachable 700-series Lucas headlight incorporating only an ammeter was used on the 1960 sport models. The lighting switch was relocated to a small mounting plate at the very front of the twin seat on the right-hand side. The TR7A Bonneville finally got a matching tachometer and speedometer as did the TR6A. Both instruments were mounted side by side on a single plate, and fastened to the top of the fork crown. The drive for the tachometer was from a geared take off on the exhaust cam sprocket and the timing cover now had the familiar bulge and relocated patent plate. As a rule the scrambler models (TR7B, TR6B) came only with a speedometer and blank timing cover, as did all home market and export Bonnevilles and Trophies.

Other differences established by then between the United States and home market machines included the handlebars and fuel tanks. The bars on sportbikes sent to America were the high-rise type (#H1179). U.K. models were fitted with the lower and more businesslike (#H1009) tillers. All Bonnevilles and Trophies used clutch and brake lever assemblies with big ball-ended blades. Without a manual spark and choke control, the T120 handle bars were less cluttered than the TR6, which still had these controls. The combined horn and dipper switch was clamped on at the far left and the kill button was put on the bar just to the right of the steering damper knob.

Depending on the Triumph dealer, some control cables were secured to the bars with black rubber ties or tape, while other shops gave

this no importance. The scrawny, checkered rubber hand-grips (#H0230) as first appeared in 1938, were emblazoned with the Triumph logo and did nothing to lessen the ever-increasing vibes ascending from the engine.

Different gas tanks were also specified between the various markets. U.S. machines came with the smaller and sportier 3.0-gallon tank (#F4700) with clip-on kneegrips. In Europe, where motorcycles were considered more seriously as transportation, a larger and more useful 4.0-gallon vessel (#F4640) was fitted as standard. This tank still retained the recesses to allow the screw-on kneegrips. All versions were still fitted with a tank top package rack, although flat-topped screws or rubber plugs were available to dress the unused holes on tanks where the grill had been removed. As in previous years, either vessel was available on demand and increasingly more U.S.-spec tanks appeared on Euro-machines.

The color schemes of both the Bonneville and Trophy models were the same in all markets. The fuel tanks were again finished in two colors, divided north from south by the cast emblem, trim motifs, and kneepads. The final line of separation at the rear of the tank was accomplished by pinstriping. The T120 tanks were in Pearl-gray and Azure-blue (bottom) although there is documentation indicating that some early models still carried the Tangerine and gray of the previous season. The TR6 colors continued in Aztec-red (bottom) and Ivory, and the hand lining on all tanks was applied in gold.

The fenders of each model continued their respective colors — ivory with an orange/red center stripe on the Trophies and gray with blue stripes on the Bonnevilles. The latter model now shared the same alloy front and steel rear mudguards as the Trophies. These fenders had no raised edge at their tips and thus the painted center stripes were applied right over the unfinished edge. Pinstriping on both was in gold.

Some U.S. bikes were still being imported with front number plates. These steel blades were finished in black enamel and had a plain

Drive side of a 1961 Bonneville with an all-black seat and battery box. The Monobloc carbs now had integral floats and the covers were still safety wired. Low bars and lonely speedometer also identify it as a U.K. T120R, but tachometers were now optional. Factory photo. *Author collection*

edge without a cast, chrome beading. Other examples arrived without the number plate and an undrilled fender. Still a third condition saw bikes with drilled fenders, but with rubber grommets to fill the unwanted holes!

The oil tank and battery box on the 650s were redesigned to agree with the new duplex frame and the froth tower moved forward. The compartments on the Bonneville were painted in Pearl-gray while the Trophy's were finished in black. The diminutive "Bonneville 120" decal was applied to the battery box lids of both T120 variants, and the "World Speed Record Holder" was sometimes omitted from the top of the fuel tank, leaving only the "Made in England" opposite the filler cap. These and all the other transfers affixed to the Bonneville were sometimes in black, sometimes in gold, while the stickers on the 1960 Trophy models remained in gold.

Completely new twinseats were supplied to both models. These were entirely covered in a coarsely textured black vinyl and trimmed with white piping around the top perimeter and a band in matching black around the bottom edge. The padding was more generous and the two-level contour stepped up approximately at the center. This seat came directly from Triumph's "bathtub" models and used the same base pan, padding, and upholstery. They were in fact the very same cushions, but were bolted in place rather than being hinged. However these twinseats were not stenciled with the gold Triumph trademark and would not be until 1966. Any restored machine, prior to the 1966 model-year, that has a stenciled seat is incorrect.

1960 Engine and Drivetrain

The power unit on both the Bonneville and Trophy 650 remained essentially unchanged

This timing side view of a 1961 U.K. Bonneville shows the Slick Shift gearbox cover and position of the oil level transfer. Sharp eyes will also see the lighting switch under the seat's nose and metal clips on the magneto HT pickups. QD headlight is also clearly visible. Factory photo. *Author collection*

from the previous year and the model's particular identity markers were maintained — the T120 cylinder continued in baked black enamel and the TR6 in hi-temp silver. The most conspicuous change around the motor of both 650s was the disappearance of the front-mounted generator. Six-volt electrical power was now supplied by the Lucas RM15 alternator that had been fitted only to the Thunderbird and Speed Twin. Like the T-Bird's, it was hung on the left-hand end of the crankshaft and used the more bulbous chaincase. All the pre-unit duplex models were equipped with alternator crank cases — earlier generator-type bottom ends will not readily fit into these frames. The sparks, however, were still supplied by a Lucas magneto.

Nineteen sixty was a year in which various carburetor experiments were tried on the Bonneville. The first batch of machines left the factory with the breathing arrangement of the previous year. The single racing-type fuel bowl, in its new position slightly forward of the carbs, was suspended from the engine torque stay by a threaded rod. But the float bowl still suffered from frothing generated by the engine's increasing vibrations. So after engine number D5975, the Bonneville got two complete Monobloc carburetors with integral fuel reservoirs, and most of the low-speed petrol problems disappeared.

Still, the factory offered no air filter arrangement for the Bonneville. A final midyear modification came in the form of a balance tube between the inlet manifolds. This fix, said to alleviate difficulties at idle and slower speeds, was also available in kit form (#CD223) consisting of two modified manifolds and a length of rubber hose. Dealers were encouraged to retrofit these to earlier models and many kits were installed.

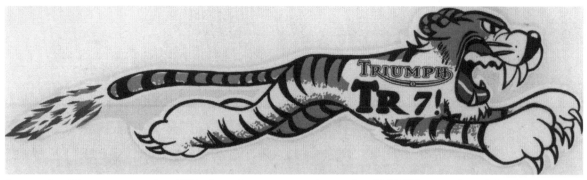

A rare decal for a rare machine! This American-generated transfer (#AD17) was offered for the redundant front number plate of 1960 duplex-frame Bonnevilles. They were made left-and right-handed so the tiger would always be leaping forward.

In concours, period accessories can mean the difference between a first- or second-place award. This 1961 publicity photo shows a U.S. T120R Bonneville with TriCor tank bag, travel luggage, and windshield. Also seen is the tachometer cable routing, black painted front wheel hub, and detachable headlight. *Author collection*

Right side of Mike Benolken's accurately restored 1961 TR6R. Sport tank and high-rise handlebars are characteristic of the U.S. variants. Position of the oil level transfer is the only apparent flaw. *Gaylin*

Because of the new frame and bulgier primary covers, the exhaust systems on all the duplex 650s had to be redesigned. Both of the American TR6A and TR7A variants shared the same downswept pipes (#E4133, E3632) and low restriction mufflers. The American TR6B and TR7B scramblers had separate (#E4177/79) high-level pipes, one on each side, and factory supplied heatshields (#E4204) for the rider. British and general export TR6 models came fitted with the familiar Siamesed (#E4125/30) high-level pipes.

A final point regarding the TR7 designation used during the 1960 model year concerns only American machines. This label was created by the U.S. distributors to distinguish the new, sportier-looking TR6-type Bonnevilles from the leftover T120s of the previous season that were being sold as 1960 models. However, all Bonneville engine numbers began with the T120 prefix, including the TR7 variants. No engine in 1960 ever bore a TR7 prefix and any surviving machine found stamped this way is

a forgery. By the end of the 1960 model year, with all the leftover 1959 Bonnevilles sold off, the TR7 designation was discontinued having served its purpose. The label wasn't used again until the 1973 Tiger 750s.

1961 Models

Nineteen sixty-one was a year of refinements, or more accurately, "reactions" to the electrical and vibrational problems of the previous year. The steering angle was steepened even further, from 67 to 65 degrees, requiring a new part number (#F4846) for the frame. Again this was done in an effort to achieve better handling.

The fuel tank was beefed at the nose bridge, but the same part number was retained. Another tank-securing strap was introduced, this time made of stainless steel. These were much stronger and stopped altogether the failures caused by the ever-increasing quivers. Two lengths were needed to fasten down two different capacity tanks — #F4916 for the 3 1/2-U.S.-gallon vessel and #F4917 for the 5.0 U.S.-gallon version.

Engine compartment close-up of a restored 1961 U.S. Trophy 650 shows the aluminum painted cylinder, tach drive details, and the very "1950s" tank badge. Period accessories include TriCor crash bars and finned rocker caps. Scripted "Made in England" transfer on front downtube is popular with some restorers, but incorrect on Triumph twins until 1971! *Gaylin*

Other mods to the running gear to counter vibration included a new toolbox design after engine number D9660.

The front forks and tire sizes on the Bonneville and Trophy remained the same, but the front and rear brakes were redesigned with fully floating shoes and a new backing plate. The C models and home-market bikes continued without tachometers and the special timing cover needed to make it happen. But the speedometers on both of the U.S.-spec T120s were changed to a type that climbed to 140 miles per hour, even though the Bonnie was unable to send the needle that far. Literature of the period also indicates that the factory was making a real effort to see that all scrambler models were sent out with skid plates, while road bikes went unprotected.

Many useful details are revealed from the driver's view of this restored 1961 U.S. TR6R. The "Made in England" (#A61) transfer and black-faced Smiths chronometrics are right on the money, while the unpainted damper knob and chrome handlebar clips aren't so close. Centrally positioned kill button is also correct. *Gaylin*

Most of the new season's tweaks were directed at the motorcycle drivetrains. This was the year that saw the alloy 650 heads recast with spacers between the outer fins to reduce buzzing noises. The remainder of the top-end, including the carburetors, went unchanged. Black rubber hoses were still used to route the fuel.

The gearbox casing and inner cover was changed to accept a larger thrust washer (#T1607)

at each end of the layshaft. The Slickshift outer cover was still used without the feature itself. The engine sprocket was reduced a tooth to 21, and the factory, for the first time, officially fitted a folding kickstart lever to the Bonnevilles.

In the electrical department, Triumph fitted an alternator of lower output in an attempt to stop the epidemic of light bulb failures. Between engine tremors and the "outlaw"

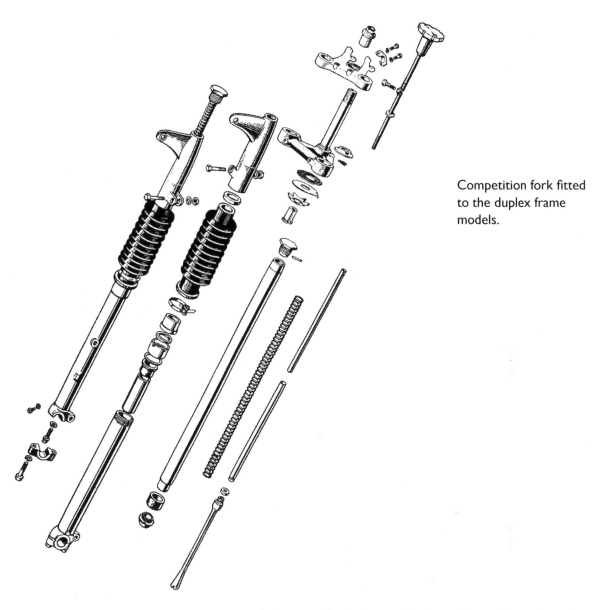

Competition fork fitted
to the duplex frame
models.

voltage produced at the higher speeds, headlight bulb replacement had become a weekly chore. Mercifully, both the T120 and TR6 models continued to use magneto ignition, with an auto-advance control now listed for the Trophy as well as the Bonneville.

Both machines saw new colors in 1961. For the Bonneville it was Sky-blue and Silver Sheen, blue being the top color on the fuel tank. The fender's main color was silver with a blue center stripe. The pinstripes on the fuel tank and fenders were applied in gold. T120s sent to America had their oil tanks and toolboxes

finished completely in Silver Sheen, but there is some evidence pointing to black-finished compartments for a small amount of U.K. bikes. As always is the case, a few of these examples may have sneaked into the United States

The Trophy models were finished in a completely new shade called Ruby-red. The metallic color was actually a genuine shade of burgundy, not the deep orange of the earlier Aztec-red. The second color, occupying the bottom half of the fuel tank and most of the fenders, was silver. Hand-lining was again in gold, but the TR6 oil tanks and toolboxes were

Front "pedestrian slicer" number plates were still being fitted to American models in 1961, although factory-made rubber grommets were available to plug any unused fender holes. Decals showcasing the model name were also offered by U.S. dealers and today make a nice touch to a restored machine. (Restored) *Gaylin*

in black. The remaining cycle parts and hardware on both models were in baked black enamel.

Note that silver was applied to both fuel tanks as a base color and then the brighter pigment was painted over the top. This practice, which became the standard procedure in Meriden's paint shop, brightened the metallic tone of the main color and helped stabilize paint finishes on machines in all markets.

In the United States, the Bonneville was no longer labeled as a TR7 and reverted back to the T120 identification in all literature and bulletins. The designation for the Bonneville with twin high pipes was T120C, and the low pipe, road model was called T120R. During the model year, Trophy engine number prefixes

began appearing with an extra "S," such as TR6SC and TR6SR. These machines are not special or exotic and are in every way identical to those not bearing the extra letter.

Apparently the additional character was thought necessary, when midway through the year Triumph announced a TR6SS for general export, the added letter S symbolizing the word "standard." This machine was the same in specification to the American TR6R except for a larger fuel tank, lower handlebars, and Siamesed exhaust system. The TR6SS also came without a tachometer arrangement. The remaining details of all 1961 Bonneville and Trophy models not pointed out in this section were as found in the previous model year.

Rare 1961 T120 Bonneville in Sky-blue and silver, restored by Don Blitz. Although it would hardly affect the value of such a desirable machine, the twinseat should be completely in black and carry no Triumph trademark. *Lindsay Brooke*

1962 Models

The final year of the pre-unit 650 engine saw fewer revisions than the previous season. It seems fantastic that by this time Triumph was finally getting the new frame and twin carburetor motor fully sorted, only to scrap everything in the following year!

Still chasing engine vibration, the factory began playing with the crankshaft balance factor. At engine number D15789, the weight was increased to a 71 percent factor. Then at engine number D17043, an altogether new crankshaft (#E4492) was introduced with pear-shaped side cheeks, a wider flywheel, and a factor of 85 percent. The shaft was still a one-piece forging with a central wheel held in place by three specially strengthened cap screws. These stabbed in toward the center from 120-degree positions.

All this engineered detuning did nothing for the 650's throttle response, but did help civilize the tremors somewhat.

The TR6 models were upgraded with Bonneville valve springs (#E3001/2). The fuel lines and fittings on the T120s were changed to allow a single petcock to feed both 1 1/16-inch carburetors, thus, for the first time, allowing a reserve tap for the other side of the tank. It was quickly realized, however, that for trips to the blurry end of the speedometer both valves had to be open! The Amal Monoblocs fitted to the Bonnevilles still were equipped only with chromed bell rings and were not shielded with air filters.

On the other end of the cylinder head, everything remained as in 1961, with the exception of the Euro-market TR6SS. The

Everything has its place on the business end of a 1961 U.S. "Trophy Bird." Dunlop K70 rear tire is inaccurate but easier to find than the correct universal pattern. Show judges should make allowances for those who actually ride their restored machines! (Restored) *Gaylin*

Sales literature image of a 1961 American market T120 Bonneville. From this angle the skid plate and carburetor's safety wiring can clearly be seen. Practically a mirror image of Don Blitz' T120 (previously seen).

Siamesed exhaust system on this model was switched to the right-hand side, which meant a redesigned muffler as well.

There were also a few exchanges in the electrical department for 1962. A new Lucas RM19 alternator was fitted to both 650 twins, but still with a low-output stator that halted the overcharging of the previous year. The QD headlight unit was discontinued on the road bikes starting with engine number D18419, and a new ammeter (#36296), not as sensitive to runaway voltage, was also fitted to the R models. And the Lucas rotary-type stop light switch (#31688) that had been giving trouble was sometimes replaced with a Wipac, pull-action trigger (#11524).

1962 Frame and Cycle Parts

The quickest way to distinguish a 1962 model from all others is by the two-toned twinseat on top of its duplex frame. This is not to say that dual-toned saddles were fitted to all Trophies and Bonnevilles during that season, but the feature was introduced from the start of production and most machines came with the new seat. The shape and contour were identical to the earlier saddle, but the top panel and ribbon around the lower edge were in gray. The piping at the top edge remained white.

Other modifications included a redesigned oil tank with rubber mountings to curb the rash of vibration-caused bracket fractures inherent on all the duplex models. The spring rate on the Girling shock absorbers was stiffened to 145 pounds per inch, but the external appearance did not change. And the rear wheel sprocket was increased to 22 teeth on the T120R and TR6R models only. The only outward change at the front of the Trophy models was an upgrade to the Bonneville 140 miles per hour speedometer.

For whatever reason, U.K. and export Bonnevilles were continued in the Sky-blue and silver of the 1961 season, while the U.S. colors were Flamboyant Flame and silver. Trophy colors in all markets were given as Flamboyant Ruby-red and silver. The T120's flame red finish was described as a reddish burnt-orange, while the TR6's pigment was the bright burgundy used the previous model year. The hand lining on the tanks and fenders was again in gold. The lower compartments on the early Bonnevilles were silver; afterwards they were painted black, as were all the Trophies.

Model designations and engine serial number prefixes for that year remained unchanged. Only the Trophies were stamped with an extra "S," making the range of labels TR6SR, TR6SC, TR6SS, T120R, and T120C.

Chapter Five

Unit-Construction Twins (1963–1965)

Author's note: From 1963 to 1970, the Triumph factory followed a program of constant change and modification to its motorcycles. Many technical upgrades were incorporated in the range as soon as production allowed, with no regard given to model year assignment. Some, but not all of these improvements were identified by engine number. The next two chapters will include many of the discernable changes deemed important for restoration purposes. For a comprehensive listing of factory technical modifications covering this period, consult the Appendix.

When most of us recall a Triumph motorcycle, we envision a machine with a 650cc engine of unit construction. In 1963, the industry trend of combining the motor and gearbox in a single case was finally adopted by the Coventry factory for its larger engines — four years after Triumph introduced the "unit" 500. This layout had many advantages over separate construction, not the least of which were speed and simplification of assembly during production.

Triumph's all-new 650 incorporated the crankcase, gearbox, and primary drive, yet through clever design retained many of the marque's pre-unit hallmarks. The timing cover kept its polished, triangular shape, complete with printed nickel patent plate. The gearbox cover was given special attention and its oval shape and underside valance did much to suggest its separated origin. On the drive side, there was a new, more modern primary cover. It had a flash extending rearward from the top of the alternator boss, emblazoned with a cast-in Triumph logo. The left side operator's footpeg was no longer supported by the outer chaincase, but was instead bolted to a lug on the lower frame rail. All outer covers on the new motor were highly polished and still held in place by Phillips-head screws.

As might be expected, the new bottom end had many internal changes. Underneath the artistic left-hand chaincase was an all new primary drive with a 3/8-inch duplex chain running between the fixed centers allowed by unit construction. Chain tension was provided by a rubber-coated friction blade that bore directly against the chain links. An extra plate was added to the clutch assembly, bringing the count to six, and the intra-hub shock absorber was changed from the previous four-paddle type to a three-chamber vane.

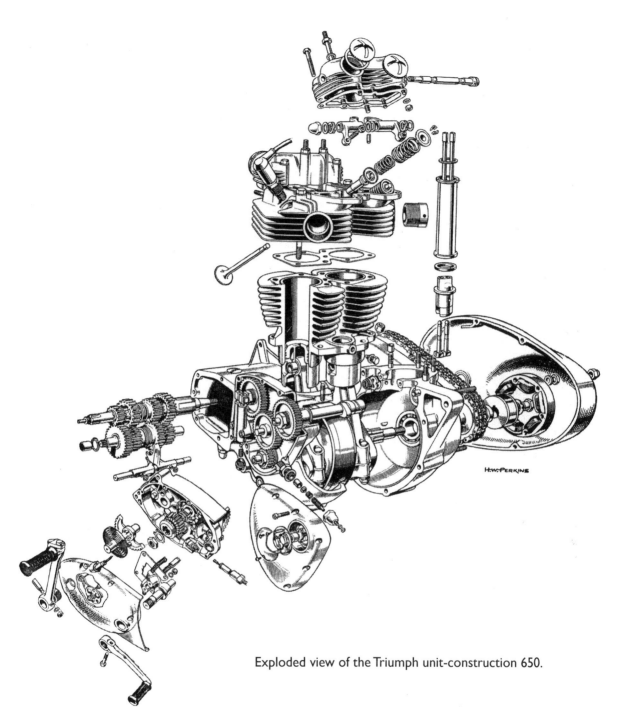

Exploded view of the Triumph unit-construction 650.

The four-speed transmission had a new clutch arm arrangement similar to that of the unit-500. The gearbox internals were basically pre-unit items, but with a new layshaft end design to allow a speedometer drive take-off. The drive sprocket on the road-going Bonnevilles and Trophies had 19 teeth, while the off-road models had 18-tooth sprockets. Under the timing cover were new camshafts (#E4819-intake, #E4855-exhaust) and timing wheels. The chambers on the oil pump were reversed, placing the scavenge side on the left, and the oil pressure indicating button was moved from the cover's chest and around the corner to face

71

Restored 1963 Bonneville street scrambler owned by Les Sumner. Road-going T120C models are considerably more rare (and desirable) than TT Specials, and this one is very accurate. Trials Universal tires, safety wired carburetors, and two-toned saddle were all part of the package in 1963. *Lindsay Brooke*

the wrath and refuse from the front tire.

The new engine featured coil ignition. Its ignition points, or contact breakers, were moved to the outside of the timing cover and driven by the exhaust cam. These cams can be identified by a star stamped into their unfinished shank. Timing access was made easy via a simple chrome-plated metal cover, screwed on to keep out the elements.

The exhaust cam also drove the tachometer, but now from the primary side of the crankcase. There was no external worm-drive box yet; the cable threaded directly into the case. When exiting, the cable looped over the outside of the left exhaust pipe (T120R, TR6SR only) and then passed under the fuel tank. It was possible to force the drive cable inside the pipe for a tidier route — but this drastically shortened its life, and the factory recommended the longer, more hazardous path. For models not supplied with the revmeter, a plug was fitted to close the unused takeoff in the crankcase. A cross was also

stamped on these cams to reveal their tach drive compatibility.

At the core of the engine, the 8.5:1 (#CP157) pistons as well as the connecting rods (#E3606) were carried over from 1962. The crankshaft was also essentially the same, but was lightened and had a modified right-hand journal to mate with a new seal in the timing cover.

A cursory glance at the new engine's top end might overlook many subtle design changes introduced for 1963. Outwardly the iron cylinder and alloy head appear the same, but the '63 Bonneville and Trophy head castings were completely new. Both had deeper finning, and on the T120s, the raw unmachined TR6 bosses finally disappeared. The mounting bolt centers were moved apart to allow more meat in the casting, especially around the valve seats which had become notorious for cracking. The wider dispersed mounting points, made possible by a ninth stud-bolt placed directly in the center of the head, discouraged warping and improved sealing.

Timing side of Sumner's 1963 T120C shows the correct front stand on the fender and unified air filter fitted to Bonneville's later in the year. Oil tank transfers were exposed – not pretty, but correct! Notice the duplex front fork held over for one more year. *Lindsay Brooke*

Another advantage of the wider bolt pattern was its facilitation of bigger cylinder bores. Triumph saw no reason to change the base of the 650 cylinders, and without much trouble they can be retrofitted to earlier pre-unit motors. Triton and specials builders worldwide can delight in the use of ninebolt Bonneville heads for their Featherbedded Tiger-110s!

The inlet porting on the Bonneville head (#E4923) remained splayed and threaded for a pair of flanged carburetor adaptors. These were steel and kept in place by jam-nuts that bore directly against the head casting. A balancing tube was still fitted that crossed between the two stubs. The Trophy head (#E4552) differed only in its parallel intake ports, tapped and machined

to accept an aluminum "Y" manifold for a single mixer.

New rocker boxes were designed which were now unpolished, but dressed in fins that matched the cylinder head. The inspection cap domes were shallower, with crossed slots and a serrated edge. Tensioned fingers, made of spring steel, were fastened to the top of the enclosures above each cap and bore directly against their rough edge, in an attempt to keep the caps from backing out under vibration.

The new Bonneville engine inhaled through the same 1 1/16-inch Monobloc carburetors (#376/257) fitted in 1962 and still without choke assemblies. The Trophy 650 was equipped with a similar instrument (#376/40), same bore,

Foot pegs bolted directly to a frame lug in 1963 only. Also visible is the new style printed nickel patent plate. (Restored) *Lindsay Brooke*

but with a choke slide, hence the different part number. And clear plastic fuel lines were now standard on the T120 and TR6 models.

For 1963, the TR6 received a simpler, pancake-shaped air filter (#F5334) that clamped directly on the carburetor. Access to its circular-shaped, removable felt or pleated paper elements was much simplified over the previous D-shaped cleaners that had been buried between the toolbox and oil tank. The T120 models started the season without protection for its twin carbs, wearing only the chromed bell rings. But late in the season, U.S. machines came equipped with a single housing (#F5262) that served both instruments. Unlike the Trophy filter, it attached to the frame and was coupled to the carbs through rubber adaptors. The ends of the perforated box were rounded to continue the theme of the TR6 item, and the entire unit was finished in black enamel.

The previous season's exhaust pipe patterns were continued, including the right-hand Siamese pipe for the TR6SS and separate high-level tubes (#E4884, E4886) for the American TR6SC and T120C. The latter models were still equipped with a single pair of chromed heat-shields (#E4204) for the operator only. Although all the exhaust plumbing across the range appeared similar, routing around the new motor meant slightly different bends, plus new

part numbers. Note that late pre-unit (1960–62) exhaust pipes will not interchange with those used on the unit-construction motors.

Muffler dimensions were also completely new, mostly owing to hanger bracket relocation. There was now a pair of detachable solid plates that screwed to the lower rear subframe from which the passenger footrest and mufflers were supported. On the road models, longer resonator-type silencers (#E4949) were fitted on each side that made the neighbors happier without affecting performance. However, the heavy-looking muffler's appearance seemed to contradict the Triumph twin's emerging athletic image and worked against the new engine's beauty! The silencers (#E4132-L, E4184-R) fitted to models with upswept pipes were not changed significantly and retained their pleasing teardrop form.

1963 Frame and Cycle Parts

The unit-construction engine was given a new frame all its own. The three-year-old duplex design was replaced by an overall sturdier frame with the traditional single front downtube that was thicker in section (1 5/8 inch) than even the 1959 chassis. The head casting was more substantial and kept the 1962-type steering angle. The front pipe split at the base into a conventional duplex cradle under the motor and continued rearward, straddling the seat post and tying to the lower subframe. Skid plates were clamped to the frames beneath the engines of the TR6SC and T120C off-road models.

Rear section rigidity was much improved by uniting the new swingarm pivot casting at the base of the seat post with the rear of the engine through a mounting plate on each side. The plates also joined the lower section of the rear subframe and supported the rear brake pedal, but the footpegs for this year (1963) only were bolted a frame lug beneath the crankcase. Wrapped around any powerplant, the new chassis would have been an improvement. But combined with the unitized engine, Triumph's big twins were now as sturdy as any in the industry.

To control the rear swinging fork, enclosed Girling units were again fitted, but with varying spring rates to suit the different markets. All U.K. and general export roadsters, including the T120R and TR6SS, were equipped with suspension units (#64054506) with the heavier spring rate of 145 pounds, while all U.S. machines came standard with the softer 100-pound shocks (#64054164). Both hydraulic suspension units had adjustable preload settings.

The front forks on both 650 models were much the same as supplied in 1962. Changes included new fork crown castings that incorporated a pair of rubber-bushed holes for single-stemmed handlebar clamps. The rubber fork gaiters were also changed to a more muscular-looking bellows — still clamped at the bottom only, but molded in stronger, if duller-looking rubber.

Bonneville and Trophy 650 handlebars in 1963 were reduced in diameter to 7/8-inch, and shims were used in the single-stemmed P clamp mounts to allow the use a 1-inch bar if desired. American models were assembled with high-rise bars (#H1511) while home and export machines came with the lower (#H1484) handles. Control layout remained as in 1962, but the T120 twistgrip now reeled in two separate

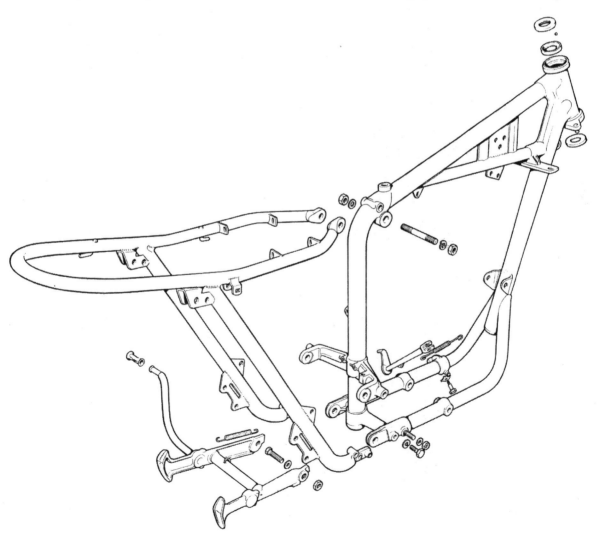

General arrangement of the new unit 650 chassis. Early serial numbers were stamped horizontally on the stirring neck, some without model prefixes.

Engine view of a restored 1963 T120C Bonneville showing details of the exhaust pipe brackets and standard skid plate. Metal straps are correctly used to secure the cables to the front down tube.
Lindsay Brooke

cables without the earlier troublemaking inline junction box. The handgrips were changed to an Amal item. These were shorter, made of plastic, and had a simple checkered pattern without the embossed Triumph logo. There were still no factory straps or ties provided to secure the cables to the handlebars, and many dealers simply taped them after assembly.

Triumph fitted Smiths chronometric instruments to its machines for the last time in 1963. U.S. models were equipped with a black-faced 140 miles per hour dial (#SC5301/23), illuminated for night riding. The matching 10,000-rpm tachometer (RC1307/01) fitted largely to U.S. roadsters was also lighted. The scramblers, as well as the standard Trophy model TR6SS, came only with a Smiths chrono speedometer. This was an illuminated 120 mile-per-hour clock, part number SC5301/03.

U.K. models T120R and TR6SS had their front wheel sizes reduced in 1963. The rim was now listed as an 18-inch WM2 and was covered

Catalog image of a 1963 U.K.-spec T120R. From its inception, the unit-construction Bonnevilles were equipped differently in each market. In Britain where motorcycles were used as serious transportation, larger fuel tanks were fitted. Contradictory to this notion, however, was the complete absence of factory-supplied air filters until the late 1960s. Other differences from American models were the low handlebars and lack of a tachometer.

by a 3.25x18 Dunlop highway rib. The drive wheel was also an 18-inch WM-3, skinned with a Dunlop highway universal. Wheels on the U.S. models remained unchanged — 3.25x19-inch (WM-2) front and 4.00x18 (WM-3) rear. Dunlop highway patterns were fitted to the roadsters and Trials Universals to the scramblers. At the front, the rims were laced to 8-inch full-width hubs with floating brake shoes. The spokes were (dull) cadmium-plated, and the hubs were no longer finished in black. At the back, a 7-inch cast-iron brake drum was screwed to the hub with eight bolts, and the entire assembly was finished in black enamel. The quickly detachable rear wheel was still listed as an option, but was available (in the U.S.) only on request.

With the new-series frames came all-new fuel tanks and mounting arrangements. The

front of the tank now rested on both sides atop a flat bracket that extended off the lower frame rail at the very front. It was fastened by shouldered screws reaching up from beneath through rubber bushings. The rear of the tank had a flanged tab that rested on the top tube just above the seat post. The frame was tapped to accept a single screw threaded down between rubber bushes, which held the rear of the tank in place. This mounting configuration proved largely fault-free and remained unchanged until the Umberslade twins appeared in 1971.

The overall shape of the new fuel tanks maintained their previous form. Capacities were again available in 3 1/2 gallon (U.S.) for American machines and 4 1/4 gallon for British and export models. "Waffled" emblems were still fitted and on the smaller sport tanks, the clip-on kneepads were retained as well as a pair of trim

This sanitized sales image of a 1963 western-U.S. TR6SR has had the tachometer cable removed. These models differed from the general export TR6SS in having twin instruments and different wheel sizes. Passenger safety straps were sometimes as slack as the one appearing here.

motifs for each side. The larger Euro-tanks were increased in the knee area and new rubber pads were molded that were wafer-thin in section but much larger in area. On these tanks, only the forward trim motifs were possible - the kneegrips were cemented in place, allowing no attachment point. Both fuel tanks incorporated recessed wells on the underside for the two Lucas ignition coils now fitted.

The 1963 Bonneville paint scheme was Alaskan-white, the fuel tanks being completely finished in this single unexciting color. The presence of a gold center stripe on the T120's white fender has led many to wonder if this color wasn't also intended for the tank in a two-tone scheme but somehow omitted by the factory. Perhaps it was due to indecision over where to divide the colored panels. This theory is bolstered by Triumph's use of identically finished fenders in 1964, which complement that season's gold-and-white two-tone tank finish.

At any rate, the fender's gold stripes were bordered in black pinstriping. On the Trophies, the striking combination of Regal-purple and

Silver was continued along with gold lining to separate the colors. Front fenders on both models were still listed as the same component (#F1294), but the new-generation frame mandated a new rear fender (#F5579) — still a steel pressing with a raised center rib. The tips of both fenders were not rolled or hemmed, allowing the painted center stripes to be carried right over the end.

The remaining cycle parts that were not plated, were dipped and oven baked in black enamel. These included the frame, engine plates, brackets, and fender braces. The oil tank and left side panel on the 650s were also painted black, but these critical surfaces were sprayed instead of immersed, to give a smoother finish.

The new frame mandated a redesigned oil tank and a matching left-side cover. Both were artistically curved to follow the contour of the twin seat. The oil tank was fastened to flanged tabs that were welded to the inside of the upper subframe — these also doubled as a fixing point for the metal battery carrier straps. The bottom of the tank screwed to the swingarm pivot casting on the frame's front section. All

Trophy TR6SS models were not officially listed for the American market, but some trickled in from Canada and others were sent directly as substitutions for unavailable TR6SRs. This unrestored example from 1963 has had a tachometer added to it somewhere along the line. Dangerous drive cable route outside of the exhaust pipe is correct. *Gene Knapp*

attachment points were rubber bushed in an attempt to isolate the tank from the shakes.

The oil filler neck and froth tower on both 650 models moved inside the frame rail and were now obscured by the dual-level seat. The latter was now hinged on the left, allowing right-side access to the tank's filler cap as well as the battery — an arrangement that was tidier and much more convenient. The twin seat's upholstery contours and dimensions still appeared identical to the earlier "duplex" and "bathtub" component, but its relocated hinge points meant a new part number.

The seat covering was still a two-tone vinyl skin, gray with black side panels. White piping was used around the upper perimeter and a gray trim strip was sewn on around the lower edge. American West Coast models were fitted with a safety grab strap.

The left enclosure was redesigned to match the oil tank and incorporated separate keyed ignition and lighting switches in its upper left corner. In this location, functional improvement was negligible from the right-hand spot used the previous season — the operator no longer had to remove his hand from the throttle, but

Drive side of Gene Knapp's unrestored 1963 TR6SS Trophy 650. Lengthy resonator silencers were standard on all unit 650s including the Bonneville. Rear fender details can also be seen. A nice genuine original! *Gene Knapp*

left-handed explorations behind the leg (now required) were still awkward, especially when in motion. This switch panel was securely fastened and was not intended to be quickly removed.

The electrical system underwent radical change in 1963, losing its magneto ignition but continuing in 6-volts. Twin Lucas MA6 ignition boosters were rubber mounted to the front frame section's lower frame rail and nestled in the aforementioned fuel tank recess. The engine's Lucas alternator was fitted with energy-transfer windings that were supposed to produce enough juice to fire the engine in case of a flat battery.

In the lighting department, a standard (non-QD) Lucas 7-inch headlamp was now fitted to all sport 650s, including the Trophies. These

were chrome-plated and incorporated a 2-inch Lucas ammeter. All switchgear was mounted back on the machine's left-hand side panel, the lighting switch placed above the keyed ignition. A new Lucas plunger-type brakelight switch was screwed to the sheet metal chain guard and was activated by brake rod travel. The Lucas 564 rear light fixture was unchanged and combined both lighting and stoplight circuits.

As on earlier Triumphs, the wiring harness was linen clad, but the exposed section of wires passing through the fork crowns to the headlight was given its own plastic sleeve. The Lucas 8H horn was moved to a lower spot in front of the battery and was screwed to a welded tab on the frame's seat post.

A partially restored 1964 U.S. T120R owned by Triumph specialist Tim Savin. A solid example of an uncommon model year. Trim motif was omitted behind the tank badge and color separation was moved to the lower tip. New beefier front forks kept earlier internals. This was the last year for the resonator mufflers in the United States. *Gaylin*

Decals and their locations on the new unit-construction models went virtually unchanged. The scripted "Bonneville 120" sticker (#A57) was placed in the center of the left-side enclosure but the oil recommendations/instruction transfers (#A40/A44) began appearing on the side of the oil tank, still at the top but in plain view. The new oil tank design allowed no room for them under the seat. The fuel tank still sported the "World Speed Record Holder" (#A56) and "Made in England" (#A61) stickers in a balanced position opposite the filler cap, but examples of these in black traded off with gold ones during the year.

The 1963 model designations also remained as before. The Bonneville models were stamped as either T120R or T120C, although early ones may have had no distinction and were marked simply with T120. Evidence suggests that some 1963 Bonnevilles left Coventry marked with engine prefixes T120SR and T120SC. But these are not special machines and are identical in every way to those not bearing the extra letter.

No 650 engine carried the T120TT prefix code until midway through 1966, and any machine bearing such an ID before then is a counterfeit.

The Trophy 650 designations were TR6SS, TR6SR, and TR6SC. The latter model was available in California as a street scrambler or a single carburetor version of the TT Special. Further details of the western U.S. Trophy Special or TR6C can be found in Chapter 7.

1964 Models

Variations between the Eastern and Western U.S. machines became so numerous by 1964 that a separate parts book supplement was issued by the factory to detail them. The differences outlined in this supplement are mainly between the western off-road racers and eastern scrambler models. The next two sections of this chapter will touch on a few of these. For a more comprehensive description, consult Chapter 7. The bulk of Bonneville and TR6 refinements for the 1964 model year were in the cycle parts. New telescopic forks had shortened external springs that surrounded the upper stanchions, rather than hiding inside them as before. The lower end of the coils sat inside an enlarged, chrome-plated cup that also served as the slider cap, while the top of the spring pressed against the lower lug casting of the fork's triple-tree. Wider rubber gaiters were designed to conceal them and these were now clamped at both top and bottom. The larger slider caps allowed a new and theoretically better double oil seal arrangement, but further design work would be needed before this happened.

As before, sheet metal headlight support arms enclosed the upper stanchions between the fork lugs. The fork still had the traditional

Rider's view of Savin's restored 1964 Bonneville. The barely visible tank top decals (#A56, A61) were changed to black for this very reason. Smiths chronometrics were replaced by magnetic versions. Notice anti-clockwise rotation of tachometer. *Gaylin*

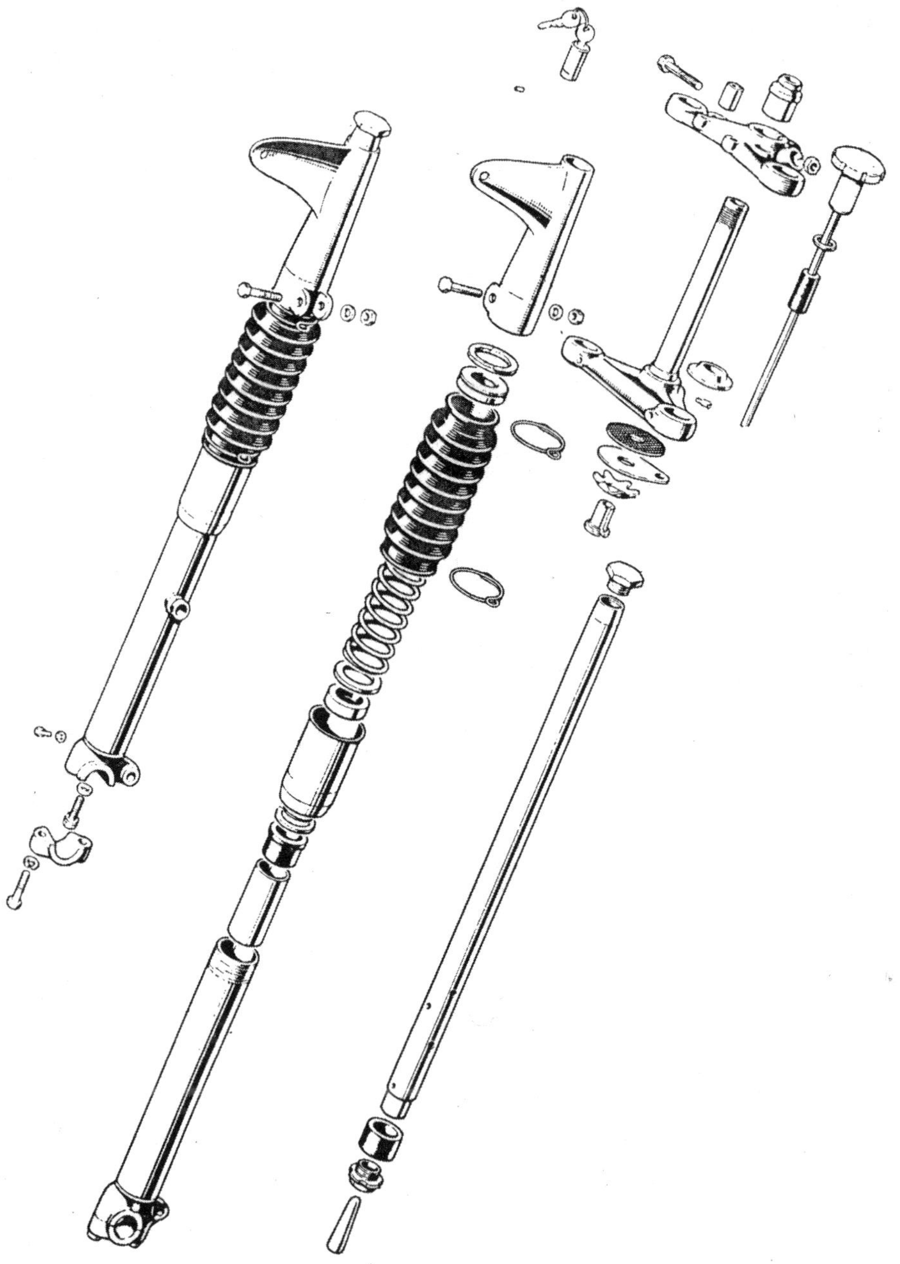

Exploded view of the
new-generation front
fork introduced during
1964.

damper knob and rod, which was now kept in check by a rubber collar inside the stem. Convention was also maintained at the bottom end of the unit, where the wheel axle was held in place by detachable caps. The sturdier new design was an improvement and its muscular look did much to enhance the sporting image of the Bonnevilles and Trophy 650s.

The front fender brace arrangement was also redesigned. A teardrop-shaped bracket fastened on an angle to the inside of the lower slider, providing an attachment point forward of the tubes for the two top stays. This design allowed wheels of varying diameters and fender heights by simply inverting the flat bracket or attaching others with differing slot angles. Triumph's official 1964 spares catalog depicts in error the earlier flat central brace that supported the guard from below. The fenders on the 1964 sport models were instead supported in the

Front clip of a restored 1964 U.S. T120R. Details of the full-width brake hub and fender stripe can clearly be seen. Hard rubber handgrips are from 1966, but were Triumph's most attractive. Inlaid paint is missing from tank emblem and lower fender brace should be the wider type that doubled as a front stand. *Gaylin*

The 1964 catalog cover.

Drive side close-up of a restored 1964
Bonneville reveals obstructed switches behind
the air filter can. Footpegs now extended from
the rear engine plates and diminutive scripted
Bonneville decal (#A57) was still specified. Float
bowl cover screws were still being safety wired
in 1964. *Gaylin*

center by a traditional tubular stay that bridged across the tubes from above in plain view. The lower fender stay continued to double as a stand and was screwed to the very bottom of the slider as before.

On top of the forks, new magnetic Smiths instruments replaced the previous chronometrics. While the scrambler models (Eastern U.S.-style T120C and TR6SC) were listed only with a speedo, 125-mile-per-hour speedometers (#SSM5001/00) and 10,000-rpm tachometers (#RSM300l/02) were standard on the road-going Bonnevilles and Trophies. The off-road Trophy and TT Specials came only with a revmeter. When a single instrument was fitted, they were fastened to a single L bracket

(#H1668) that could swing the gauge left (tach) or right (speedo) simply by flipping it over.

There were no listed modifications to the 650's frame other than the relocation of the footpegs from lugs on the lower rails to the rear engine plates. A rear brake pedal redesign was needed for this, and the routing of the brake rod was changed to the inside of the left-hand Girling suspension unit. There were, however, several improvements made to the chassis hardware, including a longer (and stronger) brazed centerstand lever. A new chain guard was fitted with deeper enclosure and the front skid plate was dropped from all but the off-road models.

The oil tank now was equipped with its own drain plug and supported from below by a curved steel pedestal. It was also rubber bushed at the point of contact with the tank. The tank's froth tower was linked via a black rubber hose with the timed crankcase breather on the end of the intake camshaft. A larger vent tube ran back from the tank on the right-hand side and was clipped to the inside of the rear fender.

Tire sizes remained unchanged, but Dunlop K70 Universals made their first appearance on the rear wheels of the T120R and TR6SR road models. These were sometimes supplanted by Avon Speed-masters on U.K. and general export machines only. When this happened, Avon ribbed tires would also be fitted as original equipment on the front wheel. The T120C and TR6SC street scramblers were still listed with Dunlop Trials Universals, but the TT Special was kitted with K70s front and back. The front tire size for this competition model was increased to 3.50x19. The 3.25-inch section tire mistakenly fitted by many restorers is easily noticed and appears anemic on the broad-shouldered Bonneville TT Special.

The dual-level seats supplied on the 1964 sport models were the same two-toned gray and black benches of the year before. But before the end of the season, seats covered completely in black vinyl began appearing on both 650 models. These were still trimmed with white piping around the upper edge and a black

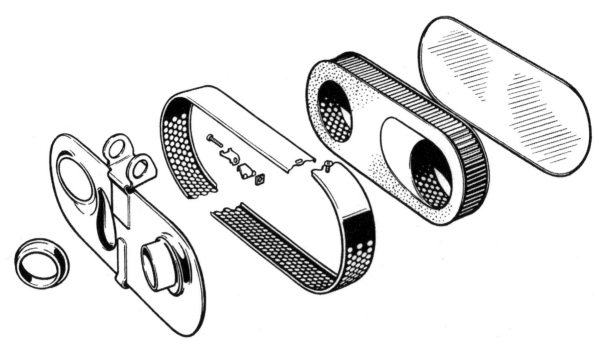

Assembly order of the Bonneville and TT unified air filter.

A beautifully restored 1965 U.S. TR6SR owned by Triumph expert Bob Sullivan. The pinstriping used to separate the colors was applied in baby-blue to distinguish tanks and fenders from the 1964 T120. Lucas horn remained unpainted until 1967. Two-tone twinseat is correct for this street model. *Gaylin*

Sullivan's restored 1965 Trophy 650 seen from another angle. Tachometer cable's harsh U-turn is tidier but was considered destructive by the factory. Handlebar choke lever and tank top transfers are missing. *Gaylin*

ribbon along the bottom. The black safety strap found on California bikes was very useful and became desired by eastern U.S. riders as well. Conversions to the western seat were sometimes made after retail delivery, but often they were shipped on new machines from the factory. The fuel tanks of all the 1964 Bonneville models, including the TT Special, were finally finished in the gold lacquer (upper) and Alaskan-white. Matching fenders were finished for the T120Rs

only. These were painted in white with a gold center stripe and pinstriped in black. Both front and rear mudguards on all the U.S. off-road and scrambler models (T120C, TR6SC, and TT Special) were now unpainted aluminum, polished to give a satin finish. The Trophy 650 color scheme was given as Flamboyant Scarlet (upper) and silver. Meriden painters first finished the entire tank in silver and then applied the red section topcoat to give a metallic glint. The TR6SR and TR6SS fenders were in silver and red to match, but with gold lining.

The line of demarcation between tank colors was also changed on 1964 machines. The dividing line at the front of the tank was still the tin strip running forward from the center of the grilled emblem. Behind the tank badge, the trim motif was omitted on all tanks including the smaller sports version. The color separation now began at the lower trailing edge of the emblem and swept rearward under the kneepad, dropping off the tank altogether before passing the rubber. Pinstriping completed the division — black on the Bonneville, gold on the Trophy.

The only decal change for the model year was to the pair found on the Bonneville tank. Made necessary by the tank's color, these remained in black all year. The "Made in England" box was a smaller version (approximately an inch in length) and had its own gold background to match the tank. The part number for this unusual transfer is unknown. Model designations and stamped engine prefixes remained the same as in 1963.

1964 Engine and Drivetrain

Engine modifications for the 1964 650 models were minimal. The crankcase was redesigned around the sump plug to allow an increase in the filter screen size. Alterations to the gearbox included a new seal around the kickstarter shaft and a few internal simplifications to speed assembly. The gearbox counter sprocket had 19 teeth on the road models and one less on the scramblers and TT Specials. And the clutch cable connection was simplified and slotted directly into the inner lever, after engine number DU66246.

On the top end of the Bonneville motor, the inlet valve was increased to 1 19/32 inch and the exhaust to 1 7/16 inch. The Amal 389 Monobloc carburetors fitted to both 650 models had their bores increased to 1 1/8 inch. Period photographs reveal that the factory was still safety-wiring the float bowl cover screws on the twin-carb models and they were still without choke assemblies. The intake stubs on the Bonneville were fitted with a balance tube and

the long single-unit air filter was now listed for all U.S. T120s. The Trophy 650 carb continued with the pancake-shaped can.

The exhaust systems on the sporting 650s also remained unchanged. The road machines were again aesthetically lumbered with the long resonator mufflers, but the T120C and TR6C models still wore a separate high-level pipe on each side with short teardrop-shaped mufflers. Elliptical, chrome-plated heat shields were provided, but again for the operator only.

1965 Models

Modifications to the engine and drivetrain were again few and subtle for the new model year. Triumph's method of timing the unit-construction motor made finding the exact position of top dead center critical. In order to remove any error, 1965 powerplants had a plugged, threaded boss in the right-hand crankcase just behind the cylinder block. When the screwed plug was removed, a small metal plunger could be threaded in which engaged a

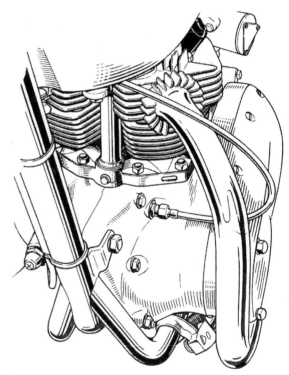

Front engine view showing vulnerable path of the tachometer cable.

Engine view of a restored 1965 U.S. TR6SR. The busy looking fuel lines are correct, but the "Trophy Sports" transfer (#D678) is from 1968. Ignition key tag and large Champion spark plug caps are very authentic. Did they ever look this nice?

notch on the flywheel when TDC was reached.

The drive side of the crankcase was not modified and earlier left-hand cases can be mated with a 1965 timing side, although this is not recommended. But any motor today bearing this plug in the right-hand crankcase and showing 1964 (or earlier) serial numbers has been fabricated.

The factory also made a change in the control of crankshaft alignment by fitting a new drive sprocket that mated directly against the face of the main bearing. Coupled with the crankshaft's shouldered journal, this allowed positive lateral location on the drive side. On the opposite end, this arrangement was reinforced by a new timing pinion that butted up to the outer face of the right-hand bearing. The aim was to halt premature primary chain wear and occasional main bearing failures.

Improvements to the 1965 transmission and clutch included a felt washer behind the gearbox sprocket as a barrier against grit. On later machines, a rudimentary internal oiler for the drive chain was provided by a small hole in the circular cover plate behind the clutch. But without any metering, more than the chain got

Triumph fitted this odd-looking taillight to U.S. models during 1965 only. A special mounting base was made to attach the Lucas 679 lamp to the standard number plate. On this restored Trophy-650 the fender tips unfinished edge is correct but the Triumph transfer (#D68) is missing from the number plate's base and stenciled trademark on the seat is premature by one model-year. *Gaylin*

This revealing peek at the battery compartment of a 1965 Trophy divulges many secrets. Oil tank breather hose is directed to the wrong side of the fender but scavenge line is correctly routed above the nose of the seat rail. Transfers are accurately positioned on the oil tank and dead-ended fender stripe is right on the money. (Restored) *Gaylin*

lubed! Soon, Triumph issued a service bulletin directing how to properly close the hole. The kickstarter received a shorter ratchet and spring, as well as a new facing washer that was hoped would keep the lever from hanging up. And the oil pressure indicator button was deleted, replaced by a simple release valve assembly that was capped by a cadmium-plated domed nut.

The cylinder head received aluminum exhaust stubs after engine number DU22682. The metal stubs had become notorious for working their way free, and it was thought that by matching the expansion properties of

the aluminum sleeve with an alloy head, the problem could be solved. But the aluminum stubs wouldn't behave either and metal versions would return the following year. The year 1965 also saw Champion spark plugs (and end caps) become original equipment on 650 models in all markets, and the factory was still safety wiring the carbs' float cover screws.

The exhaust pipes on the T120R and TR6SR were restyled with a more rearward sweep, and now incorporated a welded tab just above the bottom bend. A chrome-plated crossover strap reached between the tabs and did much to steady

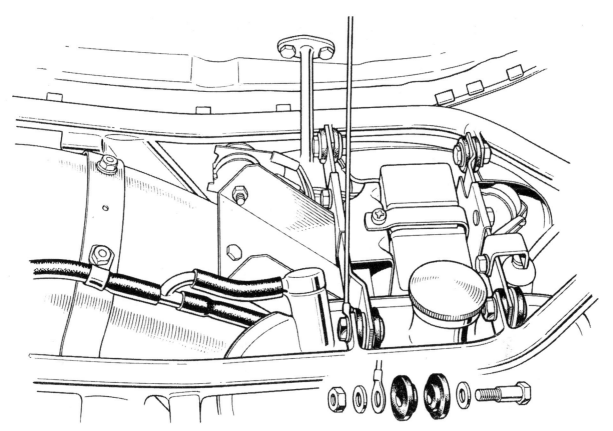

Factory drawing of the battery compartment arrangement.

the new tubes. These pipes (#E5957/58) became preferred and would fit the earlier (1963–1964) models. Although many were retrofitted, they were not introduced until 1965. The long resonator silencer continued on U.K. road models with a crossbrace at the front clamp. But the American T120R and TR6SR models received a shorter and more pleasing teardrop-shaped muffler (#E5866) with straight-through internals.

1965 Frame and Cycle Parts

The front forks were redesigned for 1965 and fitted to 650 twins beginning with engine number DU13375. These were still hydraulically damped telescopic, but with revised internals to give a more progressive response. Longer fork travel was granted because of slightly longer stanchions, sliders, and springs. Even the damper knob was beefed up at the lower end.

On the outside, the lower sliders were now extruded from a single piece of steel. Gone were

the brazed-on split lugs at the fork's base - the detachable caps were now machined. The front axle was reshaped to agree with the fork lowers, and the rubber boots covering the springs received closer pitched bellows and a cleaner appearance. As indicated, the new fork was incorporated into the range after production began, and the exploded diagram in the official parts catalog for 1965 was carried over from 1964. It does not illustrate the changes for the new season.

Both the front and rear wheels were fitted with new grease retainer rings and felt collars for grit protection. But along with the dirt, the felt rings also trapped moisture, and in the U.S. market, where a motorcycle's use was more occasional, this sponge effect promoted rust around axles and sealing rings.

Upgrades around the 650 frame included a reorientation of the swingarm pivot bolt (flipped over) to the right-hand side, where it could be

The rolling legs of a restored 1965 Trophy 650. Front view shows proper fender bracing and 3.25 x 19-inch Dunlop K70 tire. The molded rubber gaiters were also cleaned up that season. Front brake drum would soon be expanded. *Gaylin*

Rear view accurately showing no speedometer drive on the axle. 1965 was the last year for the gearbox speedo drive. The 18-inch Dunlop K70 is also correct. *Gaylin*

A 1965 T120R Bonneville in western U.S. trim. First year for the classic sport muffler, but the last for the larger sport tank and package rack (on the T120R). Pacific-blue and silver color scheme was one of the prettiest for the twin-carb model. A very desirable year. Catalog image.

An extremely rare 1965 Bonneville T120C model restored and owned by Tim Savin. There were precious few of the twin-carb street scramblers made during their last year and you will find its image in no sales catalog. One of the most sought-after Triumphs ever made! *Gaylin*

In 1965, the all-black saddles were intended for the off-road models including the T120C. The twinseat on this restored example is a reproduction. Taillight wire is correctly routed through a grommetted hole in the rear fender, but the high-level exhaust pipes are missing their chrome heat shields. *Gaylin*

Front view of Savin's 1965 C-model Bonneville. Dunlop trials tires were specified front and back but period K70 patterns make better sense for street riding. Exhaust pipe brackets are clearly seen and should be turned with the flats toward the top. *Gaylin*

withdrawn with less fuss. The kickstand angle was relaxed to allow machines to be parked parallel to streets with rising crowns. This also made for more fearful lean angles when the prop stands were used on perfectly flat surfaces. And the "flexible" cranked brake rod was straightened out and routed behind the rear subframe and engine plate. The brake pedal now pivoted in a welded collar on the engine plate, and a keyed arm tugged on the rod from behind.

In the electrical department a new, larger Lucas L679 taillight and lens was fitted but to an earlier style rear number plate. This light unit would continue on Triumphs, with various mountings, until 1974. The Lucas 8H horn was finally moved from the inaudible spot under the seat to the front of the machine where it was screwed to a bracket and hung from the lower frame rail. Here it was more effective but now an unpainted eyesore. The wiring harness was suitably modified to correspond with the hooter's new location.

Back under the seat, when the battery cradle straps were over-tightened, the rubber mountings became ineffective, allowing ruinous vibration through to the not-so-sturdy storage cell. To prevent this, metal distance collars were inserted into each mounting bolt. A final change came to the upper fork covers, which were given longer headlight support arms to allow more vertical adjustment.

Twinseats fitted to Bonnevilles and Trophy 650s were unchanged from the previous season. In fact, they were basically the same item that had begun life on Triumph's bathtub models in the late 1950s. Seat coverings for 1965 alternated between the all-black vinyl and the two-toned gray and black. The dual color saddle had been intended for the more flamboyant western United States, but given the complexities of production, faithful adherence to specific markets with respect to seat colors would have been difficult at best. This is supported by period photography which reveals both seat conditions in the eastern and western United States.

Tire sizes and patterns on all 650s also remained the same for 1965. On the road bikes, Dunlop K70 Universals were specified for the rear and ribbed treads for the front. The C model street scramblers were still skinned with Dunlop Trials Universals at both ends. These were also fitted to the off-road TR6SC Trophy Special, but the Bonneville TT Specials came with a pair of K70s. One other obscure departure from factory specs was the appearance of German-made VDO speedometers on some road-going U.S. T120C and TR6SC models. These models came standard with speedos only but matching VDO tachometers were made available.

The 1965 Bonneville fuel tank paint scheme was a rich Pacific-blue (top) and silver. The models with painted fenders had them in silver with a blue center stripe. Pinstriping on the tank

Control layout of a restored 1965 T120C. Single instrument and missing choke lever are correct. Decal placement is accurate but "Made in England" transfer should be smaller, with black lettering and a gold filled background. Handsome grips are from 1966. *Gaylin*

Drive-side engine view of the 1965 Bonneville scrambler. Horn was liberated from behind the left side panel and moved in front of the motor. Black paint wouldn't come until 1967. Fuel-line routing is accurate as is the black inlaid trademark on the primary cover and small skid plate. The only nits to pick are the unpainted center and side stand return springs. (Restored machine) *Gaylin*

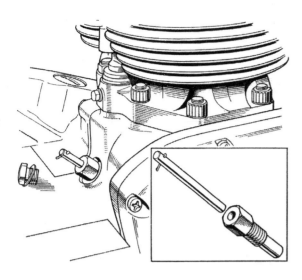

Right-hand crankcase location of the T.D.C tool in 1965.

From this perspective one can appreciate the intimate relationship between the upswept exhaust pipe and the chain case of the 1965 T120C. The air filter box made switch panel access almost impossible. A beautiful restoration by Tim Savin. *Gaylin*

and mudguards was applied in gold. The Trophy 650 tanks were in a lustrous Burnished-gold over Alaskan-white, and the mudguards finished in the complementary scheme of white with a gold stripe. To distinguish the 1965 TR6 colors from the similar T120 scheme of the year before, the pinstriping was executed in a baby blue.

The array of fenders fitted to the 650 models during 1965 is somewhat confusing. All the Bonneville and Trophy street models — or simply anything with a headlight, including the T120R, eastern-style U.S. T120C, TR6SR, and eastern-style U.S. TR6 — came with painted steel fenders. The off-road U.S. TT Specials and TR6SC Specials were equipped with polished aluminum guards, but only the first batch of 50 eastern-U.S. TT Specials came this way. Afterwards they were shipped with painted alloy (front) and steel (rear) fenders. The TR6SC Trophy Special was not generally available in the eastern United States, but any of this model would have been fitted with the polished alloy guards.

Decals and their locations remained relatively unchanged for 1965, although the

TR6 transfers, like the T120 the year before, were in black to contrast their gold background. The black-and-gold "Made in England" box continued on the Bonneville as well as the Trophy, but the gold background looked out of place on the deep blue T120 tank and didn't quite match the top color on the TR6s. And the Bonneville's "World's Speed Record" transfer was switched back to gold. Model designations and engine prefixes are believed to have remained the same.

Chapter Six

Unit Construction Twins (1966–1970)

Beginning in 1966, the Triumph factory began to concentrate its output on the U.S. market. This is reflected in the official spare parts manual for that year which gave U.S. models precedence and now used American terms such as gas tank (petrol tank) and fenders (mudguards). It was at this time that the slimline fuel tanks, wide handlebars, and cowboy color schemes were introduced.

Many consider 1966–1970 to be Triumph's zenith years. For this reason and because of the machines' similarities in style, they are grouped together in a single chapter. But even limiting focus to the 650 twins, space does not permit a description of all the modifications introduced during this five model year period. Instead the chapter will examine only the more important and visible features that restorers will find essential. For a more thorough listing of factory changes, please consult the Appendix.

The 1966 model year was a major one of changes and upgrades for the Bonneville and Trophy 650, many being introduced during the course of the season. It can be safely said that no group of T120s or TR6s leaving the factory that year were the same as any other.

Beginning with the powerplant, the crank-shaft was trimmed by more than 2 1/2 pounds but still retained an 85 percent balance factor. The lighter flywheel naturally improved throttle response to the delight of wheelstand junkies everywhere. The crankshaft bearing and sprocket sequence were altered again to give positive location on the timing side and, for the first time, a beautiful roller bearing on the drive side.

Lessons learned at the race track showed how to squeeze out more ponies by installing sport cams (#E4819 intake, #E4855 exhaust), racing type R tappets (#E3059R intake, #E6490 exhaust), and shorter valve springs and cups. The new bits, installed in both 650cc models, allowed longer valve openings and much more torque. And with the addition of higher-compression 9:1 pistons (#CP206) and eventual 1 3/16-bore carburetors, the Bonneville was transformed into a 53-horsepower firebreather. But the downside to all this development was the inevitable by-product: increased vibration.

To lessen cam and tappet wear, the timing-side case was given drilled passages that delivered a pressurized supply of oil to these components. The new plumbing included a modified timing cover and a hollowed dowel in the cylinder-to-crankcase joint. This arrangement routed the lubricant internally to the exhaust tappets and guides, themselves modified to pass the oil. Additional plumbing, beginning with engine number DU27893, came in the form of another hollow dowel for a back-up supply.

Other engine mods included chrome-plated "C" range (500cc-type) pushrod enclosures (#E3547) with straight tubes and flanged ends. These nestled in new silicone rubber rings top and bottom, a setup that the factory hoped would provide a better oil seal. Revisions in the primary case included a wider chain tensioner blade and trunnion arrangement at serial number DU22590. A larger pressure adjustment screw was used on the clutch rod at engine number DU31168, and the hidden drive

chain oil hole remained in place until number DU27893, when it was replaced by a metered feed from the oil reservoir.

The gearbox lost its speedometer drive gearing and takeoff within the inner cover. The drive (D373) was now relocated alongside a modified rear wheel hub where it would be unaffected by ratio changes and easier to service. A longer speedo cable was also specified. The tachometer drive was still driven from the exhaust camshaft, but a new right-angle reduction drive unit (#E5756) was fitted on the crankcase where the cable had threaded in previously. The new arrangement cut the revolutions in half, making the final ratio at the magnetic tach 4:1. The new tach drive also

A faithfully restored 1966 U.S. Bonneville with new slimline fuel tank and "large eyebrow" emblems. Chrome exhaust pipe brace reached across in front of the motor to grab the left-side tube. These would be replaced by L-brackets to the crankcase in 1967. Scripted "Made in England" transfer on front downtube is five years premature. This beautiful example is owned by long-time Triumph dealer Bob Worden. *Gaylin*

Drive side of Worden's T120R. 1966 was the last year for the old-style two-tone seat and carburetor screws were no longer safety wired on U.S. bikes. New tachometer drive box (seen just above primary cover) reversed the cable's direction and cut rpm in half. It also permitted a straight path to the instrument head. (Restored) *Gaylin*

allowed a more civilized cable routing, straight up the front frame tube to which it was secured with metal straps. One final transmission change of note was the lengthening of the kickstarter lever at engine number DU25497. This helped with the T120's increased compression, though it was fitted to all 650 models.

The Bonneville started the year with 1 1/8-inch bore Monobloc carburetors, but at engine number DU29738, these were replaced by thirstier 1 3/16-inch instruments. The flanged intake stubs were still balanced with a crossover tube, but the float cover screws were set flush and no longer safety wired. The throat measurement of the single mixer fitted to the Trophy 650s remained at 1 1/8 inch.

Exhaust pipe and muffler specifications remained relatively untouched. The long

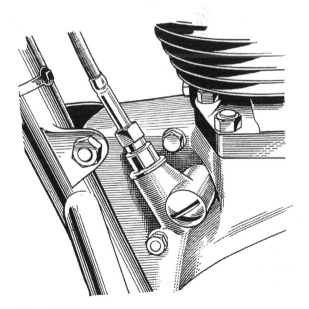

The 1966 Tachometer drive arrangement.

resonator silencers fitted to the U.K. road machines could be swapped with the shorter and louder American (#E5866) straight-through units. The screwed-in alloy exhaust ports reverted back to steel at engine number DU39464. And for the first time, western U.S. TR6C models were equipped from the factory with high-level pipes, both exiting on the left side. These were without mufflers and found only on the western off-road models. The eastern-style U.S. TR6C street scrambler still came with separate upswept tubes, one on each side, and wore mufflers for street use. Exhaust systems on the other 650cc models remained as in 1965.

Rider's view of a restored 1966 U.S.-spec Bonnie. Correct gray-faced magnetic instruments both with clock-wise direction. Stripe widths on the tank are accurate but "Made in England" decal should be joined above by the "World Record Holder" (#A56) and both moved closer to the center. Kill button is also missing from the handlebars. *Gaylin*

1966 Frame and Cycle Parts

A major change to the frame was made in the steering head. It was found that at very high speeds (90 miles per hour or more), the 65-degree head angle could cause dangerous oscillations. The angle was thus reduced to 62 degrees, by fitting a new cast-iron head lug. However, this feature wasn't implemented until engine number DU25277, and some early 1966 650s were assembled with the older chassis.

The new frame is easily identified by the appearance of small horizontal bosses on the front of the steering neck that were offered as attachment points for police and touring fairings. Other features at the steering head included the continuation of the sturdier upper fork lug (#H1287) for the TR6C and TT models, that incorporated a solid clamping boss for the handlebars. The top lug also remained the same for the road bikes, but a plastic damper sleeve was substituted for the alloy spacer at engine number DU31119 on all models. Steering lock was increased at engine number DU27672, when a new bottom fork lug was made to capitalize on the slimmer fuel tanks now fitted.

At the back of the frame, the swingarm was moved out slightly on the right side to allow the use of wider section tires. The slotted Smiths speedometer drive and the non-QD rear brake drum now came with a bolt-on, 46-tooth sprocket to facilitate ratio changes. The front braking surface was increased by almost 50 percent by widening the drum. This was accomplished by moving the right-side spokes out onto a raised flange. This design change allowed a wider brake shoe and actually strengthened the wheel.

Tire sizes and tread patterns were unchanged for 1966 except for an optional 4.00x18-inch Dunlop monster "knobby" for the rear of the TR6C models.

The transition to 12-volt electrics and other improvements brought about a great deal of change in the Bonneville and Trophy 650 midsection. The battery cradle was increased in size initially to hold two linked 6-volt cells.

Up close and personal with a 650 twin! This view of Bob Worden's restored T120R shows correct routing of the fuel lines. Separate pancake-type air filters made their appearance on later 1966 Bonnevilles allowing better access to the lighting and ignition switches. Lonely "Bonneville 120" transfer continued through 1967. *Gaylin*

This lasted until engine number DU34174, when a single Lucas 12-volt battery was used and the carrier modified again. A larger (but still too small) tool tray molded in gray plastic was fitted in behind the power cell. When subjected to constant engine heat, particularly in warm weather, these trays would warp under the weight of the tools.

The battery carrier support straps at the top were changed on the left and rolled into sleeves that fitted over protruding pegs on the upper subframe. These also received the necessary rubber bushings. From the bottom of these sleeves dropped two threaded studs that held the left side panel in place. On the T120R and the TR6R road models the panel still housed

two separate switches in the upper left corner, but the ignition switch was now a cylinder type with a "real" key and not the stamped metal joke of before. A Zender diode was used to divert the surplus juice going to the battery and was mounted on a separate plate that hid behind the left panel.

The off-road models and TR6C scramblers now came with a plain enclosure (#F6962) without switch provisions. No battery was specified for their AC ignition.

Electrical improvements were not confined to the battery compartment. At engine number DU31565, a new 700-series Lucas headlamp (#59655A) incorporated an ignition and high beam warning lamp, one on each side of the ammeter. But the red (ignition) and greed (high beam) lights were so far down on the shell as to be completely obstructed by the instruments and were utterly useless. On the eastern U.S. TR6C models, a smaller Lucas MCH66 headlight

New polished aluminum housing was introduced in 1966 for the Lucas 679 taillight. Notch in the casting allowed it to mount over the support rail. License plate obscures stainless steel fender tip which had a bare edge and was unfinished. 1966 was also the first model-year for the stenciled Triumph trademark on the twinseat's posterior. (Restored) *Gaylin*

(#58395) was fitted for the first time. The shells of these were painted black and housed the ignition and lighting switch relocated from the side panel.

In the United Kingdom, a Lucas 564 rear lamp still sat atop a large black number board, but the American models were treated to a new cast housing in polished aluminum for the L679 light that straddled the rear fender support. U.S. registration plates were now fastened to a single flat metal strap that screwed to the fender below the lamp.

A mammoth kill switch (#35601) was now specified and clamped to the handlebars on the right side. The button was housed in an imposing chrome plated tower that seemed to suggest the machine would be uncontrollable without it! On the road models with battery ignition, the button was brown and differed in its operation from the black kill buttons (#31071) used on the AC-ignited TT Specials and TR6Cs. (For restorers, the switch with the brown push button will function on all models, but black button components will not kill the engine on battery-ignition bikes.)

The standard combination dipper switch/horn button (#31563) was screwed to the bars over a rubber pad on the left side, on all but the TR6C, which used a headlight with only a single bulb. These models came only with the simpler clamped-on horn button.

Any discussion of 1966 Triumph 650 handlebars must include the Amal hard rubber handgrips (#366-011/2) introduced for that model year. These were fluted and slightly belled, and when compared to the black grips of previous years, were often referred to as being white. But even when brand new, the 1966 grips were actually a light gray. They were not liked by dealers or owners because they were easily smudged. Factory correspondence shows that only the early batches of 1966 machines left Coventry fitted with gray grips. Afterward, identical versions in black were fitted with no change in the part number. Restorers of 1966 machines with later engine numbers often incorrectly fit the gray examples, or agonize unnecessarily when they can't find them.

Elsewhere on the frame, the oil tank was redesigned and its capacity increased to 3 quarts.

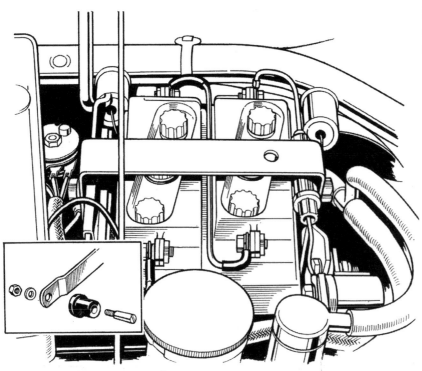

Early 1966 under-seat arrangement with two 6-volt batteries.

The Dunlop ribbed front tires were still standard on 1966 road bikes. The one on this restored bike looks new-old-stock. To increase brake surface the wheel hub was given a raised flange to relocate the right-side spokes. *Gaylin*

Front and rear stainless fenders were specified for the 1966 U.S. Bonnevilles, but not for the TT Specials until the following year! Restorers often pay little attention to fender bracing and often get it wrong. An intimate tire and fender relationship like the one seen here signals the correct items. *Gaylin*

Machines after engine number DU27893 were fitted with tanks equipped with a metering screw in their filler neck that controlled oil flow to the drive chain. Other significant frame changes were peculiar only to the American TR6C and TT models, such as folding footrest, skid plates fitted as standard, and the total omission of the centerstand. These items could still be ordered for the Trophies, but the tucked-in exhaust pipe path on the TT Specials denied their use. And VDO instruments were still being used on some U.S. scramblers and off-road models.

For 1966 there were new fuel tank shapes for all markets. The U.K. T120R and TR6R tanks (#F7004) retained their larger capacity of 4 1/4 (U.S.) gallons, package racks, and cemented kneegrips. However, the big news came in the American tanks that were offered in two forms. The TR6R container (#F7003) was still 3 1/2 (U.S.) gallons and fitted with the chromed tank top package rack. And the kneepads were no longer fitted over a separate metal plate but were glued on, as per U.K. specs.

The Bonneville and TR6C tanks (#F6728) were radically resculpted into a very pleasing teardrop form that tapered off dramatically at the rear. There is no place for function in the universe of art, and the capacity of these small tanks was reduced to a meager 2 1/2 (U.S.) gallons. The parcel grid was finally removed, but the kneepads were still thought necessary and were also glued in place. The new "slimline" tank,

The 1966 American TR6R as pictured in the Johnson Motors catalog. Larger tank still with parcel rack, in blue-and-white finish. The center stripe on the painted front fender can just be seen. Smudge-prone gray hand grips were not liked and usually switched for the black versions as soon as they became available. West Coast safety strap doesn't appear to be fastened.

as it was known, failed in every duty except one: No other single feature sold more Triumphs in the United States than that sensuous fuel tank.

The 1966 Triumphs wore a redesigned tank emblem. The new diecast badge was much cleaner and more contemporary than the busy-looking "harmonica" emblem of 1957–65. Again, it emphasized the Triumph "sweeping-R" trademark. The logo was filled in black with a raised chrome outline and set on a white background. Above the trademark a large chromed "eyebrow" swept forward to join a short horizontally ribbed wing. Even today, the "large eyebrow" slimline tanks from 1966 to 1968 seem to exude subliminal signals that would have gotten Triumph dealers burned at the stake during another time!

The graphics and two-tone color demarcations on the larger TR6 and Euro-tanks were basically the same as 1965. The forward line of color separation went straight forward from the tip of the eyebrow to the container's edge. The rear borderline swept back from the lower rear corner of the emblem, falling off

the tank completely, below the rubber knee-pad. The boundaries were again defined by gold pinstriping.

The U.K. Bonneville tanks were finished on top in yet another shade of orange, dubbed Grenadier-red (Dupont #4602H), which contrasted with an Alaskan-white bottom scallop. The upper tank color on the Trophy 650s was a medium shade called Pacific-blue, also with white for the bottom. Painted steel mudguards were specified for the U.K. 650s and the U.S. TR6R. These were in white with either a red or blue center stripe, lined in dark gold. Home market bikes were still equipped with front number plates painted in black that skipped over the forward stay. The remainder of the machine's cycle parts were either finished in black enamel or chrome-plated.

The U.S. slimline tanks fitted to the Bonneville and TR6C models were painted in a solid color and a contrasting three-part racing stripe applied directly up the center. On the T120, the main color was Alaskan-white with Grenadier-red stripes, while the TR6 tank was a solid Pacific-blue with white stripes. The stripes in both paint schemes were bordered in dark gold lines, and a chrome-plated styling strip was used to cover the centrally welded tank seam.

Front and rear fenders on these models were polished stainless steel with rolled edges only on the flanks. The black enameled stays at the front provided a satisfying no-nonsense look. On the U.S. models, the lower brace that had doubled as a front stand was now changed to a simpler fender support.

The hinged twinseat used on the 1966 models was basically the same affair as before and still used a version of the bathtub base pan. But it was given a new part number because of a new cover and padding that kicked up slightly at the rear to show off the new gold Triumph logo stenciled on the back panel. The front of the seat was also altered to integrate it with the new tank profiles. Safety straps were specified for western U.S. machines but were widely seen on eastern U.S. seats as well.

The two-toned (gray top, black sides) saddles were intended for the road bikes and the all-black upholstery was specified for the off-road and TR6C scramblers. But adherence to this scheme wasn't religious and there were some black-seated 1966 Bonnevilles, two-toned TT Specials, and other variants. There were no new transfers introduced for 1966. The small scripted "Bonneville 120" decal was still fixed to the center of the left-hand sidecover. Tank top stickers were placed opposite the filler cap. These were still in black, to contrast against the white background. And the new oil tank allowed room for the lube recommendation transfers to be moved back under the seat, out of sight.

The letter "S" was officially dropped from Trophy 650 designations, although some early machines leaving the factory still showed it. The sport models were now identified as T120R, TR6R, and TR6C. The T120C prefix stamped on the motors of TT Specials was replaced by T120TT after an initial run of machines with the earlier designation. The street scrambler version of the Bonneville was discontinued altogether. In the eastern U.S., TR6Cs were road-going street scramblers with lighting, mufflers, passenger pegs, and so on. The western TR6C was a desert animal with no road provisions, but engine number prefixes did not differentiate. More on this model can be found in Chapter 7.

1967 Models

Drivetrain modifications were not as numerous as those made to the cycle parts in 1967, but they were no less important. Triumph, until then, had forged and machined their own pistons, but at engine number DU44394, the tradition came to an end when Hepolite pistons were specified as original equipment. These were followed by beefier con-rods at number DU47006.

The intake camshaft was changed again to the Q racing-type E3134 item (same as exhaust) and copper-plated. The 3/4-inch R tappets were kept, but another revision was made in the oil supply to the exhaust cam and followers. This was a new metering plug in the forward timing cover dowel which contained a wire screen filter and a trembler pin in the metering jet. But all this was scrapped at engine DU63043, when timed tappets were fitted that opened to oilways in the tappet block. Shortly after, at number DU63241, rubber O-rings were fitted at the base of the tappet blocks. Restorers should be aware that if newer (#E8801) exhaust tappets are fitted to engines prior to #DU63043, the metering plug must be removed and replaced by the hollow T989 dowel. The oil pump was also modified with a larger scavenge side plunger.

The Trophy 650 cylinder heads were treated to Bonneville-spec valve diameters, 1 7/16-inch exhaust and 1 19/32-inch intake, and the compression was raised to 9:1. And with the bore on the single Amal Monobloc carb opened to 1 3/16 inch, the TR6 engine specifications became identical to the T120s in all but the single carb and inlet tract. The U.S. Bonnevilles adopted the Trophy-style circular air cleaners and pleated filters, while U.K. T120s came standard with only the bell rings at the carb mouths.

An award winning 1967 U.S. TR6R owned and ridden by Bill Ferriell. This example has been restored but still has its original twinseat. Dunlop tires have been replaced by modern K81 equivalents but fenders are correct in solid green, without a center stripe. The 1967 & 68 TR6R models are thought by many to be the best "riding" Triumphs ever made. *Gaylin*

The 650s started the production run with 389 Monobloc carburetors and main jets increased to 240. But at engine number DU59320, Amal's new Concentric carbs made their appearance. As the name implied, the new 30 millimeter instrument had a narrower body with centrally mounted float bowl. The design promoted even carburetion at any lean angle and allowed adjustment from either side. High-tensile studs and self-locking nuts were used to hold the carbs to their respective adaptors. With the change to the new Concentrics, the Bonneville finally received choke slides and the accompanying lever on the front brake lever base.

Nineteen sixty-seven was the year that Triumph began changing fasteners from British Standard and CEI threads to the Unified thread form being adopted on both side of the Atlantic (see chart next page). The transmission was one of the first areas of the machine converted, and at the engine number DU48114, it was fitted with a longer mainshaft that allowed a self-locking nut and plain washer on the clutch hub. This arrangement replaced the earlier tabbed washer which sometimes freed itself from captivity while spinning. Shortly after, at number DU48145, the entire gearbox was switched to Unified threads.

There were also a few revisions to the 1967 exhaust systems. The resonators still came standard on the U.K. 650s, but smaller sport mufflers were becoming a popular switch. The stays on the front down pipes on the road bikes were changed to two separate chromed L brackets that fastened to the nose of the crankcase. And the eastern U.S. TR6C models were now fitted with two upswept pipes, stacked in staggered fashion on the left-hand side. Small teardrop-shaped sport mufflers with offset inlet ports were hung on the end. The operator was protected by a pair of moveable chromed elliptical heat shields that clamped over the pipes. The new arrangement was much more stylish than the earlier separated system and did much to revive the model's appeal.

The 1967 U.S. Trophy 650 in Mist-green and white. There seem to be as many versions of the green as there are TR6s. The large rubber kneegrips were borrowed from U.K. models in 1966. (Restored) *Gaylin*

Threads Per Inch

Size	Cycle Engineers Institute (CEI)	Unified Fine (UNF)	Unified Coarse (UNC)	British Standard Fine (BSF)	British Standard Coarse (BSW) Whitworth
1/4 inch	26	28	20	26	20
5/16 inch	26	24	18	22	18
3/8 inch	26	24	16	20	16
7/16 inch	26	20	14	18	14
1/2 inch	20	20	13	16	12
9/16 inch	20	18	12	16	12
5/8 inch	20	18	11	14	11

1967 Frame and Cycle Parts

Another area of the 1967 machines gaining the new fasteners was the rear frame section. Other modifications included a new brake torque stay and rear brake adjuster nut. At engine number DU53772, the take-off below the oil tank was reintroduced to send lubrication to the rocker spindles.

On the front of the 1967 Bonnevilles and TR6Rs there was a new upper fork lug incorporating a proper cylinder-type security lock. The bolt was received by a drilled lobe hanging off the upper head stock and only the key was removable. The fork stops on the lower end of the steering head were now threaded pins and could be removed. The strap clamps at the ends of the rubber fork gaiters were replaced with tensioned, black-painted wire clips.

Handlebar detail changes included the debut of fat, squishy plastic Gran Turisimo grips. Clutch and brake levers fitted to the U.S. models were still the ball-ended type, while the home market bikes continued with plain blades. Models with choke assemblies, including Bonnevilles after engine number DU59320, still had the control lever piggy-back mounted on the base of the right brake lever. And photographic evidence confirms that some U.S. dealers were placing the kill button on the left-

Another wheel close-up, this time from a restored 1967 TR6R. Rubber gaiters were given less noticeable wire clips, otherwise the same front end as 1966. *Gaylin*

Twinseats fitted during the 1966 model-year were the first to be stenciled with the Triumph logo. Left photo shows the simplified design used from 1966 to early-1969 (1969 shown). After production began in 1969, the more detailed, bordered trademark (right photo) was applied and continued until 1983, always in gold and 5-1/2 inches in width. Both seats pictured on this page are original factory items and NOT reproductions! *Gaylin*

Drive side of the 1967 American TR6C. Lovely high-level exhaust system is shown without heat shields in this sanitized factory photo. Upper edge seat piping appears white, but trim on all the solid color benches was done in black. A very desirable model!

Offside of a restored 1967 U.S. TR6C. Self-positioning rubber fork gaiters are premature. Most C-model headlight buckets were chrome-plated and K70 tire option wasn't available until the following year.
Lindsay Brooke

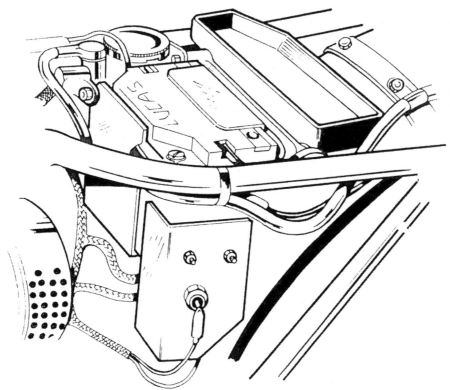

A 1967 electrical compartment showing Zener diode location, Lucas PUZ5A battery, and cross-frame tool tray.

hand bar when assembling the machines from the crate. The 650s were also treated to new Smiths 150-mile-per-hour (#SSM5001/06) speedometers.

Wheel sizes and tire sections remained mostly the same from 1967. The British market Bonneville saw its front wheel change from 3.25x18 inches to 3.00x19, while the TR6R there stayed with the smaller size. The quick-detachable rear wheel remained a popular option in the home market where motorcycles were used as transportation and tire punctures more common. In America, the QD wheel was thought an unnecessary feature and was only available by special order. However, the Dunlop 4.00x18-inch knobby rear tire was considered a more valid option, especially on the western U.S. off-road models.

There were also a few electrical tweaks given to the 650 twins for the new season. At engine number DU58565, new encapsulated alternator stator windings were specified for all models. The three-position lighting switch found on the Bonneville and TR6R was moved from

the side panel and to the back of the chromed headlight shell below the ammeter. The twist switch, as well as the warning lamps, were thoroughly obstructed by the instruments and their use could have been made easier. Without the lighting switch, the left side panel now had only a single opening for the keyed ignition. The front brace of the panel was also welded in place rather than being fixed with screws.

The Lucas horn was replaced with a louder unit and painted black but remained unchanged on the U.S. Trophy sport model. The smaller headlight bucket fitted to the TR6C was now chrome-plated and the AC ignition still meant no battery. Both U.K. 650cc models still wore the large rear number board and Lucas 564 taillamp, while U.S. twins boasted the handsome polished cast-aluminum housing and L679 taillight.

To say that the 1967 fuel tanks underwent a color change would be an understatement. Beginning with the home market Bonneville, the paint was Aubergine (a regal shade of purple) applied over Alaskan-white with gold pinstriping. The Trophy 650 in all markets was finished

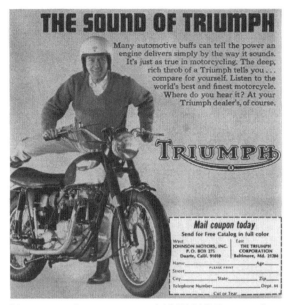

Magazine advertisement of 1967 U.S. Bonneville with late condition tank décor in Aubergine and white.

in Mist-green over Alaskan-white. Fenders on both U.K. models and the U.S. TR6R were painted steel.

British market T120 mudguards were white, with a purple center stripe lined in gold, but the green fenders on all TR6 models were solid, not striped. This might have had something to do with the mismatched fenders being used — the front guard (#F1677) had a bare unfinished tip as before, but the rear fender (#F6965) fitted to U.S. TR6R models and some U.K Trophies now had a rolled edge at the end.

The lower white accent on the fuel tank wasn't flashy enough for U.S. Bonnevilles and was painted at first a bright gold instead — the boundary defined in white handlining. The new graphics emanating from the top of the Triumph emblem were at first identical on both American and British road models. At the front tip of the badge, the main color curled up and back on each side to meet on top of the tank, forming a V just beside the filler cap. The lower edge of the colored flash started at the top rear corner of the emblem and traced the upper contour of the kneepad, until curling completely under its back corner and falling off the tank above the carburetors. Yet another variation saw the top color fall away from the kneepad at the rear corner, ending under the nose of the seat.

The TR6C and TT Special fuel tanks were accented in the manner found on the 1966

This retouched image of a 1967 U.S.-spec Bonneville with early two-toned twinseat and gold fuel tank with Aubergine (purple) upper accent. Most American models came with all-black saddles that year.

No matter how it appears in this advertising rendition, 1967 U.K. Bonnevilles were finished in Aubergine and white, with gold lining. White fenders were given a purple center stripe bordered in gold. Two-tone saddle was more common on British models. Note the resonator mufflers and unprotected carburetors.

TR6R, with the lower color sweeping down from the ends of the tank emblems and the back edge curling underneath the kneegrips. Their fenders, as well as those fitted to the U.S. Bonnevilles, were polished stainless steel. When it was discovered that the gold paint was bleaching out before the bikes even left U.S. showrooms, the paintwork on the slimline T120R tanks was changed to the more protective layout found on the competition models. Finally at engine number DU48157, the gold paint was replaced altogether with Alaskan-white. This made a total of three different paint schemes for the American T120R, all in a single season!

Two things should be pointed out here. First, Triumph's paint shop normally used the secondary accent as a base color, with the main finish being applied afterward (over top). In the Bonneville's case, this meant that when the change was made from gold to white, the Aubergine became a lighter shade of purple and lost much of its original metallic shimmer. Secondly, all these changes in the U.S. Bonneville's paint came early enough in the season to see most T120s finished

in Aubergine and Alaskan-white. Restorers seeking authenticity should check their engine numbers prior to refinishing any tank.

All fuel tank sizes and capacities remained the same in all markets. The mounting studs were eventually converted to UNF threads and self-locking nuts. The old chromed package rack was still fitted to all but the U.S. slimline forms, and all tanks came with glue-on rubber kneegrips.

The tank transfers returned to gold on all models and the "Made in England" box reverted to the larger 2-inch version. The diminutive "Bonneville 120" (#A57) scripted in gold, continued on the left side panel for its last season, and there is no evidence to support that any other design was used during the year.

After seven years, the twinseat form that began on Triumph's bathtub models was retired on the 650cc range. The new 1967 saddle was more modern in appearance and seemed a perfect mate to the sculptured fuel tanks. The top panel now had a cross-ribbed, pleated pattern that was designed to keep the rider from sliding back and forth under hard acceleration, braking, and wheelies. The twinseat was tapered and narrower at the nose and was given a subtle hump halfway back to separate the seating areas. At the rear there was a small bump stop which also served as a billboard for the Triumph trademark stenciled in gold. A safety strap was still a part of the seat design for the western United States and anyone else who sought its utility.

As before, the seat was at first offered in two versions. The saddle (#F7776) intended for the T120R and TR6R models was given a light gray panel at the top and flanked all around by black. These were then trimmed in white piping around the top edge and a gray strip around the bottom. A second version (#F7482), assigned to the competition and off-road models, was upholstered completely in no-nonsense black. But from the beginning, black saddles were

dispersed to all models during 1967 production, and by the end of the year the rather gay two-toned form was completely displaced (in America).

Model designations and engine prefixes remained the same for 1967. The street version of the TR6C was officially discontinued in the western United States. A memo sent to U.S. dealers on June 19, 1967, included the sad news that the Bonneville TT Special would no longer be produced. The approximately 1,100 examples offered in 1967 were the last.

1968 Models

In 1968, the Triumph Bonneville and TR6 Trophy models reached what many consider to be the pinnacle of their development. The 650cc vertical twin engine had been poked and prodded to yield as much horsepower as it ever would, and the running gear, which was the real

With the introduction of the twin-leading shoe front brake and Amal Concentric bowl carburetors, many consider 1968 to be the best year for the Bonneville. The only detectable flaw in this otherwise perfect Rob Frick restoration are the later condition float bowl drain plugs (sorry Rob!). Early TLS brake had some teething problems. *Gaylin*

Drive side of Frick's 1968 T120R. Twinseat is not a reproduction or recovered — there's no mistaking an original! Saddles fitted later in the year came with a chrome grab rail at the back. Gimmicky front wheel cover was not liked. *Gaylin*

story for that year, was finally able to handle the challenge.

Motor changes for the new season were many. At engine number DU79975, new design Hepolite pistons were fitted. These had a modified crown and more material added behind the ring grooves. New outer valve springs were specified that allowed a higher lift but retained original valve loadings when fully closed. And at engine number DU79965, the rocker arms were strengthened simply by leaving them undrilled — reserving more oil for the exhaust cams which still didn't have enough!

Moving down the unit engine, 12-point cylinder base nuts became standard at number DU75452, finally allowing a proper amount of clearance for a wrench. On the crankcase just below the cylinder, the TDC access hole disappeared at engine number DU66246. Meriden had been stroboscopically timing the 650cc engines at the factory for a couple of years,

but now used the position of 38 degrees BTDC directly. The flywheel location on these motors (from DU66246) was taken from the block under the front engine mount and was fitted with the necessary access plug. These machines were shipped from the factory with a special yellow sticker on the points cover declaring the factory "strobe job."

When Triumph realized the new location was better for draining crankcase oil than locating a flywheel position, the original timing socket reappeared behind the cylinder. The first batch of machines after the change had both positions in the case, as well as two matching notches in the flywheel. But after engine number DU74052, the front access was eliminated, leaving only the plug position behind the cylinder. The flywheel retained both notches (at TDC and 38 degrees BTDC), meaning three different 650 crankcase and flywheel conditions for the 1968 model year.

Bonneville

Stylish Bonneville decal used only during 1968.

This view of a restored 1968 Bonneville shows the correct width of the silver tank stripe. Scripted "Bonneville" decal is accurately applied diagonally, opposite the filler cap, and completely out on the Hi-Fi Scarlet finish. This transfer was also applied horizontally to the toolbox cover. Quilted top seat panel was not aerated until the following model year. *Gaylin*

This close-up shows one of two different cleaning instruction stickers used on air filter covers from 1967 to 1970. Oil tank transfers and proper hose clamps at the bottom can also be seen. This photo could have been taken in 1968. (Restored) *Gaylin*

Stroboscopic timing was facilitated by a detachable circular inspection plate on the primary cover, directly over the alternator. This was fastened by three screws and carried an integral Triumph trademark inlaid with black paint. When a special timing ring (D1825) was substituted for the cover plate, a strobe light could be used to synchronize the timing mark on the rotor with the appropriate line on the ring while the engine was running. The new method of verifying BTDC obsoleted the old timing disc (if one could acquire an ignition strobe light). For those that could not, the primary cover was further modified with its own BTDC static pointer at engine number DU83021.

Engine timing was also made easier by mounting the Lucas 6CA contact breakers on separate adjustable plates, allowing independent positioning and timing of each cylinder. To permit this, the condensers had to be moved and were located beneath the fuel tank's front mounting bracket. But even without the condensers, the redesigned points assembly required a deeper chamber, necessitating a new timing cover. All the breaker assembly screws had Unified threads, and at engine number DU82146, felt lubrication wicks were added to reduce wear on the nylon heels.

There were numerous gearbox revisions for 1968 as well. A new mainshaft with Unified threads was fitted to permit a better sealing arrangement at the primary inner wall. The oil retainer seal now bore directly against the shaft itself, rather than a bushing. A new gearbox camplate plunger and holder made smoother shifts, and the outer cover got a flushed screw-in filler plug. The shifter rubber became a plain bulb without the molded Triumph logo. Mods to the kickstarter included Unified threads for the mainshaft nut and washer, and the familiar open-ended type foot rubber.

The 30 millimeter Amal Concentric carburetors underwent a few minor internal changes during the year to prevent slide sticking and low speed coughing. There was still a cross-over tube between the intake stubs on the Bonneville. The air filter cans on the T120s were given threaded flanges that allowed them to screw directly to the mouth of the mixing chamber, while the Trophy models continued with the earlier split flange and clamp arrangement. Incredibly, the filters were still optional on the home market bikes.

Exhaust pipe and muffler alterations were minimal for 1968. The U.S. sport mufflers required a redesign at engine number DU75452 to prevent baffle detachments, and after serial number DU82574 the TR6C model's twin upswept pipes were coupled with an H fitting just ahead of the silencers. And in the United Kingdom, where it was considered cooler not to boast your speed, the effective resonators were still standard on both 650 models.

1968 Frame and Cycle Parts

Of all the improvements announced for 1968, the really big news was the twin leading

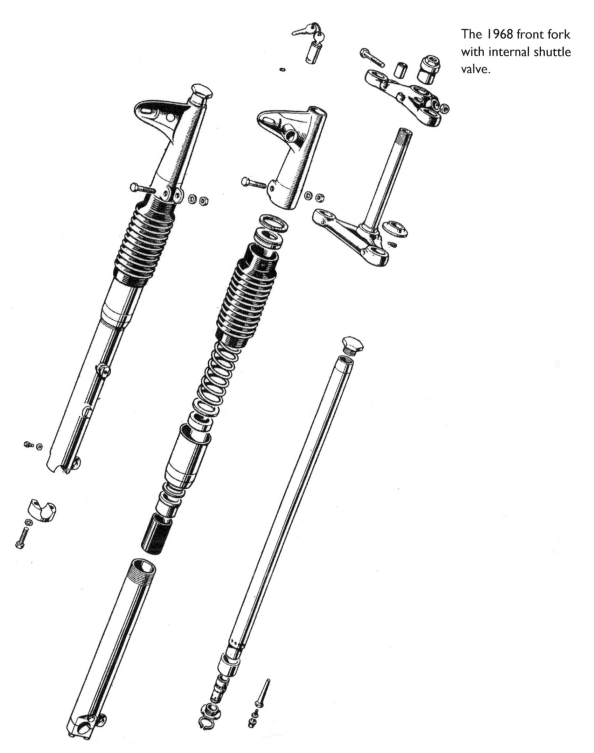

The 1968 front fork with internal shuttle valve.

shoe (TLS) front brake. The brake drum was still an integral part of the 8-inch full-width hub, but was now modified to accept a larger backing plate. Two identical shoes were spread apart at each end by two cams and levers, joined outside the backing plate by an adjustable rod. The plate was cast aluminum and included a large, functional ventilating scoop that was protected by a heavy, chromed wire mesh screen. At the rear there was an exit vent and the brake plate's perimeter was given a raised polished surface that made the unit very attractive and appear larger than it actually was!

The TLS brake control cable threaded through and pulled against a cast-in abutment in the backing plate. When out of adjustment, the cable could jump out of the boss, so at engine number DU70083, the casting was drilled and a cotter pin inserted to prevent this.

The new brake's Achilles' heel was the control cable, or more precisely, its length and the path it had to take to actuate the lever. After tucking in behind the headlight, the long cable was clipped to the rear of the front fork's lower lug pinch bolt and then to the fender through a new oblong nylon guide fitted for the purpose. The cable was then tied to the lower fender stay on its way to finally reaching the brake. Under heavy, hard braking, the long cable jacket allowed an alarming amount of flex in the lever. The cable's routing also allowed it to be trapped by the rear edge of the fender when the fork was compressed.

1968 was the last year for the "large eyebrow" tank emblem. Nylon guide on the front fender didn't keep the cable out of trouble and a new design came in 1969. Notice the deeply finned heat sink under the headlight for the Zener diode. Engine sounds as good as it looks! (Restored) *Gaylin*

Under-seat view of a restored 1968 U.S. TR6R. Rubber padding over the battery was (and is) a common safeguard. Mylar self-adhering stickers are most noticeable over dark colors as seen here by the oil level decal. Water slides are better on the black surfaces. *Gaylin*

A longer front guard, introduced during the year, solved the dangerous "trapping" problem. But more work was needed to cure the spongy lever. The left side brake drum cover was redesigned to suggest radial ventilation. Ten slots and hooded louvers were stamped into the chrome cover around its periphery. The cover was held in place by three screws and extended past the edge of the drum, giving Triumph's desired effect of increased diameter. But the cover also looked "cheesy," resembling a metal trash can lid!

This aside, Triumph finally had a brake to match the performance of the 650 engine. So strong a sales feature was the new brake that the factory made available a kit to retrofit them to

unsold 1967 machines still sitting in showrooms. Restorers of 1967 examples with high engine numbers might want to reconsider replacing a TLS front brake fitted to their motorcycle.

Internal improvements to the front fork for 1968 were a direct result of Triumph's successful production racing program. A new oil shuttle valve, screwed to the bottom of the fork stanchion, allowed precise two-way damping. The innovation meant civilized rebound damping and all but eliminated pitching when cranked over in a hard turn. The new stanchions can be identified by eight bleed holes at their base, but once assembled, the modified fork is indistinguishable from its predecessor.

Fork threads on the TR6s were changed to Unified form at engine number DU66246; however, the Bonnevilles weren't converted

Twin-leading shoe front brake of an unrestored 1968 TR6R. After only a short period of use the cable would jump out of the backing plate abutment. To prevent this, later brakes like the one pictured were drilled for a cotter pin. Wire clips on the fork gaiters were discontinued the following year. *Gaylin*

A brand-new 1968 TR6C with blue fuel tank and stainless fenders. Six-inch headlight, single instrument, and trials tires were also characteristic of the model, but muffler heat shields shown were a TriCor accessory. Look close to see the "World Record Holder" decal on the upper fork cover. Rider looks familiar! *Gary Nixon collection*

until number DU68363. Up top, the steering damper assembly was dropped from the T120R and Trophy 650 models, replaced by a blind chrome-plated sleeve nut. But for those still requiring added stability, a damper kit was made available from the factory. Smiths 150-mile-per-hour speedometers were still specified for all models, and the Bonnevilles were fitted with a combination front brake/choke lever bracket in all markets.

Frame modifications to the 1968 650s were mostly peripheral. The steering lock ear on the steering head was fattened into a longer lip to prevent the lock bolt from being dropped in the wrong position. The troublesome kickstand was redesigned into a longer and more confidence-inspiring leg. Its new shape allowed it to be deployed without the need of a separate lever and the angle of the frame lug was changed to suit.

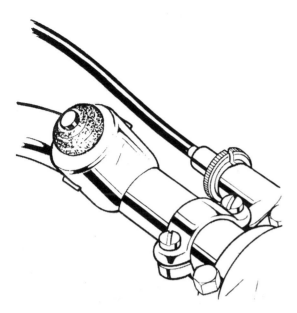

Type 151SA kill button (#35835) introduced in 1968.

There was a beefier rear swingarm pivot lug introduced at engine number DU68368, and the swinging fork itself was slightly lengthened and given thicker tubing at number DU81196. These swingarms can be identified by a stamped letter X on the pivot tube.

In the midsection of the 1968 Bonnevilles and Trophies, the left side panel finally lost all of its switchgear — the keyed ignition switch being relocated to the easier-to-use left headlight support arm. The revised side cover was easier to remove due to a threaded knob at the upper left hand corner. The rear perched on two rubber bushed pegs welded to the rear subframe. The inside of the panel incorporated a steel shelf for the tool pouch, replacing the 1966–67 plastic joke behind the battery.

When it was learned during the season that the factory had made the new panel self-detaching, a spring tension clip was placed behind a securing knob with coarser teeth. But this design wasn't 100 percent effective either, and with loud exhaust pipes, riders couldn't hear the cover (or the tools) hitting the concrete! The oil tank continued unchanged. The battery carrier was revised with sturdier sides, a rubber tray for the base, and an adjustable elastic strap to keep downward tension on the Lucas (PUZ5A) 12-volt power cell.

Other than the new TLS front brake, wheel specifications went generally unchanged for 1968. The rear wheel continued with a steel spool, 7-inch brake drum and bolt-on sprocket. The quickly detachable wheel was still an option in the United Kingdom, but with an integral drive sprocket.

There were, however, a few tire variations for the new model year. In the eastern United States, the road models began the season with Dunlop K70s on the rear and highway ribs on the front. But at engine number DU75452, the front was changed to a 3.25x19-inch K70. The Trophy 650 scramblers in the East were skinned in Trials Universals, while the western United States TR6Cs now rolled on K70s fore and aft. Motocross-style knobbies were offered as an option for either coast.

The front Dunlop ribbed tire on the U.K. model TR6 was now listed as a 3.25x19 while the Bonneville's remained a 3.00x19. Both home market 650s were fitted with 18-inch Dunlop K70s at the rear.

There were also some upgrades in the "Prince of Darkness" department. First, new headlights graced the front of all models. The Bonnevilles and TR6Rs received 7-inch buckets with the ammeter and indicator lamps repositioned for better visibility. The lighting switch was a three-position toggle with an easier to use lever. The smaller shell fitted to the Trophy scrambler was also changed to carry two indicator lights together in the center. A three-position light switch was placed on the right and dimmer switch on the left. And the headlight support ears on the fork were now slotted to allow horizontal adjustment.

The taillight fitted to American models changed again to comply with federal DOT rules. The cast-aluminum housing had the same width as the Lucas L679 lamp, from the base of the lens to the fender, and sported red safety reflectors on its flanks. On the front end of U.S. models were a pair of round amber reflectors, mounted just under the front end of the fuel tank. These were held in place by tubular sheet metal covers that fastened to the fuel tank mounts and complicated gas tank removal.

The efficiency of the Zener diode depended on heat dissipation. Its location behind the left side cover was far from ideal, as it was out of the airstream. For 1968, the diode was moved to the front fork below the headlight and given a deeply finned, cast-aluminum heat sink which made it more effective in regulating excess electrical voltage.

The 1968 colors were Hi-Fi Scarlet and silver for the Bonneville, and Riviera-blue and silver for the Trophies. In the United States, the slimline tanks were completely finished in the solid color. These were not given scalloped sections, but an approximately 2 1/4-inch-wide silver stripe on the top of the tank, bordered in gold lining. The 3 1/2-gallon U.S. TR6R tank adopted the graphics of the previous year's sport tanks. The silver section swept down from the eyebrow Triumph emblem, tapering off under a smaller kneepad that had a new cross-checked pattern. This was also the last year for the tank top package rack on all Triumphs.

The larger 4.0-gallon fuel tanks fitted to the British machines were painted the same colors as the American models, but retained the scalloped patterns from 1967. However, a smaller kneepad now meant more of the silver exposed — profile views make it the dominant color. New petcock washers fitted at engine number DU77670 were impregnated with an inner rubber O-ring. These were successful in sealing the outside of the tap, but did nothing

This image taken from the cover of the 1968 U.S. catalog demonstrates the hazard of basing a restoration on a single piece of literature. Close examination of the front machine reveals a splayed port head but with a TR6R fuel tank and fenders. Air filter has been hand-drawn in afterwards. U.S. Bonnevilles were not finished this way!

internally to keep gasoline from leaking past a closed valve. The tank's front mounting was also switched to studs and self-locking nuts beginning at the same engine number.

Fenders and finishes stayed relatively the same. The U.S. Bonneville and TR6C models kept their polished stainless guards while the U.S. TR6R had painted steel fenders in Riviera-blue with a silver stripe. In all markets, the fenders, both front and rear, gained a rolled edge at the tips — the painted stripe stopped short of the end and was squared off by gold pinstriping. At engine number DU81709, the front fenders were lengthened slightly; however, the American stainless versions were not affected. The U.K. fenders continued in silver paint with the corresponding center stripe lined in gold. And there was a new rear number plate (#F8121) design for the home market that had a wider top bridge and two fastening points.

The cross-ribbed twinseats introduced in 1967 were given slightly thicker padding and new stepped strap hinges instead of the curved rods that Triumph had seemingly used forever! Saddles fitted to the American machines were covered completely in black, while British models continued with the two-toned versions. And a bright polished aluminum edging around the bottom replaced the previous black trim. The safety hand-strap was still specified on 650s bound for the western United States, but at engine number DU75452 it was replaced by a short chrome grab-rail that fastened to the rear of the seat. These weren't supplied on eastern U.S. bikes until number DU77018, but some retrofitting was carried out by dealers. For 1968, there was a completely new range of decals developed for Triumph motorcycles. For starters, the machines that were stroboscopically tested at Meriden were given a circular yellow sticker on the outside of the chrome points cover reading "strobe tested." The reverse side of the cover received an instructional sticker (#D2138) noting point gaps, degree settings, and so on. This one became a permanent fixture until 1979 when electronic ignition took over.

On the T120s, the paired insignias that sat opposite the fuel tank's filler cap were replaced by a single gold "Bonneville" (#D680) transfer, over 4 inches long and in an exaggerated script. This decal was placed diagonally, climbing up from the left, and on the U.S. slimline tanks it sat completely out on the scarlet paint. The "World Speed Record Holder" (#A56) transfer was moved out on the left headlight support arm and the "Made in England" disappeared in lieu of the manufacturer's origin sticker placed on the steering head of the frame.

Triumph's new series of art decals introduced at this time were larger, mainly to be showcased on the side panels. So the Bonneville decal was also placed (perfectly horizontal) on the center of the left side cover and looked much more appropriate than the tiny design used before.

Early 1968 U.S. TR6R models received a pair of gold "Trophy Sports" (#D678) decals in the same style script and locations as the T120. The word "Trophy" appeared on top of "Sports," both of which were in italicized capital letters. This transfer was changed on later TR6Rs when the designation changed to "Tiger 650." The new sticker (#D1918) had both characters on the same line. At the start of the 1968 model year, the American TR6Cs were designated "Trophy Special" and given a pair of transfers (#D679) in the similar style of script and capital letters. Later in the year it was changed to a design reading "Trophy 650" (#D1920) all on the same line.

There were no known modifications to the engine prefix scheme. Serial numbers began with either T120R, TR6R, or TR6C.

1969 Models

The years 1968–1970 are widely regarded as the epitome of the Triumph 650cc twin. There may be a few arguments as to which year exactly was the best, but these debates often come down to color and what you think of tank scallops. But beyond the aesthetic changes, the factory made many subtle improvements to the Bonneville and TR6 during this period. For 1969, the parts of the engine that had not already been converted to Unified threads switched to the new order, including the crankshaft, crankcase halves, and all outer covers. At serial number DU85904, the Hepolite pistons were changed yet again, given domed crowns and fatter wrist pins. New H-section con-rods, in RR56 aluminum alloy, were introduced at serial number GC23016, with UNF bolts and self-locking nuts. Triumph engineers believed the motor had lost its smoothness when the crank was lightened in 1966, so the wider, heavier flywheel returned at engine number NC02256 but with the critical 85 percent balance factor.

One of the more significant improvements that season was the nitride-hardened camshafts (at engine number DU87105) that finally cured the cam wear problem. This process was also applied to the replacement camshafts then being made for earlier machines and many were retrofitted during overhauls. All camshafts that were nitrided, whether for production or for spares, were stamped with a capital N for identification.

The 650 cylinder head attachment points were given steel inserts to protect them during the manufacturing process, and the entire casting

received the new UNF thread forms. This included the steel exhaust stubs and carburetor adaptors. The latter item was redesigned to increase ram effect by tapering the inside diameter from 1 3/16 inches at the carburetor flange to 1 1/8 inches at the stub's mouth.

The Amal Concentrics were partially rubber-isolated in 1969. An O-ring at the carburetor joining faces prevented the instruments from being pulled in completely flush, and rubber washers under the self-locking mounting nuts gave some measure of protection at the studs. Inside, the pilot jets became fixed and the Bonneville main jets reduced from #210 to #190. And in Britain, air cleaners finally became standard on the T120s.

There was yet another pushrod tube design and sealing arrangement. The chrome-plated tubes were castellated at the top to prevent any oil trapping and sealed with black Viton O-rings at both ends. It was believed that the use of O-rings as collars around the tappet guide would be sufficient, but at engine number PD32574, a rubber washer reappeared at the bottom of the

Sanitized publicity portrait of a 1969 U.K. T120R showing exposed spring rear shocks and front wheel cover plate. Larger Euro tank wears new-generation "small eyebrow" tank emblems and kneepads. TR6 models in the U.K. had similar tank graphics and the parcel racks were now history. *Author collection*

Official press photograph of a brand new 1969 Tiger-650 taken in the U.S. Decal placement on sidecover, fuel tank and upper fork shroud can clearly be seen. Horn/dipper switch cable is unsecured.
Author collection

tappet block along with an "insurance collar" to make it behave.

Besides the UNF conversion, modifications to the timing cover included a second oil seal behind the contact breakers and new oil release valve design with Unified threads. An electric oil pressure sensor protected by a rubber boot was added and wired to the ignition warning lamp in the headlight shell. The oil pump body was changed to allow an increase in size of the feed plunger, and at engine DU88714 a shorter scavenge pipe was fitted to permit more oil to stay in the crankcase sump. Another variation came at engine JD25965 when the timing marks on the timing wheels were revised.

On the opposite side of the engine, the tachometer drive mounting was switched to a left-handed (UNF) thread to prevent its tendency to loosen up and self-destruct. Many crankcases were ruined by Saturday afternoon mechanics attempting to fit earlier tach drive units or plugs with standard threads! At engine DU86965 there was a new raised serial number pad stamped with small diagonal Triumph trademarks. The engine identification number was then added on top, in an attempt to discourage tampering. But all this did was create a black market for miniature Triumph logo stamps!

Triumph threw another midyear curve when it introduced a new serial number coding system with a two-letter prefix. The first letter in the code revealed the actual month of manufacture while the second character indicated the model

Above and left
Fuel tanks fitted to U.S. Bonnevilles in 1969 were given one of three sets of graphics, all in Olympic Flame and silver. The first was in the same solid color scheme (and dorsal stripe) as the 1968 models. The second, pictured here on an original unrestored machine owned by Doug Peterson, was a single scallop above each tank emblem. Third condition saw a silver wing added below each badge. *Gaylin*

year of the machine (not the actual year of manufacture). Engine number DU90282 was the last ID number under the old scheme.

The gearbox did not escape redesign. At engine number DU88630 a new camplate was specified, as was a new gear change quadrant at number JD26313. The transmission gears were subjected to a new hardening process, during which, not surprisingly, they changed size (diameter). So at engine CC15546 new mainshaft and layshaft diameters were specified to match the larger gears. This means that 1969 gearbox

In 1969 the U.S. DOT required a notice on every machine declaring that it complied with all federal safety standards. It is believed this transparent decal was Meriden's first attempt to satisfy the regulation. They were positioned on the frame's right-hand steering head casting. *Gaylin*

Later in the year, more impressive block stickers (with white type) were produced that carried the machine's serial number and date of manufacture. These would continue unchanged until the late 1970s. The example shown is from 1970. *Gaylin*

internals cannot be interchanged with earlier ones (including early 1969 boxes!). Another modification to the driveline came at DU88383, when the clutch housings were statically balanced. The upgraded hub can be identified by the disappearance of the cast pockets.

A more conspicuous change on the new Bonnevilles and Tiger 650s was an exhaust pipe balance tube that linked the head pipes just outside the exhaust ports. The earliest examples had separate clamping adaptors at each end, as illustrated in the parts book for that year. Later 1969 machines had a simplified crossover pipe with smaller clamps. Although the balance tube complicated exhaust removal and reassembly, the linked exhaust was noticeably quieter and improved engine performance. The reduced noise level also permitted the U.S.-style sport mufflers to become standard on the U.K. bikes, although the resonators are still shown in some of the ad literature.

The U.S. TR6C Trophy 650s received larger mufflers for their high-level system. This meant new pipe bends and fresh hardware to attach everything to the frame. There was also a massive chrome wire heat shield to cover the new system, but it completely lacked the subtlety of the earlier guards. In fact, the 1969 C-model exhaust shield looked as though it had been clipped from a shopping cart!

1969 Frame and Cycle Parts

The TR6C continued with the single Smiths speedometer, skid plate, folding footrests, and no centerstand. It could be ordered with either Dunlop K70 tires or Trials Universals and the front fork was still fitted with the rugged upper lug with integral handlebar mounts. The front fork on all the 1969 650 models had their stanchion centers spread another 1/4 inch (from 6 1/2 inch to 6 3/4 inch) which necessitated new upper and lower lugs. The brake plate

This photo of a brand new 1969 Bonneville was taken outside the building of the U.S. distributor in Duarte, California. It shows the final arrangement of tank graphics and seat-attached grab rail that first appeared on late-1968 models. *Author collection*

Drive side view of an unrestored 1970 U.S.-spec Bonneville owned by Tim Savin. Paint colors, detachable front engine plates and a grab rail now integral with the rear fender bracket are the most noticeable difference from the machine above. *Gaylin*

On the occasion when the wind-tone horns were unavailable, Meriden assemblers fitted a pair of TR6 hooters in place. Safety standards sticker is visible above the mandated amber reflector. Remarkably, even the original cover screws have survived on this unrestored 1970 Bonneville. *Gaylin*

abutment on the inside right-hand slider had to be extended, which obligated a new part number. The wider fork also meant a wider axle. The rubber fork boots were also changed to a cleaner, self-locating design, without the previous wire clamps.

The twin-leading shoe front brake received some needed attention after incidents of control cable problems and wide-spread complaints about the spongy lever. The brake cable, now with its own brake switch, was routed straight down behind the right-hand fork tube. It passed through a new cast abutment and grabbed the forward lever on the backing plate. The two brake arms were still linked, but the front lever was now bell-cranked to permit a direct upward pull. The new arrangement cured all the cable problems and finally allowed the full potential of the superior TLS brake design.

The chrome-plated cover plate on the left side of the front wheel was changed to a simpler, cleaner design with a concentric ring pattern.

The screw fastening was dropped in favor of three integral tabs around the lid's perimeter. All of the control cables on the handlebars were secured by rubber bow ties and those leaving the bars on the right-hand side passed though a grommetted hole in the right headlight ear.

There were only a few visceral modifications made to the 650 twins in 1969. Perhaps to give a more athletic look, the twin Girling shocks (#64052107) lost their shrouds and had exposed chrome springs. The oil tank filler cap was given a dipstick and the quilted material used on the top panel of the twinseat was aerated. The two-toned saddles fitted to the home market models were replaced by all black seat covers, and the rear grab rail was still a standard item on American bikes. And during the production year the stenciled Triumph trademark on the seat's stern was switched to the more detailed design with bordered lettering.

There were no changes in the Dunlop department, except for the optional K70s on U.S. Trophies already mentioned. Ribbed front tires were still fitted as original equipment on the U.K. 650s but no longer available in the United States.

Electrical modifications for the new season included dual "windtone" horns for the Bonnevilles at engine number CC14783. These had smooth, domed-shaped covers and small downward facing trumpets, and were suspended below the safety reflectors beneath the front of the fuel tank. But along with the horn relay, the new hooters proved to be too heavy for the anemic mounting bracket and a sturdier combined capacitor/horn carrier was fitted midseason (although there was no change in the part number). The Trophy and Tiger 650s continued with the single horn.

The U.S. TR6Cs were also converted to battery ignition, including a higher output Lucas RM21 alternator with an encapsulated stator. Lighting fixtures were as fitted to the 1968 models, except for a Lucas L679 taillight used on the U.K. models. This was made possible by a new number plate form. And a new wiring harness for the 650s allowed turn indicators —

if desired — as well as hook-ups for the front brake and oil pressure switch.

After only three years in production, the "large eyebrow" tank emblem was replaced by a smaller and simplified version. The new design saw the Triumph logo situated in the center of the badge surrounded with a thin chrome frame. Similar to its predecessor, the upper accent was emphasized and extended forward beyond the emblem. Although it didn't dominate the fuel tank like its larger father, it did manage to keep some of the magic and was quickly christened the "small eyebrow." The chrome package racks disappeared from all Triumph models in 1969, and at engine number DU88625 the tank's central chrome styling strip received a new hooked screw mounting at the rear.

Machine colors were Olympic Flame (dark metallic orange) and silver for the Bonneville and Trophy Red (bright metallic red) for the single carb models. Silver was the subordinate color on UK TR6 twins. The larger U.K. tanks were completed in the same style and graphics of the previous year but in the colors of the new season. The mudguards on the T120 were in silver with an Olympic Flame center stripe lined in white. To easily distinguish it from the Bonneville fender, the TR6 version was reversed to Trophy Red with a center stripe lined in gold.

The gas tanks on the American Trophy and Tiger 650 models were finished entirely in Trophy-red, without a stripe or scallop. The TR6R was given matching fenders in red but with a white center stripe lined in gold, while the TR6Cs were decked with the beautiful stainless steel guards. Stainless fenders were also being made available on Canadian market Bonnevilles.

The finish on the 1969 U.S. Bonneville gas tanks, like those in 1967, seemed to be part of some ongoing, year-long experiment. Early examples were painted in the new colors, but in the same paint scheme as 1968. The tanks were a solid Olympic Flame with a 2 1/4-inch (approximately) silver stripe straddling the length of the top seam. There were no scallops top or bottom. The second paint configuration

View from the cockpit of an unrestored 1970 U.S. T120R shows the early-year gray-faced Smiths instruments and sweeping tank scallops. Underslung mirrors are tidier than those that sprout from the top of the bars and attractive handgrips are borrowed from a 1966 model. *Gaylin*

saw Triumph's first true upper tank scallop — a thin flash of silver (now being applied on top of the main color) beginning at the top corners of the tank emblems and then curling rearward to taper into a point on each side of the top seam, well away from the kneegrip. In an attempt to maintain symmetry, the right-hand tank scallop was sent straight through the filler cap.

On the third and final 1969 T120R tank scheme, a bottom flash was added below the emblem at the bottom corners, tapering off to a point under the front of the rubber kneepad. White pinstriping divided the colors on all three paint jobs. Unfortunately, there were no engine numbers assigned to the variations, but it is believed the majority of U.S. Bonnevilles were finished in the final (twin scallops) condition. Restorers of 1969 Bonnevilles with a late sequence engine number should consider whether or not to use an early scheme.

Muscular front fork of the 1970 Triumph showing correct position (upper left fork cover) of the "World Record Holder" decal. Chrome-plated braces were used only on the painted fenders. *Gaylin*

The fenders on the American T120s wore the same finish as their British counterparts — silver with an Olympic Flame center stripe lined in white. No proof has surfaced to bolster the claim that stainless steel fenders were ever used on U.S. Bonnevilles in 1969. However, there is evidence that indicates an occasional color reversal — the body in Olympic Flame with a silver stripe. How many or how often this was done is unclear. Front supports for the stainless fenders were painted in black enamel while the braces used on painted fenders in the United States were generally chrome-plated. U.K. models were fitted with black stays, but a few American TR6Rs also came with painted braces.

Triumph's range of beautifully scripted tank and side cover decals introduced only

the year before were scrapped in 1969. They were replaced by a less artistic, but arguably more modern group of transfers in extended capital letters. The left side panels of the T120s were tattooed dead-center with a stretched "BONNEVILLE" (#D2103) almost 5 inches long. A smaller 2-inch version (#D2026) was set in the familiar place opposite the gas tank's filler cap. The TR6R, now designated Tiger 650, received a two-line decal (#D2102) which read "TIGER" in solid capitals over an outlined "650." The dimensions were 3x1 1/2 inches for the side cover sticker and 1x1 1/2 inches for the matching (#D2025) tank transfer. The U.S. TR6C model was now the "TROPHY 650" and its pair of decals (large #D2104, small #D2027) were identical in size and design to the Tiger. The "World Record" bird still held on to its spot on the left-hand headlight ear.

As required by the U.S. Department of Transportation, a sticker (#D2452) declaring that the machine complied with all safety standards and also giving the date and place of origin was fixed to the right side of the frame just below the steering head. The serial number was also added; however, the frame was still stamped on the left headstock casting in the usual manner.

1970 Models

The 1970 650cc twins were the last to be completely designed by the Triumph Engineering Company. In 1970, Coventry was selling more 650 twins than ever before, and there was still little reason to modify a motorcycle so popular. Engine revisions for the new season would be minor.

The 650 twins gained a crankcase breathing arrangement similar to that used on the three-cylinder Trident. This design vented the crank area into the primary case through small holes drilled under the main bearing. The chaincase was then opened behind the clutch area, through a flanged elbow from which extended a long D-shaped plastic pipe. A small cover plate was necessary to protect the opening behind the clutch. The D tube was clipped externally to the

A 1970 U.S. Tiger-650 restored by ex-Triumph dealer Bob Worden. The color of the tank and fenders was called Spring-gold, but it was actually a metallic avocado-green. Seat is a recover but an uncommonly good one. A well-executed restoration of a very desirable model. *Gaylin*

Flip-side of Worden's 1970 U.S. TR6R reveals no mistakes here either. Fuel tank was not a slimline but still pleasingly shaped. This was the last year for rubber kneepads on U.S. 650 twins. (Restored) *Gaylin*

Close-up view of the instruments fitted to the 1970 U.S. Tiger-650. These were changed for black-faced versions later in the year. Clear odometer warning sticker is missing from the speedometer. (Restored) *Gaylin*

Back end of a freshly restored 1970 TR6R with black and chrome grab rail. These were switched for all-chrome brackets on later 1970 Bonnevilles and TR6s, but red safety reflectors were found only on the sides of the taillight housing that year. Fender center stripe accurately stops short of the finished edge. *Gaylin*

left side of the rear fender and continued to the end of the machine.

The new layout ensured a constant level of lubricant in the chaincase, and because of the vent pipe's elevation, oil was not normally expelled into the atmosphere. The new engine breather obsoleted the timed disc (and tube) at the end of the inlet camshaft. It also meant new nitrided camshafts in UNF threads with presized bushings for the ends and, of course, new crankcase halves.

The timing gears were altered to include two tapped holes for a gear puller in place of the screw bosses in their centers, although there was no change in the part number. There was another O-ring design (#E11283) for the top of the pushrod tubes and the tachometer drive

on the TR6 and T120 used a solid take-off plug instead of the previous pressing.

The four-speed transmission underwent a few modifications, not all of them with positive results. An area for potential oil leaks was corrected by fitting a shorter selector rod in the gearbox outer cover. There was a heavier main bearing circlip installed at engine number AD37473 and at number ED51080 aluminum bronze selector forks with fixed rollers replaced the earlier steel versions. Finally, at engine number ED52044, the old cam plate, plunger, and indexing spring were changed to a precision pressing and leaf spring. All of these modifications conspired to complicate disassembly and kicked off a spate of gearbox problems that continued through ensuing model years. A much welcomed engine change came late in the 1970 season. The float bowls on the Amal Concentric carburetors were given plastic drain plugs. This minor modification eliminated the chore of having to remove the entire bowl just to drain trapped water after a storm or thorough washing. And the TR6 carbs were now O-ring mounted as per the Bonneville arrangement.

1970 Frame and Cycle Parts

The running gear received the bulk of the factory's attention in 1970. The front engine mounting frame tabs were changed to a pair of small triangulated plates fixed by sturdy UNF bolts and self-locking nuts. This facilitated engine removal, but its real importance was to speed motor installation on the assembly line. Another frame change came at the kickstand,

Drive side view of Jerry Wheeler's largely unrestored 1970 U.S. Trophy 650. By this time larger mufflers were specified for the TR6Cs. Huge wire heat shield acquired derogatory nicknames including "barbecue grill" in the United States and "chip basket" in the United Kingdom. Pictured twinseat has been recovered. *Gaylin*

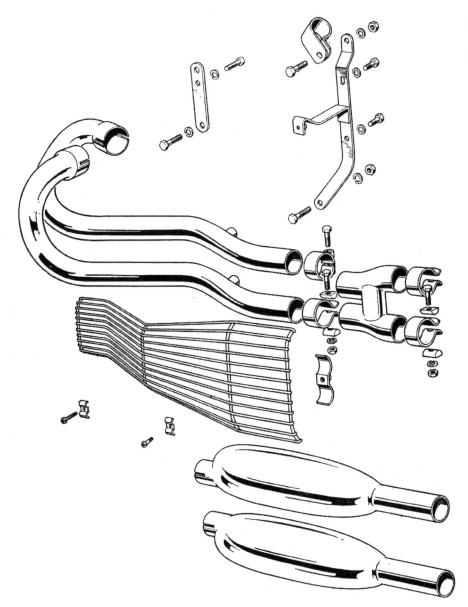

which was given a threaded adjustable stop to keep the leg from banging against the exhaust pipe when retracted.

The front fork stanchions were now hard chrome-plated, with a ground surface to extend the life of the seals. Front fender mounting was also changed on the inside of the lower sliders. Steel channels were welded on that were keyed for the teardrop brackets and captured a square nut to receive the mounting bolt. The lower front stay was modified to fasten the fender at two points on the sides, instead of the single

central screw of before. The radius and length of the fenders were now standardized between the ranges, and although the mounting holes may be in different locations, 650 twin restorers may find what they need sitting on a 500cc Daytona, albeit in the wrong color.

On top of the front forks, the same gray-faced magnetic Smiths instruments (speedo–#SSM5001/06, tach–#RSM3003/01) were specified during the first part of production. But at the approximate halfway point in the season, clocks with black-faced dials (speedo–

Left and right engine views of Wheeler's 1970 TR6C. Drive side shows exhaust head pipe routing, folding footpeg, and very top of the skid plate. Seldom seen timing side surrenders a few details including rubber boot for the oil pressure switch and painted straps used to secure the sub-harnesses to the front down tube. *Gaylin*

#SSM5007/00, tach–#RSM3003/13) took their place. There are no known engine number assignments for this change, but machines bearing late ID numbers shouldn't be sporting gray-faced instruments. On the handlebars, the base of the control levers were changed to allow the mounting of safety mirrors. Rubber "bow ties" were supplied to secure the control cables, but on the Bonneville and TR6R models, chromed spring clips were used on the left to neatly subdue the gray dipper switch harness.

On the rear of the machines, new Girling suspension units (#64052107) were fitted that employed castellated sleeves to protect the bottom adjusters from road grime and water. The rear backing plate, hub, and Smiths speedometer drive adaptor were converted to the Unified thread form, and flat stock replaced the tubular sectioned brace as the brake torque stay. Ostensibly there was no change in the twinseat from the previous year. The tapped holes at the back of seat pan that had fastened the grab rail were omitted and the base's shape was slightly changed to give a lower profile.

The only recorded difference in tire and wheel sizes for 1970 was the increase of the U.K. T120's front section to 3 1/4 inches. Dunlop highway ribs were still specified on the front of British market machines as were the optional K70 or Trials Universals (front and rear) on the U.S. TR6Cs.

The unscalloped slimline fuel tank of the 1970 Trophy 650 carried a narrower black stripe on its back than its TR6R counterpart. The Trophy 650 decal was placed out onto the green paint. Single instrument (speedo) and handlebar-mounted kill button were also features of the TR6C. *Gaylin*

In America, stainless steel fenders with black stays were fitted only to the Trophy 650 in 1970. Dunlop K70 tires were optional that year. Zener diode heat sink appears massive under the 6-inch Lucas headlight. *Gaylin*

The Bonneville was given new dome-shaped windtone horns, and at engine number ED44339, restriction plates were added to the slotted mountings to prevent poorly adjusted horns from fouling the front fender. A single Lucas 6H squealer continued to be sufficient on the TR6 models. Other electrical mods included smaller but more powerful Lucas 17/M12 ignition coils (#45223) and a slightly different (less conspicuous) exit for the alternator wires behind the clutch area in the crankcase.

Paint colors for the 1970 Bonnevilles were Astral-red (a metallic maroon) and silver. The Trophy finish was Spring-gold (metallic avocado green) and accented in black. Separations were carried out in gold pinstriping. On the American

bikes, tank art remained mostly unchanged from the year prior. The size and aspects of the slimline tank scallops were the same, but the TR6R tank was given a wider than usual central black stripe (approximately 3 inches). Fenders on the Bonneville and Tiger 650 were sprayed in the main color and striped in either silver (T120) or black (TR6R). Gold lining marked the boundaries on both bikes. The Trophy 650's slim fuel tank was also colored in Spring-gold, but with a thinner black stripe.

Sadly, the stainless steel fenders fitted to the U.S. TR6C and Canadian models in 1970 were the last seen on 650cc Triumphs. All fender braces were chrome-plated except those used on the stainless guards. These were painted in black

British Only's unrestored 1970 Bonneville T120RT, with new-old-stock mufflers fitted. The kitted 750cc twin is indistinguishable from a standard Bonneville, but subtle casting marks on the cylinder and its stamped engine number give it away. Notice the twin standard horns and taillight extension required by some state DOTs. Only 204 of the RTs were made and most were put to the whip — making this unrestored example rare in the extreme! *Lindsay Brooke*

enamel for a pleasing contrast effect.

The larger 4 1/4-gallon fuel tanks on the British market bikes were painted the same colors as their American cousins but without scallops. The Tiger 650 tank was in solid Spring-gold with matching fenders. However, the U.K. Bonneville tank was stigmatized with a two-tone finish that only a mother could love! The entire flanks of the tank, from the tunnel at the front clear to the nose of the seat, were painted in silver. The panels were then encircled by Astral-red at the edges and top where the red covered completely from side to side. Gold hand-lining was used to define the borders. The U.K. mudguards were finished in the usual complementary practice, but the fender stays were in black enamel.

The 1970 range of U.S.-market 650 twins stabilized at three machines — T120R Bonneville, TR6R Tiger 650, and TR6C Trophy 650. In the United Kingdom there were only two—T120 Bonneville and the low-piped TR6 Trophy 650. The transfer scheme of the year before was continued without change.

1970 750cc Bonneville

In the United States, a small batch (204) of Bonnevilles were enlarged to a 750cc engine displacement by fitting an aftermarket big-bore kit. The sanctioning body of American racing, the American Motorcyclist Association (AMA), required that a minimum of 200 like models (or at least the performance parts) be officially catalogued and offered for public sale before

Number:	(Twin) 5-70
Subject:	750cc Twin
USA Models:	T120RT
Date:	June 30, 1970

SERVICE BULLETIN

TRIUMPH MOTORCYCLE CORPORATION A subsidiary of The Birmingham Small Arms Company Incorporated, Verona, New Jersey

Duarte, Calif. 91010, P. O. Box 275   Towson, Baltimore, Md., P. O. Box 6790 21204

THE BONNEVILLE 750

The "Bonneville 750" was approved for competition by the American Motorcycle Association on June 26, 1970. The 750 is basically the same as the "Bonneville 650," except for displacement, bore, and B.H.P. The cylinder bore was increased 5 mm (from 71 mm to 76 mm), while the stroke of 82 mm remains the same.

All parts fitted to both the 650cc and 750cc Bonnevilles are identical, except the following:

E6304T7	Cylinder block (cast iron)
* E9488T7/8	Piston c/w rings and circlips (.008" o/s), 10.5:1 ratio
E9488T7/32	Piston c/w rings and circlips (.040" o/s), 10.5:1 ratio
* CD460T7/8	Ring set (.008" o/s)
CD460T7/32	Ring set (.040" o/s)
E6869T7	Circlip (install with opening at top - sharp edge outward)
E4547T7	Gasket, cylinder head (radius bore edges by hand)
E4771T7	Center head bolt
S25-3T7	Washer (for head bolt)
E8751T7	Plug, tappet feed
E6309T7	Gasket, cylinder base

*NOTE: E9488T7/8 (forged) piston (.008" oversize) was fitted to the original engines. The registered cylinder bore of 76 mm plus .008" equals 3". This means that the standard cylinder is .008" over the registered size of 76 mm. When fitting E9488T7/32 piston, bore cylinder to 3.032", which is equivalent to 76 mm plus .040". Always mike each piston and bore cylinder for running clearance of .0045" to .005" (with honed finish). Hone pin hole for "easy push fit." Head gasket must also be bored when fitting oversize pistons.

FOR COMPETITION USE in A.M.A. events, only the cylinder listed above has been approved. 650cc cylinders must measure not less than 71 mm nor more than 71 mm plus .045". 750cc cylinders must measure not less than 76 mm nor more than 76 mm plus .045".

TRIUMPH USA

SERVICE BULLETIN

TRIUMPH MOTORCYCLE CORPORATION   A subsidiary of The Birmingham Small Arms Company Incorporated, Verona, New Jersey

Duarte, Calif. 91010, P. O. Box 275   Towson, Baltimore, Md., P. O. Box 6790 21204

SPECIAL BULLETIN

IMPORTANT!   IMPORTANT!

USE OF THE 750 BONNEVILLE IN COMPETITION

1. The Bonneville 750 (750cc) has been approved by the American Motor-cycle Association for use in competition. However, its use must be as outlined in the Rules and Regulations of the A. M. A.

2. The A. M. A. Rule Book states: " . . . and the manufacturer's crank-case, cylinder, and cylinder heads from the approved model must be used . . ."

    As the crankcases and cylinder head as fitted to the approved models of the Bonneville 650, Bonneville 750, and TR6 650 are the same, the only question of legality arises in the use of the cylinder as fitted to the approved model of the Bonneville 750.

3. The only cylinder approved for competition is the cylinder listed in Service Bulletin (Twin) 5-70 which listed the part numbers of all parts fitted to the Bonneville 750 that were different from those fitted to the Bonneville 650.

4. Specifically, cylinders supplied through accessory houses were not fitted to the Bonneville 750 when submitted for approval and are therefore not legal for A. M. A. competition.

                              *
                              *
                              *
                              *

they could turn a wheel on a race track. Under AMA rules, major performance modifications had to be of factory origin.

The AMA's 750cc rule was approved for the 1969 dirt track season, but Triumph didn't get around to homologating a 750 twin until early 1970. The program began in the racing shop of Triumph's eastern U.S. distributor (TriCor), which did its best to make the big-bore Bonnies look like they came straight from Meriden. The kit TriCor developed in conjunction with Sonny Routt, a respected American supplier of Triumph speed equipment, consisted of only nine components, including new pistons, gaskets, an Allen-head center head bolt, and the cylinder barrel. It was intended that the conversion of 200 bikes be done rapidly; burlier connecting rods and proper crankshaft balancing would have meant engine removal, so these were left alone.

The kit's Routt cast-iron cylinder barrel looked very similar to the stock Triumph 650cc item. Cast by Motor Castings of Milwaukee, Wisconsin, the barrel had the corresponding amount of fins and shared the same contour. To make it look even more like a Coventry item, the corner mounting holes at the base were fly-cut to simulate the Triumph process.

According to AMA and Triumph memoranda, 145 standard 1970 Bonnevilles were converted to 750cc at the Triumph Corporation in Baltimore, Maryland, and 55 were upgraded at Triumph's western U.S. distributorship in Duarte, California. There were four extras, including the TriCor prototype. After reassembly, the motorcycles were virtually indistinguishable from the standard U.S. Bonneville 650. Only the two small Motor Castings trademarks (a small capital "C" inside a larger capital "M" and surrounded by a triangle) included on the base flange to the right of each tappet block, could give away the non-Meriden component. The part number (#E6304-T7) was also stamped into the forward face of the flange on the timing side. There were no other aftermarket cylinders used other than the one described, and any examples found today with barrels from aftermarket big-bore vendors such as MAP, Chantland, and Morgo, or without the characteristics detailed above, are probably counterfeits.

After each conversion was carried out, an extra letter T was stamped into the left-side crankcase pad, behind the existing engine number prefix, to finally read "T120RT." The conversions were executed while the machines were still strapped down in the shipping crates, which made it impossible to stamp the frame with a corresponding "T." Anyone intending to acquire one of the 204 should steer clear of any machine bearing a frame stamped "T120RT."

Because of the nature and the low numbers of this special model, official sales literature was never produced. However, the western U.S. distributor did print a leaflet that was nothing more than a standard T120R Bonneville flyer — with the 750 bore and stroke typed at the bottom.

Chapter Seven

TT-Specials (1963–1967)

Author's note: The TT Special was a variant of the standard Triumph Bonneville and as such shared the same cycle parts and paint finishes. For descriptions of general items such as frames, forks, colors, tank graphics, decal placement, and so on, the reader should refer to the general narrative that chronologically pertains to his or her motorcycle. Chapter 7 will focus only on those features specific to the Bonneville TT Special.

There is an old joke that seems to apply specifically to the Triumph Bonneville TT Special. It goes something like: "Of the 3,500 or so examples built, only 4,000 have survived!" Today many, many T120TT Bonnevilles are entered every weekend in concours across the country, but unfortunately, not all are the genuine item. Many are fudged around an orphaned motor or frame, perhaps found at a swap meet. Others are complete fabrications from scratch, with no honest claim to the heritage. Others still are the real deal. The TT buyer should really beware today — particularly at auctions!

Another problem adding to the universe of surviving TT Specials is misidentification. Because the Bonneville street scrambler shared the same engine prefix code (T120C, from 1963

to 1966) with the TT Special, many people make the mistake of assuming their discovery to be a TT and steer their restoration on the basis of the engine number alone.

Whether through ignorance or unwillingness to believe otherwise, thought is rarely given to the trials tires, lighting equipment, and speedometer that is discarded during a tear down. This is very unfortunate, as road-going T120C Bonnevilles have become exceedingly rarer (and more valuable) than the TT Specials.

The Bonneville TT Special was originally created for western U.S. off-road and steeplechase-style TT racing, hence its name. It quickly became a favorite of California desert racers as did the TR6SC Trophy Special, a single-carb version of the TT. Although not the first high-piped off-road versions of the Bonneville, the TT Special was born with the unit-construction motor in 1963. First year examples were really just stripped-down Bonnevilles with very few special parts.

The engine was listed with a 12:1 compression ratio in western U.S. distributor Johnson Motors' literature, but in reality it was 11.2:1. The 1963 TT motor came with the same racing inlet and sports exhaust cam as

Bob Sullivan's beautifully restored 1963 T120C TT Special. Basically a stripped Bonneville with higher compression and lower gearing. Straight-through high-level pipes make an unbelievable sound! Frame-mounted footpegs were a one-year feature. Scripted "Made in England" decal is inaccurate and twinseat should probably be two-toned. *Gaylin*

the Bonneville. But larger than normal 1 3/16-inch Amal 389 Monobloc carburetors were fitted with 330 main jets. There were no choke assemblies and the fuel lines were in clear plastic.

Champion N58R racing spark plugs were also specified, but these were often the first thing switched by the owner. The twin high-level exhaust pipes (#E4884/6) were the same as T120C street scrambler items but with chrome straight pipe extensions (#E4183/4) in place of the mufflers. Sales literature created the illusion that these pipes were one piece — they were not! A pair of chrome elliptical heat shields of minimal proportion were also provided for the rider.

1963 Frame and Cycle Parts

The TT's frame was a stock Bonneville item and included both centerstands and kickstands, but no passenger pegs. The operator's footrests were nonfolding and a TR6-spec skid plate was

an option. The AC ignition meant special E.T. (energy transfer) ignition coils and no battery (or battery carrier). The wiring harness was borrowed from the T100SC model, also with an E.T. system.

A TR6-type sport fuel tank painted in white came with clip-on kneepads and a chrome package rack, but most owners quickly discarded the latter, filling the holes with rubber plugs made available for this purpose. Blanking buttons in black rubber (#F5427) were also listed for the unused switch holes in the left side panel. In all factory and period literature, only the two-toned gray-and-black seat is shown, and it is unclear if any TT Specials were sent out with all-black saddles in 1963. However, some western TT's came without the safety straps.

Wheel sizes were given as 4.00x18-inch for the rear and 3.50x19 for the front. Both were covered with Dunlop Trials Universal pattern tires. The white-and-gold painted fenders in

Drive side of Sullivan's restored 1963 T120C. Rubber grommets were made available to plug the unused holes in the side covers. Painted fenders are correct but only off-road trials tires were fitted to the TT Special during its first year. Centerstand is also missing, but these were usually discarded soon after delivery. *Gaylin*

1963 were the same as specified for the Trophy 650s. The rear guard was in steel with a raised center rib and the front was aluminum, without the channel. Only a tachometer (#RC1307/01) was supplied to the TT and placed in the center of the upper fork lug on a special single-instrument bracket.

Restored machines using double-clock mountings or later single brackets that swing the tach to the right position are incorrect for 1963. There was no question about the location of the tachometer on the TR6SC Trophy Special — it didn't have any instruments at all! And there is no evidence to support that anything other than the standard twin-pull Bonneville twist grip was used on the TT Specials.

The "TT Special" designation appeared at first only in West Coast sales literature and the engines were stamped with a T120C prefix code. This prefix was also used in serial numbers of the eastern U.S. street scramblers (lower compression, battery, lighting, and so on) and restorers should check the surviving features of their machine to determine which variant they have. This also held for the 1963 TR6SC models, which were desert racers in the West but a street scrambler in the East.

For a point of reference, the engine number of the first T120C Bonneville arriving at the Triumph Corporation, the eastern U.S. distributor, in 1963 was T120C DU534. The number of the first eastern machine in TT specification was T120C DU3185, proving that TT Specials did not only go to California in 1963! Decals and their locations were as described for the standard road-going Bonneville.

1964 TT Specials

For 1964, the Bonneville TT Special's engine specifications remained relatively unchanged. A new cylinder head (#E5727) allowed larger carburetor adaptors with 1 3/8-inch threads. In

Tank top racks were part of the 1963 TT Special package, but most were removed on the first day. For this, Triumph made rubber plugs to close the unused holes. Large handlebar kill button is premature and double instrument mounting bracket is incorrect. (Restored) *Gaylin*

addition, the TT's carbs were also given special insulating blocks and face gaskets. Restorers should note that the float bowl screws were still being safety wired on all Bonnevilles, including the TT Specials. The single-unit air filter was now an official feature-the same black case with curved ends used on the T120R. The gearbox counter sprocket on both the TT and TR6SC had 18 teeth, and the drive chain made a link shorter than the road models.

1964 Frame and Cycle Parts

The TT's footpegs now sprouted from the rear engine plates but were still fixed. The bikes were shipped with both stands in place as well as a skid plate.

The TT Special inherited Triumph's new generation forks with external springs, but there was also a TR6 top lug (#H1287) with integral handlebar mounts and steering damper knob. Wide U.S. handlebars (#H1511) were standard. There were new upper covers (without headlight ears) and an L-shaped tachometer bracket (#H1668). The traditional location for the tach was on the left, but when the new mounting was used correctly (curved lip facing down) the instrument was placed on the right. This bracket was used more often for single speedometer mounting on road models and this is the presumed reason for the right-hand position. On the left handlebar, a towering new Lucas SS5 kill button was clamped that differed internally from the stopper that would be fitted to the battery models in 1966. The Smiths chronometric tachometer was now replaced with a magnetic instrument, its part number RSM3001/02.

At the back of the frame, TR6 suspension units (#64054164) were specified on both the TT and T120C models. The tire patterns were changed to Dunlop Gold Seal K70s on both ends but in the same sizes as 1963. Restorers often mistakenly fit a T120R tire (3.25x19) at the front instead of the 3.50 specified, and the difference is easily noticed. Trials Universals were kept for the TR6SC Trophy Special. Polished alloy fenders, front and rear, became standard for both off-road models, and the wide lower stay that double for a front stand was switched to a narrower sport brace.

The TT's gas tank color changed along with the other Bonneville models to gold and white, there were now flush head screws (#F3026) in place of the rubber plugs for the unused package rack mounting holes. Officially, all the TT twinseats were now solid black, while two-tone covers were cataloged for the T120C models. But these sometimes got switched around and restorers of both are safe with either seat! Transfers and decals were as applied to the 1964 Bonneville.

Engine view of a restored 1963 T120C. Lovely upswept pipes made contact breaker access a chore. Stylish heat shields were marginally effective. Most first-year examples were sent out without air cleaners as shown. However, later in the year the single box filter was fitted to TT Specials and road-going Bonnevilles. *Gaylin*

1965 TT Specials

For 1965, new piston and rings were fitted that lowered the TT's compression ratio to 11:1. A small number of eastern U.S. TT Specials were given experimental "Tuftride" camshafts. The engine numbers of these were listed from DU18838 to DU18880.

But the big news for 1965 was the appearance of the beautifully sculptured downswept TT exhaust pipes (#E5959/61). These were 1 3/4-inch racing pipes with finned header clamps and an expanded end to slip over the steel stubs. After leaving the splayed ports on the cylinder head, they immediately turned down and

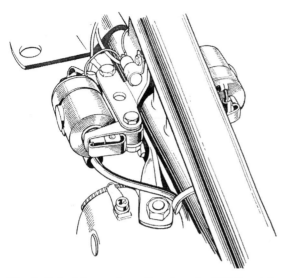

The A.C. ignition coils as fitted to the TT Specials and TR6SC models.

converged at the base of the front down tube. Continuing rearward, the pipes spread slightly apart, but remained neatly tucked under the frame precluding the use of a centerstand.

Halfway down on the forward bends there were (welded-on) threaded bosses that fastened the pipes to the front of the engine with flat straps painted in black. And at each pipe's terminus, there were two chrome ring clamps to secure them to the underside of the frame. So popular were the TT pipes that they became an immediate switch by owners of new and old 650s alike, and many aftermarket suppliers rushed to offer copies.

The 1965 TR6SC and T120C models continued with the high-level pipe arrangement as before, with straight-through extensions

The 1964 Bonneville TT Special as pictured in the Johnson Motors catalog with street tires and unpainted alloy fenders. New generation front fork and air filter can are also shown. Note solo top (front) fender brace and handlebar shims. All-black seat is pictured, but two-toned saddle was often substituted.

A beautifully restored 1964 TT Special. Package rack has been removed and mounting holes filled with optional rubber plugs. Decal is missing from the side panel but the hard-to-find switch hole grommets are in place. Centerstand also remains. Fenders appear to be stainless steel and should be aluminum. A very desirable machine! *Joe Lemay*

Sales literature image of the 1964 Trophy Special incorrectly shown with side panel switches. Photo retoucher took a little license with the exhaust pipe heat shield — they were never curved. Alloy fenders and narrow, lower front brace were now standard. This model was preferred over the TT for desert racing.

SUPPLEMENT TO

REPLACEMENT
PARTS CATALOGUE
No. 2

650 c.c. MOTORCYCLES
SUPPLIED TO THE UNITED STATES

In 1964 the Triumph factory issued this 4-page supplement to the standard B-range (650 twins) parts catalog that outlined special components fitted only to US models. This addendum also detailed the variations between the American East and West coast T120C and TR6SC models. Rather than page numbers, the supplement corresponds to figure illustrations within the spares catalog. However the TT Special was made available on both coasts in it's offroad form and the "E" and "W" classifications are somewhat misleading. Users of this chart can identify TT Special part numbers wherever the letter "W" relates to the T120C column, while the letter "E" indicates a component for the Bonneville street scrambler. The same method can be employed to separate the Trophy Special part numbers from those of the TR6SC street model.

Fig. 1

Item	Part No.	Description	E/W	6T	TR6R	T120R	TR6C	T120C
13	CP201	Piston 11.2 C.R.	W	–	–	–	–	2
20	E5450	Engine sprocket, 29 teeth Duplex	W	–	–	–	1	1
21	E4912	Distance piece	W	–	–	–	1	1
—	E4913	Dowel	W	–	–	–	1	1
23	54215824	Rotor, type RM 19	W	–	–	–	1	1

Fig. 5

Item	Part No.	Description	E/W	6T	TR6R	T120R	TR6C	T120C
9	E5727	CYLINDER HEAD ASSEMBLY	W	–	–	–	–	1
12	E5351	Carburetter adaptor, left	W	–	–	–	–	1
13	E5352	Carburetter adaptor, right	W	–	–	–	–	1

Fig. 6

Item	Part No.	Description	E/W	6T	TR6R	T120R	TR6C	T120C
11	47602	CONTACT BREAKER, type 4CA	W	–	–	–	1	1
29	45149	IGNITION COIL, type 3ET	W	–	–	–	2	2
—	F6112	Coil bracket	W	–	–	–	4	4
41	F1756	Bolt ($\frac{3}{4}$ in. U.H.)	W	–	–	–	2	2
—	W932	Bolt (1 in. U.H.)	W	–	–	–	4	4
—	F6125	Returner	W	–	–	–	2	2
—	F6136	Retainer	W	–	–	–	2	2
—	S25-43	Plain washer	W	–	–	–	2	2
—	F879	Nut	W	–	–	–	7	7
—	E1612	Serrated washer	W	–	–	–	8	8
—	54441582	Condenser	W	–	–	–	2	2
—	DS57	Bolt ($\frac{7}{16}$ in. U.H.)	W	–	–	–	1	1
45	—	Sparking plug, Champion N58R	W	–	–	–	–	2

Fig. 8

Item	Part No.	Description	E/W	6T	TR6R	T120R	TR6C	T120C
3	T1912	Mainshaft high gear	E	–	–	–	1	–
6	T968	Mainshaft second gear	E	–	–	–	1	–
9	T974	Layshaft second gear	E	–	–	–	1	–
11	T1844	Layshaft c/w high gear	E	–	–	–	1	–
12	T973	Speedometer pinion	E	–	–	–	1	–
14	T1820	Speedometer gear	E	–	–	–	1	–
—	T1227	Blanking nut (speedo drive)	W	–	–	–	1	1
21	T1918	Gearbox sprocket (19 teeth)	W	1	–	–	–	–
21	T1917	Gearbox sprocket (18 teeth)	E	–	–	–	1	1
21	T1916	Gearbox sprocket (17 teeth)	E	–	–	–	1	1
21	T1952	Gearbox sprocket (15 teeth)	E or W	–	–	–	A	A
21	T1953	Gearbox sprocket (16 teeth)	E or W	–	–	–	A	A

Fig. 10

Item	Part No.	Description	E/W	6T	TR6R	T120R	TR6C	T120C
14	T1885	Driving plate (Bonded)	E & W	6	6	6	6	6

Fig. 11

Item	Part No.	Description	E/W	6T	TR6R	T120R	TR6C	T120C
5	D444	Rear chain, 102 links	W	–	–	–	1	1
18	47188	Stator, type RM 19	W	–	–	–	1	1
18	47162	Stator, type RM 19	E & W	1	1	1	–	–

Fig. 12

Item	Part No.	Description	E/W	6T	TR6R	T120R	TR6C	T120C
11	F5786	PROP STAND COMPLETE	E & W	1	1	1	1	1

Fig. 13

Item	Part No.	Description	E/W	6T	TR6R	T120R	TR6C	T120C
15	64054164	SUSPENSION UNIT	E & W	–	2	2	2	2
15	64054164	SUSPENSION UNIT	W	2	–	–	–	–
—	F5686	Rubber grommet (stop switch holes)	W	–	–	–	2	2

Fig. 15

Item	Part No.	Description	E/W	6T	TR6R	T120R	TR6C	T120C
1	E4884	Left exhaust pipe	E & W	–	–	–	1	1
2	E4886	Right exhaust pipe	E & W	–	–	–	1	1
3	E4501	Finned clip	E & W	2	2	2	2	2
9	E3469	Clip	E & W	–	–	–	2	2
10	TE164E	Bolt	E & W	–	–	–	2	2

Item	Part No.	Description	6T	TR6R	T120R	TR6C	T120C
11	TE164D	"D" washer	E & W –	–	–	2	2
—	TE164C	"D" Nut	E & W –	–	–	2	2
14	E4132	Left silencer	E –	–	–	1	1
14	E4176	Right silencer	E –	–	–	1	1
—	E4183	Left extension pipe	W –	–	–	1	1
—	E4184	Right extension pipe	W –	–	–	1	1
—	E4889	Sleeve nut	E & W –	–	–	2	2
—	E4887	Left stay	E & W –	–	–	1	1
—	E4981	Right stay	E & W –	–	–	1	1
—	H590	Bolt ($\frac{9}{16}$ in. U.H.)	E & W –	–	–	4	4
—	S26-3	Spring washer	E & W –	–	–	4	4
18	F5087	Left pillion footrest support	E & W –	–	–	1	1
18	F5088	Right pillion footrest support	E & W –	–	–	1	1
19	H426	Bolt ($\frac{23}{32}$ in. U.H.)	E & W –	–	–	2	2
—	S26-1	Spring washer	E & W –	–	–	2	2
20	S1-52	Nut	E & W –	–	–	2	2
—	E4204	Leg guard	E & W –	–	–	2	2
—	E4207	Clip	E & W –	–	–	4	4
—	F4715	Screw	E & W –	–	–	4	4
—	E2351	Plain washer	E & W –	–	–	4	4
—	F3799	Self locking nut	E & W –	–	–	4	4

Fig. 16

Item	Part No.	Description	6T	TR6R	T120R	TR6C	T120C
—	H1580	Steady rubber	E & W 2	–	–	–	–
—	H1581	Distance piece	E & W 2	–	–	–	–
—	F3814	Cup	E & W 2	–	–	–	–
23A	54336177	Nut, for ignition switch	E & W 1	–	–	–	–
26A	180316	Nut, for lighting switch	E & W 1	–	–	–	–

Fig. 18

Item	Part No.	Description	6T	TR6R	T120R	TR6C	T120C
1	H1716	FORK ASSEMBLY	E –	–	–	1	1
1	H1717	FORK ASSEMBLY	W –	–	–	1	1
8	H1287	TOP LUG c/w CAP	E & W –	–	–	1	1
—	H506	Cup	E & W –	–	–	2	2
—	S25-3	Plain washer	E & W –	–	–	4	4
12	H1340	Bolt (1$\frac{1}{8}$ in. U.H.)	E & W –	–	–	4	4
18 & 19	H1696	Top cover	W –	–	–	2	2
—	H1580	Steady rubber	E & W –	2	2	–	–
—	H1581	Distance piece	E & W –	2	2	–	–
—	F3814	Cup	E & W –	2	2	–	–
42	H1758	Restrictor body	W –	–	–	2	2
—	H1707	Rod	W –	–	–	2	2
—	H1764	Cup	W –	–	–	2	2
—	H454	Pin	W –	–	–	2	2
—	H452	Restrictor valve	W –	–	–	2	2
—	F879	Nut	W –	–	–	2	2
—	H1761	Restrictor body cap	W –	–	–	2	2
—	T224	Nut	W –	–	–	4	4
34	H1762	Cap nut	W –	–	–	2	2

Fig's 19 & 20

For front and rear wheels for all models *except* Eastern 6T read as for TR6.

Fig. 24

Item	Part No.	Description	6T	TR6R	T120R	TR6C	T120C
23	F5957	AIR FILTER	E & W –	1	–	1	–
23	F5693	AIR FILTER	E & W 1	–	–	–	–
24	F5694	Filter element (paper)	E & W 1	1	–	1	–
—	E5262	AIR FILTER	E & W –	–	1	–	1
—	E5267	Filter element	E & W –	–	1	–	1
—	E5268	Rubber connector	E & W –	–	2	–	2

Item	Part No.	Description								6T	TR6R	T120R	TR6C	T120C
—	F6036	Clip	...	...	...	...	...	...	E & W –	–	2	–	2
—	F5857	Cap ...	...	...	...	...	...	...	E & W –	–	2	–	2
—	F4743	Bolt (2⅛ in. U.H.)	...	...	...	...	...	E & W –	–	1	–	1
—	S26-2	Spring washer	...	...	...	...	...	E & W –	–	2	–	2
—	F879	Nut	...	...	...	...	...	...	E & W –	–	2	–	2
—	F6061	Bracket	...	...	...	...	...	E & W –	–	1	–	1
—	DS57	Bolt ($\frac{7}{16}$ in. U.H.)	...	...	...	...	E & W –	–	1	–	1
18	F4875	Tool carrier	...	...	...	...	...	W –	–	–	1	1

Fig. 25

Item	Part No.	Description								6T	TR6R	T120R	TR6C	T120C
—	F5427	Grommet (for switch holes)	...	...	...	...	W –	–	–	2
27	F5366A	TWINSEAT	...	...	...	...	...	E 1	1	1	1	1

Fig. 26

Item	Part No.	Description								6T	TR6R	T120R	TR6C	T120C
1 & 8	H1677	Front mudguard (undrilled)	...	...	...	...	E & W 1	1	1	–	–
4 & 21	H1678	Bottom stay	...	...	...	...	E & W 1	1	1	–	–
10 & 14	H1683	Mudguard bridge	...	...	...	...	E & W 1	1	1	1	1
9 & 13	H1685	Bracket	...	...	...	...	E & W 2	2	2	–	–
12	H1681	Front stay ...	...	...	...	...	E & W 1	1	1	1	1
8	H1687	Front mudguard (polished)	...	...	...	...	E & W –	–	–	1	1
13	H1688	Bracket	...	...	...	...	E & W –	–	–	2	2
21	H1273	Bottom stay	...	...	...	...	E & W –	–	–	1	1
33	F5955	Mudguard blade (polished)	...	...	...	W –	–	–	1	1
43	F3363	Number plate	...	...	...	...	E 1	1	1	1	1
43	F3363	Number plate	...	...	...	...	W 1	1	1	–	–
—	F3327	Rubber grommet (rear mudguard)	...	...	W –	–	–	2	2

Fig. 27

Item	Part No.	Description								6T	TR6R	T120R	TR6C	T120C
1	H1694	Handlebar	...	...	...	...	...	E & W 1	–	–	–	–
1	H1511	Handlebar	...	...	...	...	...	E & W –	1	1	1	1
3	313/6	Twistgrip ...	...	...	...	...	E & W –	–	1	–	1
13	18/935	Front brake lever	...	...	...	E & W –	1	1	1	1
23	18/993	Clutch lever	...	...	...	...	E & W –	1	1	–	–
23	18/993	Clutch lever	...	...	...	...	E –	–	–	1	1
23	18/942	Clutch lever	...	...	...	...	W –	–	–	1	1

Fig. 28

Item	Part No.	Description								6T	TR6R	T120R	TR6C	T120C
4	D417	Front brake cable	...	...	...	...	E & W 1	1	1	1	1
15	D528	Throttle cable	...	...	...	...	E & W –	–	2	–	2
29	H1580	Steady rubber	...	...	...	...	E & W 2	2	2	–	–
30	H1581	Distance piece	...	...	...	...	E & W 2	2	2	–	–
31	F3814	Cup	...	...	...	...	...	E & W 2	2	2	–	–

Fig. 30

Item	Part No.	Description								6T	TR6R	T120R	TR6C	T120C
22	376/100	Main jet, size 270 ...	...	...	...	...	E & W 1	–	–	–	–

Fig. 31

Item	Part No.	Description								6T	TR6R	T120R	TR6C	T120C
23	376/100	Main jet, size 310 ...	...	...	...	...	E & W –	1	–	1	–
23	376/100	Main jet, size 260 ...	...	...	...	...	E & W –	–	2	–	2

Note: West Coasts T120C has 1 $\frac{3}{16}$ in. carburetters with 330 main jet.

| 47 | E4918 | Insulating block | ... | ... | ... | ... | W – | – | – | 2 |
| 48 | E4949 | Joint washer | ... | ... | ... | ... | W – | – | – | 2 |

Fig. 32

Item	Part No.	Description								6T	TR6R	T120R	TR6C	T120C
15	54934830	Wiring harness	...	...	...	...	W –	–	–	1	1
16A	54336177	Nut, for ignition switch	...	...	...	E & W –	1	1	–	–
19A	180316	Nut, for lighting switch ...	...	...	E & W –	1	1	–	–
—	31376	Cut-out button, type SS5	...	...	...	W –	–	–	1	1
—	H1669	Cup	...	...	...	...	...	W –	–	–	1	1
—	H1670	Clip	...	...	...	...	...	W –	–	–	2	2
—	H687	Bolt ($\frac{3}{8}$ in. U.H.) ...	...	...	...	W –	–	–	1	1
—	H745	Nut	...	...	...	...	...	W –	–	–	1	1

Fig. 33

Item	Part No.	Description								6T	TR6R	T120R	TR6C	T120C
38A	D546	Rubber plug for tachometer	...	...	...	W –	–	–	1	1

A 1965 Bonneville TT Special as appearing in the JoMo sales catalog. First year for the TT pipes and lovely blue/silver color combination make it perhaps the most desirable year. Eastern U.S. examples reverted back to painted steel fenders after the first 50. Most TTs came with all-black twinseats.

on the Trophy Special and mufflers on the Bonneville scrambler. Both models also kept their centerstands.

1965 Frame and Cycle Parts

There were new front fork internals for all of Triumph's B-range, including the TT Special, that gave more progressive damping. The fork's sliders and detachable axle caps were now machined from steel billet and were much stronger. The TT came with a Smiths magnetic tachometer (#RSM3001/02) and L-shaped mounting bracket as described for 1964, but neither were yet listed for the California TR6SC models.

Mysteriously, the handlebar identification number was changed in 1965 to H1870. It is unclear how these bars differed from the earlier version, especially in light of the 1966 handlebars again being listed as H1511. All TTs as well as the Trophy Specials were fitted with new folding footpegs (#F6653/54) that collapsed at a 45-degree angle. The mounting location and rubbers remained unchanged.

In the sheet metal (tinware) department, the unused holes for the brakelight switch

on the chain guard were closed with smaller rubber buttons than those still being used on the side panel. The fenders on the California-bound TT and Trophy Specials remained (unpainted) in polished aluminum. The TT models sent to the eastern U.S. were listed with painted fenders — the front aluminum and the rear steel, with a raised center rib. However, the first 51 examples for that year arriving at the Triumph Corporation still had polished alloy guards, front and rear! The new colors for 1965 were Pacific-blue over silver and the painted fenders (silver) were given a blue center stripe lined in gold. Curiously, tank-top parcel grills were still being sent on all, including the Trophies.

Nineteen sixty-five would be the last year for the Bonneville scramblers. Few of these road-going T120C models were produced in their final season and today they are rare in the extreme, commanding great value. The engine number of the first of these to arrive at the eastern U.S. warehouse was T120C DU13515. The first recorded number for the TT Specials was T120C DU13970.

The 1965 West Coast TR6SC Trophy Special still delivered with parcel rack and center stand. Skid plate and trials tires were also standard. Publicity photo. *Author collection*

1966 TT Specials

The TT Specials incorporated all T120R improvements announced for 1966, including new high performance camshafts (#E4819– intake, E4855–exhaust.) At engine number DU31119, the exhaust cam was changed again (#E5047). The 11:1 compression ratio was still listed, as was the special E5727 cylinder head with enlarged adaptors for the Amal 1 3/16 carburetors. Individual pancake-type filters were now fitted to the eastern TT Specials, but the unified filter remained on the West Coast TT models for one more year. And the float bowl screws were no longer safety-wired and now flush mounted.

Other engine-related business saw a new external tachometer drive on the front of the motor that spun at one-quarter engine speed. This dictated a new revmeter (#RSM3003/01) for all Bonnevilles, including the TT. At engine number DU24875, the gearbox sprocket was reduced to 17 teeth and the detachable rear wheel sprocket changed to 46 teeth. There were new high-level exhaust pipes for the western off-road Trophy Specials that exited on the left

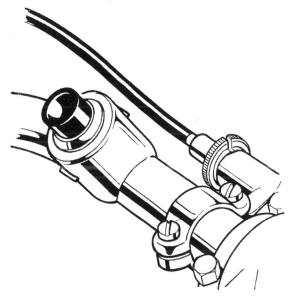

Mammoth handlebar kill button fitted to the TR6SC and TT Special.

side and stacked above each other, the right-hand tube on top. These were still open pipes and not intended for street use. The new TR6C arrangement was more stylish but by itself did not improve performance.

SUPPLEMENT TO

REPLACEMENT
PARTS CATALOGUE
No. 3

650 c.c. MOTORCYCLES
SUPPLIED TO THE UNITED STATES

In 1965 the Triumph factory issued this 4-page supplement to the standard B-range (650 twins) parts catalog that outlined special components fitted only to US models. This addendum also detailed the variations between the American East and West coast T120C and TR6SC models. Rather than page numbers, the supplement corresponds to figure illustrations within the spares catalog. However the TT Special was made available on both coasts in it's offroad form and the "E" and "W" classifications are somewhat misleading. Users of this chart can identify TT Special part numbers wherever the letter "W" relates to the T120C column, while the letter "E" indicates a component for the Bonneville street scrambler. The same method can be employed to separate the Trophy Special part numbers from those of the TR6SC street model.

Item	Part No.	Description	6T	TR6R	T120R	TR6C	T120
Fig. 1							
13	CP202	Piston, 11:1 C.R.	W –	–	–	–	2
20	E5450	Engine sprocket, 29 teeth DUPLEX	W –	–	–	1	1
21	E4912	Distance piece	W –	–	–	1	1
—	E4913	Dowel	W –	–	–	1	1
23	54215824	Rotor, type RM19	W –	–	–	1	1
Fig. 5							
9	E5727	CYLINDER HEAD ASSEMBLY	W –	–	–	–	1
12	E5351	Carburettor adaptor, left	W –	–	–	–	1
13	E5352	Carburetter adapter, right	W –	–	–	–	1
Fig. 6							
11	47602	CONTACT BREAKER, type 4 CA	W –	–	–	1	1
29	45149	IGNITION COIL, type 3ET	W –	–	–	2	2
—	F6112	Coil bracket	W –	–	–	4	4
41	F1756	Bolt ($\frac{3}{4}$ in. U.H.)	W –	–	–	2	2
—	W932	Bolt (1 in. U.H.)	W –	–	–	4	4
—	F6125	Retainer	W –	–	–	2	2
—	F6136	Retainer	W –	–	–	2	2
—	S25-43	Plain washer	W –	–	–	2	2
—	F879	Nut	W –	–	–	7	7
—	E1612	Serrated washer	W –	–	–	8	8
—	54441582	Condenser	W –	–	–	2	2
—	DS57	Bolt ($\frac{7}{16}$ in. U.H.)	W –	–	–	1	1
45	—	Sparking plug, Champion N58R	W –	–	–	–	2
Fig. 8							
3	T1912	Mainshaft high gear	E –	–	–	1	–
6	T968	Mainshaft second gear	E –	–	–	1	–
9	T974	Layshaft second gear	E –	–	–	1	–
11	T1844	Layshaft c/w high gear	E –	–	–	1	–
12	T973	Speedometer pinion	E –	–	–	1	–
14	T1820	Speedometer gear	E –	–	–	1	–
—	T1227	Blanking nut (speedo drive)	W –	–	–	1	1
21	T1917	Gearbox sprocket (18 teeth)	E –	–	–	1	1
21	T1916	Gearbox sprocket (17 teeth)	E –	–	–	1	1
21	T1952	Gearbox sprocket (15 teeth)	E or W –	–	–	A	A
21	T1953	Gearbox sprocket (26 teeth)	E or W –	–	–	A	A
Fig. 11							
5	D444	Rear chain, 102 links	W –	–	–	1	1
18	47188	Stator, type RM19	W –	–	–	1	1
Fig. 12							
11	F5786	PROP STAND COMPLETE	E & W 1	1	1	1	1
Fig. 13							
15	64054164	SUSPENSION UNIT	E & W 2	2	2	2	2
—	F5686	Rubber grommet (switch holes)	W –	–	–	2	2
Fig. 14							
13	F6653	LEFT FOOTREST ASSEMBLY	W –	–	–	1	1
14	F6654	RIGHT FOOTREST ASSEMBLY	W –	–	–	1	1
—	F6409	Left footrest	W –	–	–	1	1
—	F6410	Right footrest	W –	–	–	1	1
—	F6411	Footrest pedal	W –	–	–	2	2
—	F6655	Pivot bolt	W –	–	–	2	2
Fig. 15							
1	E4884	Left exhaust pipe	E –	–	–	1	1
1	E4884	Left exhaust pipe	W –	–	–	1	–
1	F5959	Left exhaust pipe	W –	–	–	–	1
2	E4886	Right exhaust pipe	E –	–	–	1	1
2	E4886	Right exhaust pipe	W –	–	–	1	–
2	E5961	Right exhaust pipe	W –	–	–	–	1
14	E5866	Silencer	E & W –	2	2	–	–
14	E4132	Left silencer	E –	–	–	1	1
14	E4176	Right silencer	E –	–	–	1	1
—	E4183	Left extension pipe	W –	–	–	1	–
—	E4184	Right extension pipe	W –	–	–	1	–
—	E4889	Sleeve nut	E –	–	–	2	2
—	E4889	Sleeve nut	W –	–	–	2	–
—	E5963	Stud	W –	–	–	–	1
—	S1-51	Nut	W –	–	–	–	2
—	E4887	Left stay	E –	–	–	1	1
—	E4887	Left stay	W –	–	–	1	–

Item	Part No.	Description	6T	TR6R	T120R	TR6C	T120C
—	E5964	Left stay	W –	–	–	–	1
—	E4981	Right stay	E –	–	–	1	1
—	E4981	Right stay	W –	–	–	1	–
—	E5965	Right stay	W –	–	–	–	1
—	H590	Bolt ($\frac{9}{16}$ in. U.H.)	E –	–	–	2	2
—	H590	Bolt ($\frac{9}{16}$ in. U.H.)	W –	–	–	2	–
—	S26-3	Spring washer	E –	–	–	4	4
—	S26-3	Spring washer	W –	–	–	4	2
—	F929	Bolt ($\frac{1}{2}$ in. U.H.)	E & W –	–	–	2	2
—	E5966	Clip	W –	–	–	–	2
—	T1439	Bolt ($1\frac{3}{16}$ in. U.H.)	W –	–	–	–	2
—	F4299	Plain washer	W –	–	–	–	2
—	S1-51	Nut	W –	–	–	–	2
18	F5087	Left bracket	E –	–	–	1	1
18	F5087	Left bracket	W –	–	–	1	–
18	F5088	Right bracket	E –	–	–	1	1
18	F5088	Right bracket	W –	–	–	1	–
19	H426	Bolt ($\frac{23}{32}$ in. U.H.)	E –	–	–	2	2
19	H426	Bolt ($\frac{23}{32}$ in. U.H.)	W –	–	–	2	–
—	S26-1	Spring washer	E –	–	–	2	2
—	S26-1	Spring washer	W –	–	–	2	–
20	S1-52	Nut	E –	–	–	2	2
20	S1-52	Nut	W –	–	–	2	–
—	E4204	Leg guard	E –	–	–	2	2
—	E4204	Leg guard	W –	–	–	2	–
—	E4207	Clip	E –	–	–	4	4
—	E4207	Clip	W –	–	–	4	–
—	F4715	Screw ($\frac{13}{32}$ in. U.H.)	E –	–	–	4	4
—	F4715	Screw ($\frac{13}{32}$ in. U.H.)	W –	–	–	4	–
—	E2351	Plain washer	E –	–	–	4	4
—	E2351	Plain washer	W –	–	–	4	–
—	F3799	Self locking nut	E –	–	–	4	4
—	F3799	Self locking nut	W –	–	–	4	–

Fig. 17

Item	Part No.	Description	6T	TR6R	T120R	TR6C	T120C
23A	54336177	Nut, for ignition switch	E 1	–	–	–	–
26A	180316	Nut, for lighting switch	E 1	–	–	–	–

Fig. 18

Item	Part No.	Description	6T	TR6R	T120R	TR6C	T120C
1	H1925	FORK ASSEMBLY	E & W –	–	–	1	1
8	H1287	TOP LUG c/w CAPS	E & W –	–	–	1	1
—	H506	Caps	E & W –	–	–	2	2
—	S25-3	Plain washer	E & W –	–	–	4	4
12	H1340	Bolt ($1\frac{1}{8}$ in. U.H.)	E & W –	–	–	4	4
18 & 19	H1696	Top cover	E & W –	–	–	2	2
22	H1892	Main spring (Green)	E & W –	–	–	2	2
—	H1913	DAMPER ASSEMBLY	E & W –	–	–	2	2
42	H1893	Restrictor body	E & W –	–	–	2	2
—	H1897	Rod	E & W –	–	–	2	2
—	H1764	Cup	E & W –	–	–	2	2
—	H454	Pin	E & W –	–	–	2	2
—	F879	Nut	E & W –	–	–	2	2
—	H1761	Restrictor body cap	E & W –	–	–	2	2
—	T224	Nut	E & W –	–	–	4	4
34	H1762	Cap nut	E & W –	–	–	2	2

Fig's 19 & 20

FOR FRONT AND REAR WHEELS FOR ALL MODELS
EXCEPT EASTERN 6T READ AS FOR TR6.

Fig. 24

Item	Part No.	Description	6T	TR6R	T120R	TR6C	T120C
23	F6432	AIR FILTER	E & W –	1	–	1	–
23	F6433	AIR FILTER	E –	–	–	–	–
24	F5694	Filter element (paper)	E & W 1	1	–	1	–
—	F5262	AIR FILTER	E & W –	–	1	–	1
—	F5267	Filter element	E & W –	–	1	–	1
—	E5268	Rubber connector	E & W –	–	2	–	2
—	F6036	Clip	E & W –	–	2	–	2
—	F5857	Cap	E & W –	–	2	–	2
—	F4743	Bolt ($2\frac{1}{8}$ in. U.H.)	E & W –	–	2	–	2

Item	Part No.	Description	6T	TR6R	T120R	TR6C	T120C
—	S26-2	Spring washer	E & W –	–	2	–	2
—	F879	Nut	E & W –	–	2	–	2
—	F6061	Bracket	E & W –	–	1	–	1
—	DS57	Bolt ($\frac{7}{16}$ in. U.H.)	E & W –	–	1	–	1
18	F4875	Tool carrier	W –	–	–	1	1

Fig. 25

Item	Part No.	Description	6T	TR6R	T120R	TR6C	T120C
—	F5427	Grommet (for switch holes)	E –	–	–	2	2
27	F5366A	TWINSEAT	E –	–	1	1	1

Fig. 26

Item	Part No.	Description	6T	TR6R	T120R	TR6C	T120C
1 & 8	H1677	Front mudguard (undrilled)	E 1	1	1	1	1
1 & 8	H1677	Front mudguard (undrilled)	W –	1	1	–	–
21	H1678	Bottom stay	E & W 1	1	1	–	–
14	H1683	Mudguard bridge	E & W 1	1	1	1	1
9	H1685	Bracket	E 2	–	–	–	–
12	H1681	Front stay	E & W 1	1	1	1	1
8	H1687	Front mudguard (polished)	W –	–	–	1	1
13	H1688	Bracket	W –	–	–	2	2
21	H1273	Bottom stay	W –	–	–	1	1
33	F5955	Mudguard blade (polished)	W –	–	–	1	1
43	F6435	Number plate	E 1	1	1	1	1
43	F6435	Number plate	W –	1	1	–	–
—	F3327	Rubber grommet (rear mudguard)	W –	–	–	2	2

Fig. 27

Item	Part No.	Description	6T	TR6R	T120R	TR6C	T120C
1	H1869	Handlebar	E 1	–	–	–	–
1	H1870	Handlebar	E & W –	1	1	1	1
3	313/6	Twistgrip	E & W –	–	1	–	1
13	18/951	FRONT BRAKE LEVER ASSEMBLY ...	E & W –	–	1	–	1
14	18/754	Front brake lever	E & W –	–	1	–	1
15	18/777	Lever bracket	E & W –	–	1	–	1
22	18/838	Cable adjuster	E & W –	–	1	–	1
23	18/839	Thumb nut	E & W –	–	1	–	1
28	18/952	CLUTCH LEVER ASSEMBLY ...	E & W –	–	1	–	1
29	18/752	Clutch lever	E & W –	–	1	–	1
30	18/773	Lever bracket	E & W –	–	1	–	1

Fig. 28

Item	Part No.	Description	6T	TR6R	T120R	TR6C	T120C
4	D559	Front brake cable	E & W 1	1	1	1	1
15	D528	Throttle cable	E & W –	–	2	–	2
29	H1580	Steady rubber	E & W 2	2	2	–	–
30	H1581	Distance piece	E & W 2	2	2	–	–
31	F3814	Cup	E & W 2	2	2	–	–

Fig. 30

Item	Part No.	Description	6T	TR6R	T120R	TR6C	T120C
22	376/100	Main jet, size 270	E & W 1	–	–	–	–

Fig. 31

Item	Part No.	Description	6T	TR6R	T120R	TR6C	T120C
23	376/100	Main jet, size 310	E & W –	1	–	1	–
23	376/100	Main jet, size 260	E & W –	–	2	–	2
		Note: West Coasts T120C has 1 $\frac{3}{16}$ in. carburetter with 330 main jet.					
47	E4918	Insulating block	W –	–	–	–	2
48	E4949	Joint washer	W –	–	–	–	2

Fig. 32

Item	Part No.	Description	6T	TR6R	T120R	TR6C	T120C
15	54937097	Wiring harness	W –	–	–	1	1
16A	54336177	Nut, for ignition switch	E & W –	1	1	–	–
19A	180316	Nut, for lighting switch	E & W –	1	1	–	–
—	31376	Cut-out button, type SS5 ...	W –	–	–	1	1
—	H1669	Cup	W –	–	–	1	1
—	H1670	Clip	W –	–	–	2	2
—	H687	Bolt ($\frac{3}{8}$ in. U.H.)	W –	–	–	1	1
—	H745	Nut	W –	–	–	1	1

Fig. 33

Item	Part No.	Description	6T	TR6R	T120R	TR6C	T120C
20	53973	STOP/TAIL LAMP (type 679)	E 1	–	–	–	–
20	53972	STOP/TAIL LAMP (type 679)	E & W –	1	1	1	1
21	54572932	Lens	E & W 1	1	1	1	1
23	54571677	Gasket	E & W 1	1	1	1	1
24	572289	Screw	E & W 2	2	2	2	2
26	54573248	Bulb holder	E & W 1	1	1	1	1
—	F6436	Adaptor	E & W 1	1	1	1	1
—	F6438	Distance piece	E & W 2	2	2	2	2
—	F6439	Screw (1$\frac{3}{4}$ in. U.H.)	E & W 2	2	2	2	2
38A	D546	Rubber plug for tachometer	W –	–	–	1	1

1966 Frame and Cycle Parts

The 1966 TT Specials also inherited new steering geometry and horizontal fairing mounts on the headstock introduced for that year. At engine number DU27672, the lower fork lugs were modified to take advantage of the wider steering permitted by a smaller gas tank. On the handlebars, a giant Lucas kill button (#31071) was fitted to the right-hand side. It sat atop a tall chrome shroud and was identical in appearance to the item used on the battery ignition models (#35601) except for the button's

color — black for the TT and Trophy Specials and brown for all others. There was also a new Smiths tachometer (#RSM3001/01), but the 1966 parts book incorrectly identifies the double instrument mounting bracket for the TT.

The TTs appearing in 1966 sales literature are pictured with new light gray Amal grips, but is unlikely that many T120TTs were shipped with the lighter-colored handles. By the time the models were being assembled, handgrips with the same shape but molded in black were being fitted as standard on all models. Keeping

Lee Estes' magnificent 1966 Bonneville Special restored by Britech and pictured here with the optional polished aluminum fenders. East Coast T120TTs came with painted steel mudguards in white, with a Grenadier Red center stripe. There is no evidence supporting the presence of stainless steel fenders on a new TT Special in 1966! *Gaylin*

With the arrival of the slimline fuel tank in 1966, the tank top parcel rack and its mounting holes were eliminated. From this angle, Estes' restored machine appears to be all business and no B.S.! Note the right-hand tachometer mounting and massive kill button on the bars. *Gaylin*

Meaty 3.50x19-inch front tire was standard on all TT Specials. Difficult to find, most restorers opt for the T120R Bonneville's 3.25-inch section, noticeable on the TT. Chromed earthquake-makers astride the front frame tube obsoleted the centerstand. (Restored) *Gaylin*

in mind the factory's intention to keep the lighter two-toned seats from the off-road bikes and gray grips on a TT Special become even more doubtful.

The introduction of Triumph's slimline tanks spelled the end of package racks for all the off-road bikes. The finish for the Bonneville TT was now Alaskan-white, with a three-piece racing stripe in Grenadier-red on the upper spine. The TR6SC was given a similar scheme in Pacific-blue with a white racing stripe. Like the T120R road models, there was a chrome styling strip for the raised welded seam. This was also the first year for the hypnotic "large eyebrow" tank emblem and paint-fouling filler cap with inner security chain. The kneegrips

were also increased in size and now cemented in place.

The West Coast fenders continued in polished aluminum front and rear but in the East, TT fenders were sometimes in painted steel - white with Grenadier-red stripes lined in gold. Although the stainless steel guards being fitted to the T120R might have been preferred at the time, there is no evidence supporting their place on 1966 TT models.

As indicated earlier, it was Meriden's intent to use the two-toned (gray-and-black) twinseats on the street bikes and reserve the all-black saddles for the competition models. But as long as there was a choice, anything was possible and even factory ad literature is ambivalent about this detail. Under the seat there was now a solid left-hand side panel without the switch holes or the need for blanking grommets.

The first group of TT Specials leaving the factory in 1966 had cases stamped with T120C engine prefixes. Later examples finally wore the sacred T120TT code. The not-so-sacred "S" was eventually dropped from the Trophy Special identity prefix, afterward reading TR6C. This model was still available in desert racer form in the West, but also as a street scrambler on both coasts, without a change in the TR6C engine code.

Decals used on the 1966 T120TT models were as found on the T120R Bonnevilles — still no specific stickers listed for the TT Specials. There were 798 Bonneville TT Specials made during the year.

Engine view of the Britech 1966 Bonneville TT Special. Because they are pictured in most of the factory sales literature for that year, gray handgrips are desired by many restorers. However, black versions were the reality. Unified air filter can is accurate but the Allenhead cover screws are not. Early 1966 examples carried T120C engine prefixes, later machines were stamped T120TT. *Gaylin*

1966 Trophy Special as depicted in the Johnson Motors catalog. High-level pipes now stacked on the left for a unique sonic experience. Note the complete lack of any instrumentation. What is the purpose of the safety strap when there are no passenger pegs?

A restored 1966 U.S. Trophy Special waiting the auction block at Daytona in 1995. Modified air filter arrangement was typical of these desert racers. Centerstand is long gone, but the necessary skid plate remains. *Lindsay Brooke*

The 1967 T120TT as the factory saw it, with early Aubergine and gold tank finish lined in white. The lower color on later examples was changed to white (lined in gold.) All TTs that year came with solid black seats. Note the microscopically scripted "Bonneville 120" transfer on the side panel. Publicity photo. *Author Collection*

Restorers should note that the "Bonneville T.T. Special" decal (#D681) pictured here is inaccurate on any TT model. These were created as part of a new series of transfers for 1968, when it was still uncertain whether the TT model would continue in production. As there were no 1968 TT Specials, this decal was never applied to a factory-built machine. They look great, but only the scripted "Bonneville 120" (#A57) is authentic! *Lindsay Brooke*

1967 TT Specials

There were many modifications made to the B-range motors in 1967 and the TT Special again assumed many of the improvements, including Hepolite pistons and the changeover to UNF threads. After engine number DU59320, Amal 30-millimeter Concentric carburetors were specified for all 650 twins, but it is unclear if any TT models were hung with the new mixers. If so, these would have been without choke slides. And there was still one less link in the drive chain, but it's doubtful that a concours judge would spot the difference!

1967 Frame and Cycle Parts

The chassis of the 1967 Bonneville TT Special incorporated Unified threads on the rear frame section and was given a special kickstand (#F7373) to finally compensate for the larger front tire. Tire sizes had not changed since the model's inception. The front Dunlop K70 was 3.50x19 inches, and a 4.00x18 was still listed for the rear. Skid plates were still standard, as were the retractable footpegs and TT pipes.

Two views of a restored 1967 Bonneville TT Special owned by Chuck Spilman. Stainless fenders finally appeared in 1967. Correct tank graphics but handgrips from the previous model year and a tachometer cable of the wrong length. A machine that begs to be stood on its back wheel! *Lindsay Brooke*

On the front fork there were new black wire tension clips for the rubber gaiters, top and bottom. The Amal hard rubber handlebar grips were switched for softer but chubbier Italian-made Gran Turisimos, in black only. The Smiths tachometer and right-hand mounting bracket were not changed from the previous season. And the H1511 handlebar was still cataloged.

For 1967 there was only one set of TT specifications for both U.S. coasts. For the first and only year stainless steel fenders were specified for the TT Special. The slimline gas tanks were finished completely in Aubergine (deep purple) with a small gold panel sweeping down from the tank emblem and curling under the large black kneegrip. But at engine number DU48157, the gold panel was switched to Alaskan-white. To expedite wear and scratching on the purple tank, the chained filler cap was again specified. A new-generation twinseat was introduced with a small bump stop at the tail along with the stenciled Triumph trademark that had been introduced in 1966. While a two-toned version in black and gray was reserved for the street bikes, it should be noted that all the TT seats were black.

Engines of the TT Special continued to be stamped with the T120TT prefix. The TR6C model, on the other hand, was no longer available as a desert racer and was offered only in street

Restorer's Tip: TT Decals

The final year of the TT Special used the existing set of decals from the 1967 T120R models, including the small scripted "Bonneville 120" (#A57) for the left side cover. (For more details of all the stickers, readers should refer to the general text.)

Many restorers attach an attractive "Bonneville TT Special" transfer (#D681) to the left side enclosure that is certainly more impressive. This sticker was in gold and placed the dramatic Bonneville script (from 1968) diagonally over an italicized "TT Special." But this decal was part of the new range of 1968 graphics, created after TT production had been discontinued. Restorers should be aware that A57 was the only factory applied transfer ever to grace the left cover of the TT models.

scrambler form. A confidential factory memo sent to the eastern U.S. distributor on June 19, 1967, included the sad words, "650cc 120TT are no longer being produced." According to official Meriden log books, 1,100 TT Specials were made during their last year of production — of which only 1,200 have survived, of course!

Chapter Eight

Umberslade Twins (1971–1975)

It is not the purpose of this book to offer recommendations of one model year over another. The 650cc twins produced in 1971 and 1972 have earned, unfairly or not, the reputation as being poor examples of the Triumph marque. Some of the reasons for these criticisms are obvious while others are just perpetuations of accepted opinion.

But like 'em or not, they are still Triumph motorcycles and they deserve thorough description for the purposes of restoration. This involves detailing mistakes and design weaknesses, as well as explaining the reason behind the modifications.

In 1971 a new generation chassis and accompanying running gear were developed by the BSA research and design facility at Umberslade Hall in Britain. The Umberslade effort was originally conceived to modernize the sagging BSA brand in the late 1960s. But when the parent BSA Group decided to merge the two motorcycle companies, the new frame (factory coded P39) was redesigned to accept the Triumph 650 engine as well.

The P39 frame was an all-welded design that combined a duplex (twin downtube) cradle with a large single backbone tube that doubled as an oil reservoir. Significantly lighter and stronger, the new frame replaced Triumph's proven single front downtube frame, with its brazed cast-iron lugs and bolt-on rear sub-frame, that had steadily evolved since 1963. The oil-bearing spine measured three inches in diameter. It was welded to the steering head and extended back to join the rear subframe, then turned straight down to form the seat post.

A sump plate with central drain plug and a cylindrical wire-screen filter was attached at the base of the tube by four screws. On early machines, this plate and filter were a single unit, but they later became separate components to simplify service.

The oil filler neck was originally intended to be welded on just aft of the steering head, which would have allowed more than three quarts of lubricant. But frothing problems and the need to accommodate two different engines and two sets of cycle parts forced its relocation to the bend at the seat post. In this spot, the oil reservoir held only 4 pints, a backwards step that guaranteed hotter-running engines.

The redesigned chassis mandated completely new hardware, including stepped rear engine plates, footrests (still folding on the TR6C

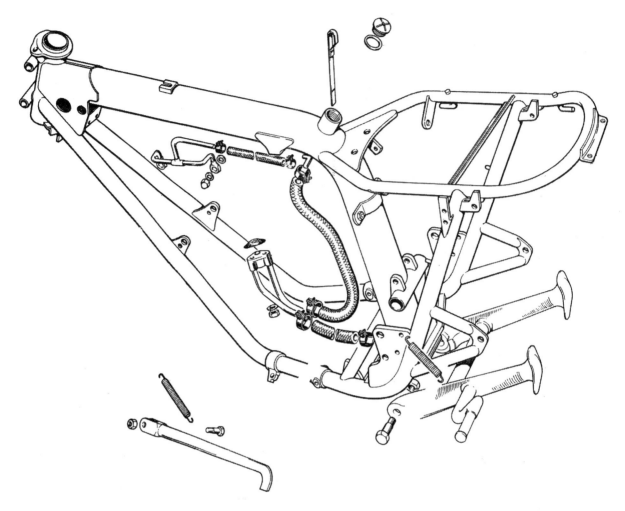

General layout of the early-type oil-bearing frame with high seat rails.

Trophy), welded brake pedal, an abbreviated chain guard, and all new stands. The centerstand swivel was reinforced after production began when it was realized the early condition caused fractures at the base of the oil bearing spine. At the rear, stiffer Girling suspension units (#64052341) with a heavier 110-pound spring rate and closer pitched chrome external springs were also specified. And the skid plate on the Trophy model also had to be reshaped.

The telescopic front fork that had undergone steady evolution through 1970 was replaced by a completely new design. The new unit looked similar to Ceriani racing forks and for the first time pivoted on tapered roller bearings. The exposed upper stanchions were hard chrome-plated and sat in unpainted alloy lower sliders with a raised rib on the outer flanks. The fork springs were internal and two-way damping was checked by a clack valve. Overall travel was 6 inches. Dust scrapers replaced the rubber gaiters and detachable axle caps secured by four studs (and self-locking nuts) returned to the bottom of the sliders. Steering dampers were no longer supplied as standard but were available upon request.

There were new fork lug castings in black enamel that contained mounting bosses (top and bottom) for a pair of bent chrome wire headlight supports. Secured by the stanchion cap nuts, chrome-plated hoops were fitted above both fork tubes to support each Smiths

"Dr. Umberslade's Frankenstein!" A publicity photo from the 1971 press kit shows the new generation oil bearing frame Bonneville in U.S. trim. Visible front end details include rubber cable gaiter between the brake arms, raised outer rib on the fork slider, and wire-mounted front fender. Tank kneegrips were not fitted to U.S. models. *Author collection*

instrument, themselves now completely encased in rubber cups. The Trophy 650 came only with a single speedometer mounted above the right tube, and U.S. sales literature showing this model with a tachometer fixed above the left stanchion is incorrect. The sealing arrangement on the early forks proved insufficient. Leaks were common, especially in the United States where neglect and infrequent motorcycle usage promoted corrosion of the vulnerable upper stanchions. Later 1971 models came with an improved seal that was only marginally better.

Style took precedence over function in many areas on the 1971 650s. The front fender was shamefully shortened in length, and its minimal support consisted of a single thin rod on each side, welded toward the tips. The rods were then clamped in the middle to tapped bosses on the inside of the lower sliders. But the fenders were not vertically braced, making them slaves to engine vibration. Most mudguards developed rod fractures almost immediately. Late in the season another rod was added in the center to keep the fender from self-destructing.

Another 1971 Bonneville parked outside the lobby of the eastern U.S. distributor. From this profile view the 34-inch seat height can really be appreciated. Unsightly gray speedometer cable and "zero tolerance" rear shocks can also be seen. Also of note are the shorter front brake arms. Period photo.
Author collection

One of the few features Triumph kept from its forced rationalization with BSA in 1971 was the scripted "Made in England" transfer (#60-3361). This sticker was found only on BSA-built machines before then but many restorers of 1950s and 1960s Triumphs incorrectly affix it to their projects. Edward Turner would not have approved! (Unrestored) *Gaylin*

On the rear fender, a chrome brace passed under the taillight and still carried a grab rail on top similar to (but not the same as) the bracket used in 1970. A red safety reflector fastened to the rail's gusset on each side and corresponding amber reflectors were attached to the frame behind the steering head.

The Umberslade designers jettisoned the BSA-Triumph twin-leading shoe front brake introduced only three seasons earlier, in favor of a new conical alloy design that resembled Manx Norton items. But this second-generation TLS design was not as effective as its predecessor. Its plainer-looking alloy backing plate incorporated a massive air scoop on the upper half and two separate grilled exit vents at the bottom. There was a rubber grommetted hole in the plate to provide adjustment access to each brake shoe internally.

Two shortened cam levers were squeezed together by the control cable and a thin rubber

The 1971 Tiger-650. Different paint and a single carburetor (and cylinder head) are all that differentiated it from the T120R. Frame gave better handling than its predecessor but the motor could not be installed with the rocker boxes in place. Publicity photo. *Author collection*

The least common of the 1971 oil bearing 650 models were the TR6Cs. This drive side view reveals the high-level exhaust system with chrome-plated "barbecue grill." Smaller 6-inch Lucas headlight was standard but the tachometer was available only as an option. Publicity photo. *Author collection*

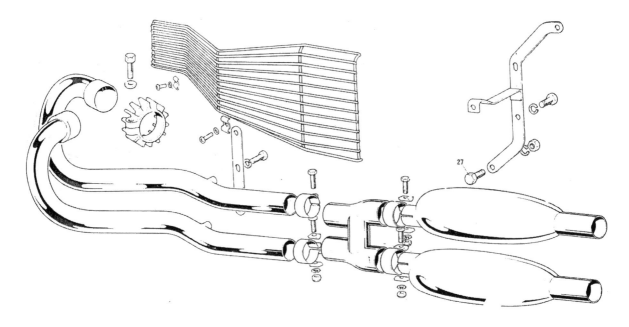

Order of assembly of the 1971-72 TR6C high-level exhaust system.

gaiter was provided for the exposed cable in between. But the inevitable flex in the cable jacket and abbreviated levers made the early production front brake trouble-prone. Later in 1971, the rubber boot was discarded and an external spring added between even stubbier arms. However, the brake still faded badly under hard use and the short-throw levers crippled the design's potential.

The 7-inch conical rear wheel was not quickly detachable, and the brake was no longer a fully floating type. Later 1971 models came with a thicker brake lining and fulcrum pads. The arm was given a heavier return spring and was reorientated toward the top, but the brake rod remained vulnerable and outside the frame. Wheel removal was made more awkward and the 47-tooth rear sprocket (increased by one tooth from 1970) made the engine work harder to achieve the same road speed.

Wheel and tire sizes on these U.S.-spec. models were the same as before, with a 3.25x19-inch front and a 4.00x18 rear. The Trials Universal option was discontinued, and all models were skinned with Dunlop K70 tires.

The new chassis' midframe enclosures were an elaborate design that began with a cast-aluminum, split air filter housing that wrapped around the seat post section of the oil-bearing spine. Two rectangular wire-screen-and-felt elements fit over locating tracks on the inner wall of the housing and were covered by black alloy covers with false louvers. (Air was actually ducted to the center of the elements from behind the frame spine.) On the Bonneville, the filtered air flowed to each carburetor directly from the outer chambers through rubber connecting tubes. On the TR6s, the cover openings were blanked off, and the air for the single carb was taken from the center of the housing through a different molded rubber connector.

To enclose the remaining area between the filter box and rear subframe, a triangulated sheet metal side panel was screwed to the back of the housing on each side. The right panel included a four-position keyed lighting and ignition switch, and provided cover for the Zener diode heat sink. The left panel was left plain, and both side covers were painted black and received the extended "Bonneville" transfers (#D2103) from 1970. The new midsection sequence made service and disassembly difficult, especially for TR6 carb removal.

This sales literature image shows the 1972 U.K.-style Bonneville still with "roof-top" seating. Larger 4.0-gallon (Imp.) tank forced relocation of forward safety reflector. Special graphics and kneepads were liked but the emblem was a tacky sticker in silver and black. Other details seen are the black finished front brake backing plate and "gargoyle" taillight.

The Lucas PUZ5A battery sat in a redesigned carrier mandated by the new frame. The power cell was joined in the cavity behind the frame spine by the Lucas 17M12 ignition coils, which were rubber bushed and vertically mounted on a separate platform behind the battery. Long high-tension leads now reached forward from under the seat, dodging the oil-bearing frame tube on each side and connected to the spark plugs through smaller Champion (WC200) Bakelite caps. However, some early 1971 machines were sent out with the larger Champion (WC548) spark plug covers. Between the coils sat the remaining electrical organs including the capacitors, rectifier, and turn signal flasher.

The Lucas headlight was changed in 1971, its chrome shell replaced by a shallow pan, now with three warning lights including an amber lens for the newly added turn indicators. These were placed on the pan's back side facing the rider. Later machines were given plastic hoods to increase their visibility in bright sunlight. The ammeter was discarded and the light switch changed to one with rotary action. The

TR6 models retained the small 6-inch lamp and toggle lighting switch, but this was now surrounded by three warning lights, as it too came with turn "winkers."

The Lucas turn signals had amber lenses and chrome housings and were mounted on hollow stalks. At the front, the stems also served as headlight fasteners and swivel-points which were threaded through the bent wire mountings. The rear signals mounted on shorter stems and threaded through the sides of a narrow sheet metal taillight housing that jutted straight out from the rear fender. (Machines sent to Canada were without the blinkers, as they were not yet required there.)

With its wider Lucas L679 light unit, the 1971 taillamp assembly looked like a church-top gargoyle, and was so nicknamed. Two sheet metal license plate brackets were screwed to the fender under the "gargoyle's" head, and in the United Kingdom a metal number board was added on top.

Other Lucas modifications included a single 6H horn that now faced forward, below

"Son of Bonneville." A fiendish slogan announcing the 1972 TR6R. Note the alternative twin scallop tank graphics.

the front of the fuel tank on all the 650s. A new plastic stop light button was fastened to the rear frame member on the left side and was activated directly by the brake pedal. And the 50/40-watt main bulb in the headlight was replaced by a slightly dimmer 45/35-watt unit.

Another big change for 1971 were the new, modern-looking Lucas handlebar switch consoles. The unpainted alloy housings combined multiple switches on the operator's side and control lever bases on the other, each clamping around the bar with four screws. The clutch and brake levers were now alloy and still retained the safety balls on the blade's tips. The lever bases were drilled for safety mirrors, but they no longer allowed a piggy-back mounting for the choke control, which had to be clamped on the bar separately on the right-hand side.

Although modern in appearance, the switch arrangement proved awkward. On the left there were two push buttons, one each above and below a flimsy-looking plastic dipper blade. The top button flashed the headlight and the bottom one "strangled the cat." On the right, the three

Two views of Greg Pound's virtually untouched 1972 American-spec T120R, with alternative tank graphics and high seat rails. Oil filler neck is clearly visible in the gap between the seat and tank. Sweeping megaphone mufflers are not unattractive and make pleasant music. *Gaylin*

position plastic blade operated the turn signals and was dangerously close to the top kill button. The remaining button underneath was a dummy — presumably it would activate an electric starter someday!

The gray, plastic-jacketed wiring sub-harnesses leading from each console to the center were tucked into the bar with chrome spring clips (#H4112), while the control cables were routed in behind the headlight without

In this close-up of the tank and engine it's not easy determining the year of manufacture. New series rocker boxes but early twin intake stubs identifies the machine as a mid-1972 Bonneville. For verification, the safely standards sticker awaits inspection on the steering head. Oil cooler is an intelligent modification by those who ride these models. (Unrestored) *Gaylin*

Control layout of an unrestored 1972 T120R. Warning lamps and lighting dial hide in between the rubber-encased instruments while steering lock lurks behind the handlebar. Infamous Lucas switch consoles and choke lever position can also be seen. Filler cap vent is useful but not standard. (Unrestored) *Gaylin*

ties to the handlebars. The front brake cable retained its troublesome inline brake switch and was clipped to the right side of the front fender with a black nylon guide.

The frame changes also mandated another seat design. The new simpler saddle was shortened, which made the 650s crowded when riding two-up. And there was no longer a center hump to distinguish the seating areas.

No longer a true twinseat, it lost its rear bump but retained the quilted, aerated top panel. The entire seat was covered in black vinyl and a gold Triumph logo was again printed on the tail section. The bench now hinged on the right (opening on the left) and pivoted on skinny welded L-brackets. It was secured on the left by an unpainted external buckle that looked like it had been ripped off a lunch box. However, the

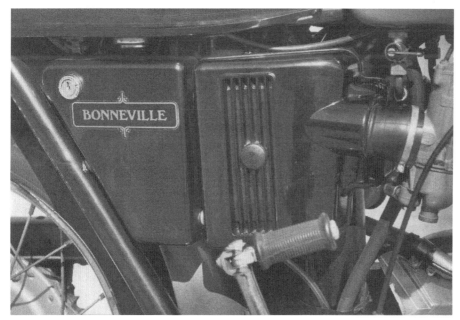

Triumph's sculpted oil tank was replaced in 1971 with a two-piece enclosure — the front section was the air filter chamber and the rear just a filler. Early filter covers were cast aluminum and later changed to plastic. Ventilation grille was purely decorative and not functional. *Lindsay Brooke*

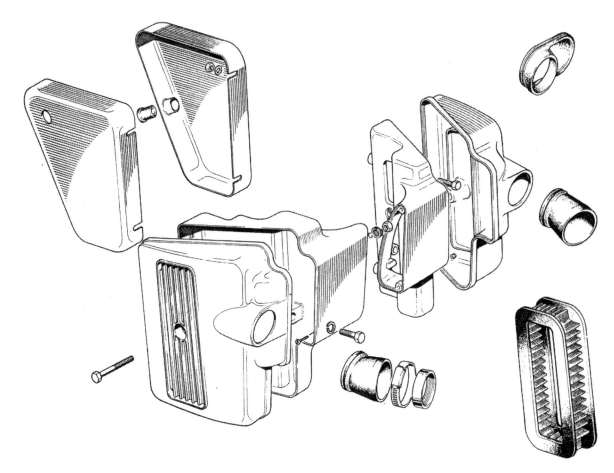

1971-72 midsection air cleaner assembly. New frame in 1972 meant a redesign of these components and later ones will not interchange.

latch did allow the use of a padlock, though there was little storage room under the seat!

The seat was thick and comfy, and with the extended front fork tubes and high seat rail, the seat height on the 1971 650s was a gargantuan 34 inches. Attempts to lower the seating height included hacking out some of the foam padding at the front by the owners (and dealers) but a factory-trimmed seat wouldn't come until later in the following year's production.

New fuel tanks made necessary by the Umberslade chassis were slightly more bulbous at the front, but were close in shape to the 1970 U.S. TR6R tank. This 3 1/2-gallon (U.S.) vessel was fitted to all 650cc models at first, including those offered in the United Kingdom. It should be pointed out here that only U.S.-spec motorcycles (small, scalloped tanks and wide handlebars) were produced until later in the season, and if a British rider acquired a new machine early in 1971, this is what he got!

Superior BSA-style gas tank mounting was adopted in 1971, with a single central securing bolt facing up through the center of the tank and two rubber collars over the frame rail to provide location and cushioning. The mounting cavity in the tank split the styling strip in two pieces. At the ends of the tank, the strips were bent over, but in the center they were held down by a matching chrome circular bead holder. A plain black rubber grommet (some improperly embossed with BSA!) was pressed in to cover the mounting cavity.

Winged upper and lower paint scallops again accented the fuel tank, this time on all three Triumph 650 models. The four scallops swept rearward from each corner of the small eyebrow tank emblems. The top flashes had a different shape than in 1969–70. They were wider and poured backward immediately from the tank emblem, rather than sweeping forward and then back. The scallops outlined the area once occupied by the rubber kneegrips, which were no longer fitted in the United States.

The Bonneville tanks were painted Tiger-gold (metallic mustard) with black scallops and bordered in white pinstripes. TR6 colors were Pacific-blue and white with gold lining. The fenders were finished in the usual fashion with the wire stays painted in the machine's primary color. Trophy 650 guards were now chrome-plated instead of stainless steel.

Later in the year, machines with lower handlebars and a new generation 4 1/4-(U.S.) gallon tank were made available in the home market. The fuel tank was rectangular in shape, with an almost flat top, and was broader at the front than in the knee area. The shape made better use of the frame behind the fork, albeit at the expense of the amber safety reflectors. Its overall form was very similar to those BMW introduced in 1974, and it had its own appeal. Later known as the "European" tank, they were fastened in the same manner as the traditional Triumph (American) versions and were finished in the same colors, although the TR6C was only available in U.S. trim.

Restorer's Tip: Made in England

Nineteen seventy-one was the first year in which the scripted "Made in England" (#D3361) transfer was applied to Triumph 650cc motorcycles by the factory. These gold decals were 4 inches long and applied halfway down on the right front down tube. Until then, this style of "Made in England" transfer was found only on BSAs, and any pre-'71 Triumph twin wearing them does so incorrectly.

The paint scheme on the British T120 tank was similar to the one used in 1970, but with different colors — flanks in Tiger-gold and surrounded in black. On top, the black area was reduced to a 4-inch (approximately) wide stripe. All boundaries were defined in white pinstriping. The Tiger tank was finished entirely in Pacific-blue with only a 4-inch white stripe on top, lined in gold. Neither model had rubber kneegrips.

The smaller cast emblems were replaced on the Euro-tanks by tacky-looking Triumph stickers, in chrome and black. The featured model transfers were adopted from 1970. The position of the safety standards decal (#D2452), first applied in 1969, was moved to the left-hand side of the steering head. The identification number was still stamped to the left side of the frame, but now at the very top of the down tube.

1971 Engine and Drivetrain

After the new oil-bearing frame was already in production, the factory discovered that the Triumph 650 engine could not be installed unless its rocker boxes were removed. But the through-bolts used to secure the boxes, as well as the cylinder, could not be inserted after the engine was in place! This meant a redesign of the rocker boxes and head bolt arrangement.

The new rocker boxes were internally milled for clearance and featured four new access holes on the sides to facilitate valve clearance checking. The screw-in caps also doubled as another escape for engine oil.

The four through-bolts were staged. The lower section was Allen-keyed and torqued down on the cylinder; the upper stage secured the rocker boxes by threading into the lower part. And finally, the cylinder head was given four new locating pins.

Other changes to the engine top end included yet another pushrod tube design. The tubes were no longer castellated; instead, drainage "portholes" were added above an integral collar that compressed the O-ring. The bottom of the tube was given a double O-ring and sealing ring combination that sat inside a pressed-in collar.

Few changes occurred to the 1971 engine's bottom end. The flywheel attaching bolts were strengthened and given flat washers. There was a new engine sprocket that omitted the oil seal and a modified distance piece to allow drive side shims. On the timing side, metric-sized main bearings were substituted after engine number GE27029, when the standard component fell in short supply. To adapt, the right-hand crank journal and timing gear nut had to be modified. Main bearing failures as a result of this change were as high as 30 percent by one estimate, and replacements for the standard bearing became nonexistent!

The oil pressure release valve and filter were now condensed into a self-contained assembly that could also be safely retrofitted. In April, five-speed gearboxes designed by aftermarket specialist Rod Quaife were made optional and a "Quaife 5-speed" sticker was placed on the outer transmission cover on the bikes so equipped. The five-speed cluster was a tight fit in the 650's gearcase. It used a roller race for the sleeve gear but could be retrofitted to earlier boxes with a little finesse. There was also a three-ball clutch lever mechanism designed to stop excess play.

There were no carburetor changes for 1971, although the pair of 30-millimeter Amals fitted to the Bonneville were given new part numbers. Outwardly there seemed to be no change in the exhaust pipes; however, they actually had new bends to cope with the oil-bearing frame. The T120 and TR6 head pipes retained their balance tubes, but new pseudo-megaphones replaced Triumph's trademark bullet mufflers. The Trophy 650 kept its left-hand high-level system (with "chip basket") but with slightly different bends and new numbers.

A final point concerning these early oil-inframe 650 twins is that Triumph produced over 30,000 of them between 1971 and 1972, making these twins the most numerous of all model years. Consequently there are more survivors from these two seasons than any other, and restorers should have no problem finding donors for replacement parts. But consider also whether or not a restoration should be undertaken at all, when there are so many surviving examples still in original condition today.

1972 Models

In 1971, Triumph tooled up to produce more 650cc twins than ever before. Because of their late arrival in the United States, however, and the unexpected sales resistance once they had finally landed, Meriden was forced to delay desperately needed modifications until the bulk of the 1971-style engine and frame stocks were depleted. So the factory added to the mountain of unsold '71 models with 1972 versions that were little changed.

Engine modifications in 1972 were slight at first. The hastily installed metric timing side main bearing remained, but there were new wrist pins on the connecting rods as well as revised cap nuts on the big ends.

Later in the year, the cam pinions were switched to solid (thicker) full-width items with opposing tapped holes for extraction. Also at this time the oil pressure release valve reverted back to the two-part assembly. There were no recorded changes for a trouble-prone gearbox that was in desperate need of attention. The internal three-ball clutch lever continued, as did the five-speed option on all 650s.

By the winter of 1971/72, all the first edition 650 motors had been used up, and at engine number XG42304, a new cylinder head design (originally intended for all the 1972 models) was finally introduced. The exhaust stubs were now eliminated and the ports machined to accept push-in head pipes. Without the need to fit over the stubs, the ends of the push-in exhaust pipes were now consistent in diameter. More to maintain a traditional appearance rather than anchoring the pipes, smaller cast-aluminum finned clamps were fitted at the junction. On the back side of the Bonneville cylinder head, the screw-in intake stubs were also replaced by separate bolt-on cast-aluminum manifolds for each carburetor. These were still connected

Details of the 1972 twin-leading shoe brake with short levers and no rubber gaiter in between. The brake worked well but wasn't as efficient as the one it replaced. Auxiliary wire fender support behind fork slider looks like the afterthought it was. (Unrestored) *Gaylin*

The "gargoyle" taillight used the Lucas 679 unit and was fitted to Triumph motorcycles from 1971 to 1973. Rubber beading provided a uniform joint and protected the fender. Also of interest is the shortened turn indicator stems, lowered safety reflectors, and the printed logo on the seat bump. (Unrestored 1972 T120R) *Gaylin*

with a balance tube. The 30 millimeter Amal Concentrics remained unchanged.

A new rocker box design was also introduced that put an end to the separate inspection caps. The access areas were now unified on each side and entry was through a single finned cover plate, rounded at the ends and fastened by screws. This was certainly a more sensible arrangement, although still not ideal for maintaining oil-tightness. There were also new two-piece through-bolts to hold down the rocker boxes, as well as four inner head bolts.

1972 Frame and Cycle Parts

The Triumph factory was well aware of the problems (and lost sales) caused by the tall oil-in-frame chassis, and prepared a new, lower design to replace it. But before the new frames could be produced, the company had to get rid

of a warehouse full of the leftover tall frames.

To lower the seat height on the leftover frames, Meriden narrowed the saddle's nose and shaved away some cushioning at the front, albeit at the expense of rider comfort. The front fork was shorted by pruning the stanchions and suspension springs. The thread pitch on the stem was also changed (from 16 to 24 UNF) to allow finer adjustments of the Timken tapered roller bearing head races. These measures succeeded in reducing seat height to 32 1/2 inches. Unfortunately, the shorter fork caused the machine to cant forward, subtracting usable fuel tank capacity, especially on the U.K. models. The centerstand, too tall to begin with, was remade to accommodate the shorter forks.

The Lucas handlebar switch consoles were reversed in 1972. The turn signal blade, headlight flasher, and kill button were on the left, while the dipper switch and horn push were placed on the right. The lower right-hand button remained functionless. Other electrical mods for the new season included a louder Lucas 6H horn that was mounted on rubber bushings and Trident turn signal stalks that became shorter at the front. And the sheet metal taillight housing on some of the road machines began appearing in black paint instead of silver.

The U.S. Trophy models were still equipped with the 6-inch headlight and skid plate. Only a speedometer was specified as standard and factory sales literature showing the TR6C with two instruments is erroneous, although a tachometer could be fitted. There were no further modifications to the front brake beyond the 1971 midseason upgrades, except that some U.K. and general export machines had their front backing plates painted black.

By spring 1972, Triumph's 650 production finally depleted stocks of the taller frames and beginning with engine number CG50414, the fix was in! The new chassis had the rear subframe welded to a spot almost 3 inches lower on the oil-bearing spine.

Reducing the seat rail height in this fashion meant a complete redesign of the machine's rear half. Under the seat was a new battery carrier, coil platform, air filter box, and outer covers. The side panel front sections on the TR6Rs were now molded in plastic, in place of aluminum. The seat hinge position was changed and a plunger-type seat latch replaced the 1971 "ammo box" buckle. The rear fender position was naturally affected, as were its attachment points. There was a new cross brace under the seat and the chrome grab rail also had to be changed, which included repositioning the red safety reflectors onto welded tabs below the rail.

Shorter Girling suspension units were fitted. In fact, the only parts of the bikes' rear section to escape change were the swingarm assembly and rear wheel. Virtually every other item cannot be interchanged with the earlier machines. With only slight modifications, this would become Triumph's last chassis design for the B-range twins.

Colors for 1972 remained almost unchanged. The Bonneville stayed in Tiger-gold, with the second color switched from black to Cold-white. The TR6 models were again finished in Polychromatic-blue and white. Pinstriping on all fuel tanks and fenders, including the T120, was now black.

The 3 1/2-gallon American-style tanks were finished in two different styles. The first and most widely seen version was a two-tone scheme resurrected from the mid-1960s. The color division was centered at the small eyebrow tank emblem — the front boundary went directly forward from the badge's tip and the rear separation swept down and back from the lower corner, as though outlining an imaginary kneepad. The main color was placed over white on all versions, and black pinstriping defined the divisions.

The second condition employed twin scallops that recalled those used during 1969–70. On these, the top wings leaving each tank emblem swept slightly forward before turning and tapering back along the top. The bottom scallop followed the now familiar practice of sweeping back immediately from the lower edge of the badge. But this tank was larger than the 1970 version and without kneepads, the effect was not the same.

Very late in the 1972 season, a 2 1/2-gallon (U.S.) slimline fuel tank with the same outside dimensions of the 1970 item was made available as a sales tool to U.S. dealers. These smaller tanks still used a raised top seam, but with central BSA-type fastening and a front underside securing strap between the two chambers. They were sent to dealers unpainted and any surviving finish today did not originate at the factory.

The slab-sided U.K. tanks were not changed, but they were given triangular glue-on kneegrips. The graphics were only slightly altered from 1971, in that the lower border, now in white, was increased in thickness to approximately 2 1/2 inches from the bottom. And the painted trim on the blue-and-white Tiger 650 tank now had the same appearance and dimensions as its twin-carb brother. Even with cheap-looking trademark stickers for emblems, the Euro-tanks

An unrestored 1972 U.S. Bonneville with tank scallops. The high seat frame and separate rocker caps marks this machine as an early-year example. The Triumph factory produced more machines in 1971 and 1972 than any other model year. *Lindsay Brooke*

seemed to have an air of legitimacy that the U.S. versions lacked in 1972. It should be noted that the U.S-style tanks were available in the home market and vice-versa, although Euro versions were very uncommon in America.

The painted fenders were the same in all markets. The guards and their wire stays were painted entirely in the main color of either Tiger-gold or Polychromatic-blue, with a white center stripe applied over top. Lining was black. Chrome-plated mudguards were specified for the Trophy 650 models as well as the Canadian market Bonnevilles. And all front fenders now came with the extra wire brace welded in the center.

The side cover decals were changed in 1972 to a style of lettering and decor that could have been taken from a Boot Hill tombstone. The model designations were still in gold capitals but were now placed on the same line. The surrounding gold borderline formed a rectangular box with squires placed centrally above and below the name. Models with the five-speed gearbox option were given the Roman numeral 'V' below the designation. (The part numbers for these decals as well as the plain four-speed versions are listed in the specifications Appendix.)

These were not transfers, but transparent pressure sensitive decals, and restorers can avoid a tacky appearance by trimming the stickers as close and as even to the design as possible. The later five-speed machines were also given a separate circular sticker (#D3748) in gold, black, and white, advertising the feature. This replaced the transparent Quaife five-speed sticker but was applied at first to the taillight housing, and then directly on the rear fender in subsequent model years.

1973 Models

Engineers at Meriden had worked feverishly during the previous season to salvage Dr. Umberslade's Frankenstein and the resulting 1973 models recaptured much of the old Triumph magic. Had it been these machines unveiled in 1971, Triumph executives (and BSA shareholders) might have had a longer dance in the disco decade! With the discontinuation of the TR6C Trophy 650 and enlargement of the

Exploded view of the 1971-73 front fork.

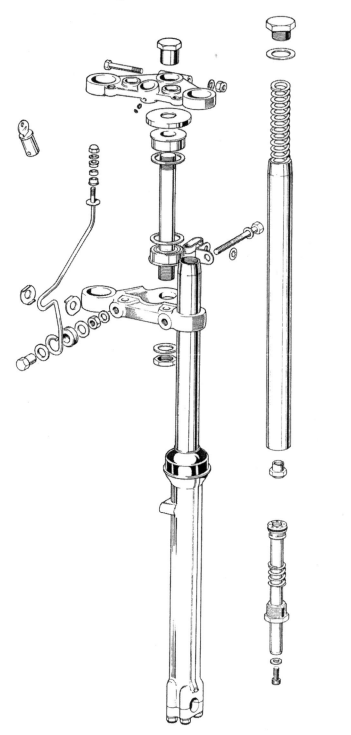
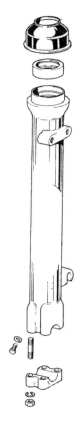

new B-range engines to 750cc, the following text focuses on these models — the T140V Bonneville 750 and TR7RV Tiger 750. Note, however, that the 650cc T120R and TR6 continued in production.

There were so many revisions to the 1973 twins that it's hard to believe they were all implemented in a single season. Initially, at engine number JH15435, the displacement was boosted simply by bigger bores in the existing cylinder block (#713335). With the original 85-millimeter stroke of the 650 engine, the wider 75-millimeter bore actually yielded a capacity of only 724cc.

These barrels used two different thread types to fasten the cylinder head - the four outside head bolts were British 3/8–26; the four inside studs were 3/8–24 UNF. At engine number XH22019, a new cylinder casting (#71-3679) debuted, allowing a 76-millimeter piston and a 744cc displacement. This cylinder block was shorter, as were the accompanying connecting rods, which meant the rocker boxes could be left in place during installation or removal. The thread form for the cylinder head bolts was converted to UNF. The final 750 cylinder block (71-4005) came at engine number CH29520 and kept the 76-millimeter bore. And the drilled oil passages were opened up on all the 76-millimeter cylinders, to increase flow.

The center head bolt now had a brother, and the pair moved slightly apart to dodge the larger cylinder bores. This brought the bolt count to ten, all of them made of material with the same expansion properties as the head casting. There were new valve guides and locating pins for the valve covers to keep them from walking. To ease engine removal and installation, the top torque stay was simplified to a simple flat strap that picked up the center rocker box studs, then reached back to grab the underside of the top tube.

The Bonneville carburetor manifolds were changed once more. A balance tube was still fitted, but its inlet diameter was a straight 1 1/8 inches. A tapped mounting boss was provided for the choke lever mounting bracket, on the left-hand adaptor only. Amal 30-millimeter concentric carburetors were fitted to the 750 Bonneville, with 210 main jets.

In the lower end, the con-rods were shortened by almost half an inch and beefed up, along with the wrist pins, to cope with the increased stresses. There were thicker crowns on the lighter-weight Hepolite pistons, and the bottom oil control ring was now a three-piece Apex-type component.

The crankshaft balance factor was lightened to 74 percent, and there were new flywheel bolts. Otherwise, the crank itself was little changed from the 650 item. The Q-cams were replaced by milder versions (inlet #71-3011, exhaust #71-3010). Nitride-hardened, timed tappets were still fitted but their radii changed to 3/4 inch for the inlet and 1 1/8 inch for the exhaust pair. There were also new pushrods and chromed pushrod tubes.

The crankcase aperture was widened to receive the bigger cylinder barrels and strengthened around the bearing housings to withstand the increased loads. There was also a bigger timing side (metric) main bearing. The duplex primary drive chain introduced in 1963 was replaced by one with 3/8-inch triplex links, and the chaincase and cover redesigned to allow more room. The rotor inspection cover was retained and the Triumph logo was still inlaid with black enamel. The clutch springs were stiffened and the shock absorber vane modified, all to handle more stress from the 750cc top end. This primary drive arrangement also appeared on the 1973 T120s.

A five-speed gearbox became standard on the 750 twins (still optional on the 650s) and there was a new layshaft and gear assembly. But the transmissions continued to give trouble. False neutrals and unwanted (sudden) ratio changes were characteristic. So a gear conversion kit (CP1000) was made available later in the season that included new first, second, and third gears; a layshaft selector fork; and a driving dog. Another midseason gearbox modification was the switch from leaf spring indexing to a T150-style camplate and plunger. By the beginning

The three faces of Bonnie! The 1973 U.S.-spec Bonneville 750 with lower seat, high-rise handlebars, and slim line fuel tank. Front disc brake was long overdue. This press kit photo is unusual in that it shows a deployed kickstand. Had this been the model unveiled in 1971 things might have been different. *Author collection*

The 1973 U.K.-spec T140V with lovely Euro-tank and knee pads, low bars, and fork gaiters. Also visible are the second series mufflers fitted to 750 twins in all markets during the year, and upper fork covers in black. Rear number board was standard only in the home market. Publicity photo. *Author collection*

Canadian market Bonnevilles in 1973 were similar to the American variant but with fork gaiters and black fork covers. This factory photograph reveals a machine without the turn signals — not yet required by the Canadian government. The chrome front brake cover (over the Lockheed caliper) was also omitted on many Canadian models. *Author collection*

of the 1974 model year, all these transmission remedies were incorporated and the shifting problems cured.

The 750 twin's exhaust system mufflers underwent constant evolution during the year. Early production models were equipped with the chromed megaphone-shaped silencers (#71-2382) from 1971 to 1972. At engine number AH22965, a longer unit (#71-3723) with a curved, welded-in reverse cone was fitted, giving the silencer a pleasant appearance similar to (but not the same as) the Norton peashooters. Late in 1973 production these were again replaced by units (#71-3999) with a wider opening at the exit and a slighter, straight tapered end cap. Mufflers in this form served the 750 twins until their end at Meriden.

1973 Frame and Cycle Parts

A brand new hydraulically damped front fork was fitted to the 750 twins that was interchangeable with the Trident. The modern-looking polished aluminum lower sliders traveled up and down on new chrome-plated stanchions, anchored in all-new top and bottom iron yokes. The top casting incorporated splits behind the tubes to allow clamping (with Allen screws) of the stanchion tip and an inner cap nut. Chrome hoops for the rubber-encased instruments sat above the upper lug over each tube and were secured by an outer chrome cap nut. The top lug also included a boss for the brake line's first junction off the master cylinder.

Between the yokes, traditional sheet metal covers returned to headlight support duty, but the projecting arms were rubber mounted and detachable. The left-hand support was again the home for the keyed ignition switch. On American machines, these two-piece arms were chrome-plated while on British, Canadian, and general export models, they were painted in black. U.K. and Canadian bikes were also given clipless rubber fork gaiters, to cover the stanchion between the lower lug and slider. These boots were more for style than function, as the fork springs had been internal since 1971. The stanchions on U.S. bikes were left naked, with only a rubber dust scraper on top of the sliders.

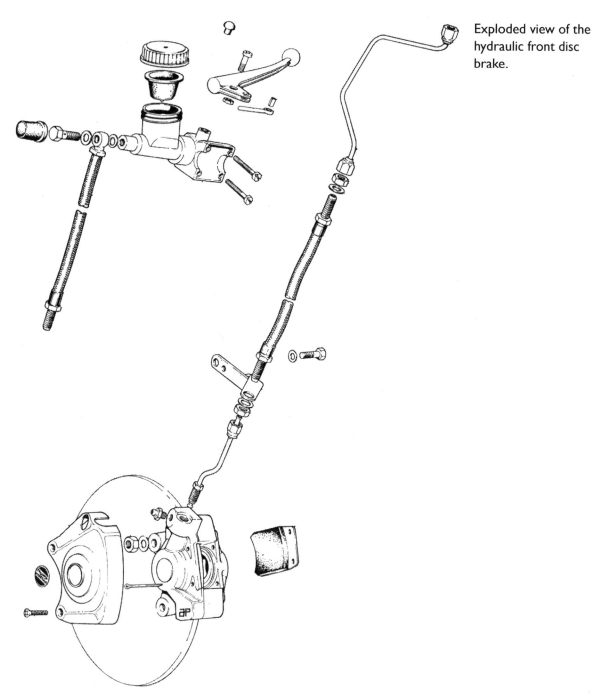

Exploded view of the hydraulic front disc brake.

Perhaps the biggest news was the Lockheed hydraulic disc front brake. A single caliper was mounted behind the base of the left-hand slider, on an integrally cast support lug. The cast-iron caliper pinched a 10-inch, chrome-plated iron disc. The reservoir/master cylinder unit clamped to the right-hand side of the handlebar, which was reshaped to suit. Steel brake line and pressurerated hose (at the flex points) carried the fluid down to the binders.

The calipers were given an attractive chrome cover and small circular decal that read "Triumph Hydraulic," although some early machines were shipped without the cover (and sometimes without the decal). The brake's performance was superior to the previous drum, as long as the disc plating didn't deteriorate — the resulting exposed iron would wear down the brake pads. Restorers shouldn't fit pads with sintered composition (such as Dunlopads) that

A 1973 front fork with redesigned LH slider.

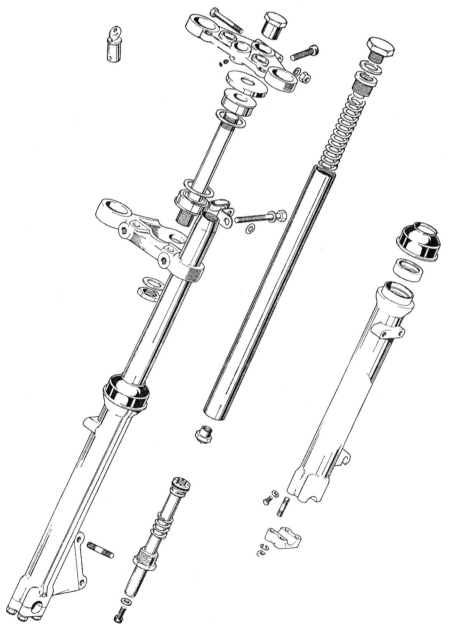

This unusual angle of the 1973 U.S.-spec Tiger-750 reveals the lumpy twinseat and leftover 1972-style mufflers. In this view the American "ape-hanger" handlebars and troublesome Lucas switch gear can be appreciated, but a very nice machine overall! Factory photo. *Author collection*

In 1973, 264 BSA-badged Tiger-650s were produced for an institutional customer in the Middle East. This factory photograph shows the machine, but with Triumph TR6 colors (blue and white) and badges. Notice the 1969-70-type TLS front brake and hand-drawn Tiger-650 side cover emblem. Factory photo. *Author collection*

A rare factory photo of a 1973 T120R made available in Canada and Great Britain. These were basically leftover 1972 models but with tanks finished in (1970) Astral-red and silver. Chrome fenders and no blinkers mark this as a Canadian model. *Author collection*

will quickly scrub off the chrome.

Handlebars fitted to both British and American T140Vs and TR7RVs had new bends that permitted a relatively level position for the front brake fluid reservoir, without completely abandoning rider comfort. In response to American dealers, the 30-inch wide bars on U.S. machines (#97-4411) were radically changed and given an 8-inch rise. Although chopper-type "ape-hangers" might have been desirable in the western United States, they were not preferred in the East, and many were replaced with lower handles at the dealership. The low, narrow U.K. bars (#97-4300) were offered as an option in America, but were considered too extreme and never really caught on.

The dreaded Lucas switch consoles continued to amuse in 1973, although the clutch and brake lever blades were fashioned once again in chromed steel. The choke levers on both 750cc twin-cylinder models were relocated to the carburetor area. On the Bonneville, a mounting bracket was screwed to the left-hand carb adaptor, while on the TR7, the lever assembly fastened directly to the forward left face of the air filter box. No changes were listed for the Smiths speedo and tachometer fitted to all models. The twin-seat was reprofiled, flipping up slightly at the rear and giving the tail section a softer curve for the gold-printed Triumph trademark. The top panel was still ribbed in aerated material and a subtle hump midway reappeared to delineate separate perches. Coarser textured vinyl was used on the seat's side panels and bright chrome trimming returned to the lower edge. The saddle swung open on sturdier hinges that were moved back to the left rail, yielding access to the battery compartment from the right.

The two-piece side panels were simplified by the removal of the decorative louvers on the front section which were molded in plastic on the Bonnevilles as well. The tombstone-style decals were discontinued and replaced with a chrome bezeled name-plate that spanned the covers and helped mask their piecemeal nature. An embossed sticker in the center of the badge was color-keyed for either model — red (#60-4148) for the Bonneville and blue (#60-4169) for the Tiger 750. (All other transfers from 1972 remained in use.) Right-hand panels were cleaned up by the relocation of the keyed ignition switch to the left headlight support arm.

Other 1973 electrical revisions included the return of a traditional teardrop-shaped 7-inch Lucas headlight bucket. All three warning lamps were retained, but the lighting switch was changed back to a three-position toggle type. At the rear, a new cast-aluminum taillight

housing that included a larger Lucas L917 lamp replaced the tin "gargoyle." The polished lamp assembly gave a handsome impression, rather like an enlarged 679 unit that had been fitted to the 1966-67 models. The circular black and gold five-speed sticker was moved to an exposed part of the fender above the taillamp, and the rear

Because of the factory work stoppage begun in September 1973, very few 1974 B-range twins were actually produced. This sales literature image shows the U.K. Tiger-750 intended for that year but without much change. Jade-green (and white) tank and later mufflers are the only indicators. *Author collection*

This rare, unrestored U.S.-spec T120V was one of the hostages released during the temporary lifting of the Triumph factory blockade in the summer of 1974. Identical in every respect (but displacement) to the 1973 750s, only its engine prefix code and purple fuel tank give it away. Owner has replaced the lost Bonneville 650 side cover stickers with 750 items. Leftover 1972-style mufflers are accurate but the tires are not. *Gaylin*

turn indicators were moved to the gusset plate on the chrome grab rail. From this position, blinker visibility was improved without lengthening their stems, but the front signal stalks had to be extended to achieve the same prominence. Canadian Triumphs, however, were unaffected as "winkers" were not yet mandated.

The front disc brake assembly included a new two-piece aluminum hub, machined to mate with the 10-inch rotor. At the rear, the 7-inch alloy conical hub and drum was retained but with a polished, clear-coated finish to replace the previous silver paint. On British T120s and T140s, the tire sizes were not changed: a 3.25x19-inch Dunlop K70 up front and a 4.00x18-inch K70 at the rear. U.S. models kept the same size K70 pattern in front, but switched to a meatier 4.25x18-inch Dunlop K81 for the rear of both 750 twins.

There were few amendments to the final-edition 1972 chassis with the lowered subframe. The fairing lugs were removed from the steering head at the front and the seat hinge pins were moved to the left rail as related earlier. The oil tank filler neck remained at the bend of the seat post, but the dipstick shank was taken from the tool roll and permanently attached to the filler cap.

Fuel tank shapes and capacities remained unchanged in all markets, but there were new graphics for all in 1973. The 2 1/2-gallon seamless slimline tanks standard on all U.S. models were decorated with a single pair of winged scallops above each Triumph emblem. Their shape was a pleasant compromise between the 1970- and 1971-type scallops — the wing now creeping slightly forward before arching back on top. The chromed tank top bead holders and styling strips disappeared. Instead, the mounting well was covered by a single black rubber grommet and a decorative white plastic badge with a raised Triumph logo in gold.

The larger home market tanks also received the dorsal decor as well as new painted accents for the sides. The forward flanks were outlined (around a new cast Triumph trademark) and filled in with the secondary color - the top tapering off into a thin wing over the rubber kneepad. The overall effect was that of a large "comma," and along with the rubber kneegrips, successfully transformed the boxy appearance into a very pleasing tank design.

Model identity colors were applied only to the fuel tanks in 1973 and all the fenders, except for U.K. 650s, were chrome-plated. The T140V colors were Hi-Fi Vermilion (deep tangerine) and gold, pinstriped in white. The TR7RV tanks were painted Astral-blue and Alaskan-white with gold lining. British-market 650 twins continued in the 1972 colors, but Canadian-market T120s were finished in Astral-red and silver and the TR6s in Spring-gold and black. The pinstriping on these odd ball models was applied in gold.

There were new chrome fenders for the 750 twins, sized adequately for weather protection. The front guards were now supported by traditional U-shaped chrome brackets — two for the top and a single loop for the bottom — and screwed to brackets on the inside of the lower fork sliders. The top stay was fastened inside the bracket while the forward brace went outside of the strap. The lower brace reached into the axle caps on the bottom of the fork legs.

U.K. T120 and TR6 models continued with 1972-style mudguards and were painted as before. These leftovers were also offered in Canada but with TR6C-style chrome-plated fenders.

As related, the 650cc twins continued to be available in home and general export markets as the T120R (T120RV with five-speed option) and TR6R (TR6RV with five-speed). These motorcycles were really the result of unused stocks of high-seat frames and earlier engines, but by the end of the model year, both machines

were being assembled with the improved motor and chassis.

Commencing at engine number JH15101, a small batch (264) of TR6 engines were thrown into U.K.-spec TR7 running gear, given BSA tank badges, and were designated as 1973 Thunderbolts (T65). The front disc brake was traded for a 1970-style TLS drum but finished in black, and the lower fork legs were reworked to accept. There were cast BSA emblems for the large 4-gallon tank and a tank finish the owners manual called "Hi-Gloss Jet" (deep purple). Thunderbolt-650 transfers (#604145) were fixed to the side covers and the Triumph patent plate was stricken from the timing chest. It is believed that these rare birds were dedicated to an institutional customer in Africa or the Middle East, but a few examples are known to have stayed in the United Kingdom.

1974–1975 Models

Production of the 1974 Triumph models had just started up when the assembly line ground to a halt due to a workers' strike that eventually lasted until spring 1975 — almost 18 months! This closure also meant a shipment blockade (by the workers) of completed machines. However, in late summer 1974, the blockade was lifted sporadically for a couple of months and small batches of motorcycles were released. Most of these were 1974 American-spec T140V and T120V Bonnevilles that were being assembled when the strike began. They were little changed from 1973 specifications, partly due to the fact that there had been little opportunity to change them!

Pesky rocker box oil leaks forced a redesign of the inspection covers which were given two additional attachment points and improved gaskets. There was a finer wire screen filter for the oil pressure release valve and a new nylon-loaded pressure indicator switch with a revised rubber boot. The flanged fitting on the back of the primary that connected the engine breather hose was changed to a black plastic item. And the outer face of the gearbox drive sprocket was modified to allow a new lock washer and

1974 U.K.-spec T120V Bonneville. Few were produced due to the 18-month factory shut-down. The folded prop stands and polished carburetors reveal the embellished nature of factory publicity photos. *Author collection*

oil seal O-ring. Besides a choice of compression ratings of 7.9:1 and 8.6:1 (the latter standard in the United States), there were no other recorded changes to the 750 engine.

1974-1975 Frame and Cycle Parts

The circumstances at Meriden also prevented any major revisions to the 1974 running gear, not that there was a pressing need for any. The front fender mounting brackets were strengthened to halt a rash of fractures and the steering damper kit was no longer listed as an option. And the embossed color-keyed model stickers on the side panels were rationalized to emblems with gold lettering on black backgrounds on all models.

The fuel tank graphics went unchanged, but there were stunning new tank colors for all models in 1974. The T140V was painted in Cherokee-red (maroon #83-5413) and white, while Jade-green and white was selected for the TR7RV tank (#83-5414). The 650 Bonneville (T120V), which now shared the same cycle parts as its bigger brothers, was finished in

purple and white. Gold pinstriping was applied on all models.

Surviving 1974 Triumphs are rare. To give the restorer or would-be owner an engine number reference point for authenticity, the machines released during the temporary blockade lift carried serial numbers from JJ58080 to NJ60032. When the Meriden workers' cooperative was established and production resumed in spring 1975, a few more Bonnevilles (in both engine capacities) bearing 1974 engine numbers were produced — the highest recorded number being NJ60083. As indicated, these were both 650cc and 750cc Bonnevilles, but the T120 is the more unusual machine.

Triumph's 1975 production period was short, just over two months. The motorcycles were identical in specification and color to the 1974 versions and can be sorted only by engine numbers, which ranged from DK61000 to GK62239. Triumphs with these numbers are no less desirable than 1974 examples.

Chapter Nine

Meriden Co-op 750 Twins 1976–1979

Outwardly, 1976 Bonnevilles and Tiger 750s exhibited no difference from those bearing engine numbers from the previous model year. Even the same fuel tank colors were carried over from 1974 and 1975. But they can be readily identified by the left-hand gear change lever. The repositioning was accomplished by sending the new control shaft through the back of the gearbox and interrupting its course with a crank to jump over the clutch assembly. The splined foot change spindle now emerged in the center of the primary cover and the toe lever was made shorter by 3/4 inch.

The new mechanism meant revisions (and new part numbers) to the inner and outer gearbox covers, shift quadrant, kick-start axle, clutch lever, and, of course, the cases and primary cover. The latter lost its rotor inspection plate and was replaced instead with a flush screw-in plug with crossed slots and a fixed pointer inside the case. The integral Triumph trademark reverted back to the earlier condition with a sunken outline, but was now inlaid with gold paint instead of black.

Other drivetrain tweaks included a new O-Ring for the oil pressure release valve to end its role as an "oil release valve." The Spanish-made 30-millimeter Amal carburetors were given an extended tickler button, and washers were no longer specified under the cylinder base fixing nuts. Although appearing unchanged, the muffler cans were modified internally to absorb more noise and the end plates given a slight concave dish. And the silencers' uniform hanger brackets were changed to accommodate a hydraulic brake hose on the right.

1976 Frame and Cycle Parts

The other prominent tell-tale feature for 1976 was the right side hydraulic rear disc brake. An all-new wheel spool replaced the conical hub and was screwed to a 10-inch iron rotor, 0.235 inch thick. (The thickness of the front disc was similarly increased for standardization.) A swingarm modification was necessary to allow attachment of a single underslung caliper and room for the master cylinder. The brake pedal was reordered to pivot on the right engine plate (also changed) and the keyed control arm repositioned downward to actuate the brake cylinder.

The fluid reservoir was remotely located under the seat and the related parts modified to make room, including the battery tray, coil

It's here.
The Legendary Bonnie.
TRIUMPH Bonneville for 1976

platform, and tool shelf. The rear fender also underwent surgery for the new system. The new brake worked well (when dry), but wheel removal was complicated by the caliper position. British-made Dunlop K70 tires were again fitted to all Triumph twins, front and rear.

The previous left-and right-handed footpegs were standardized for either side and assigned a single part number (#83-7040). Another change mandated in the American market was repositioning the passenger footpegs at 45 degrees. In this attitude, their folding base allowed them to (sometimes) retract, rather throw off the rider when encountering an obstacle.

The U.S. Department of Transportation also required clear labeling of all small controls and switches. The Lucas left-hand handlebar console was changed to a more user-friendly layout with cast-in labeling. The switch blade (and buttons) on the right remained the same, but now had

transparent decals to indicate positions. Stickers, in black with silver lettering, were placed on the headlight shell above the lighting switch (#60-7005) and warning lamps (#60-7004). A third label (#60-7003) was placed above the ignition switch boss on the left headlight ear.

The DOT stickers looked like the afterthought they were, and the black ink wore away quickly in the elements or when polished regularly. Many original examples today wear these blank silver squares. Other changes involving the cockpit included new faces for the Smiths speedometer and tachometer, without the NVT logo, introduced late in the season. And the throttle reverted to a single rotor twistgrip and inline junction box on the cable run.

The twinseat's padding was thickened considerably for 1976, and a new black vinyl cover was fitted. Black piping returned to trim a more pronounced upper edge all the way

By 1977, single-carb twins had become an uncommon sight even in Triumph showrooms. This otherwise completely original U.S.-spec Tiger-750 has been fitted with a retro exhaust system and lacks its turn indicators. (Unrestored) *Gaylin*

around the saddle. The aerated top panel was still cross-ribbed, but the broader flanks were now of smoother material. And at the bottom edge, the chrome trimming was embellished with black rubber boarders. A less conspicuous seat revision was the reformed base pan to allow uniform hinges. The 1976 parts book recorded no change in number for the new saddle, and restorers of 1973–74 machines are often mistakenly sent this item (#83-7065) by parts suppliers unaware of the difference. Conversely, the earlier condition seats don't belong on 1976 Bonnevilles.

The Triumph factory was no longer offering 650cc twins (for the general public) and the original B-range dwindled down to only the 750 Bonneville (T140V) and Tiger 750 (TR7RV). Fuel tank colors were unchanged from those announced for 1974. You could have any color you wanted as long as it was a Cherokee-red and white (#83-5413) Bonneville or a Jade-green and white (#83-5414) Tiger. As ordered by the

U.S. Department of Transportation, the two fuel taps on American models were given marked settings (on/off and reserve/off). But the valve barrels were now plastic and suffered from prolonged fuel exposure. Most leaked profusely and were quickly replaced by the owner.

In early spring 1976, a small quantity (120) of British-style Bonnevilles, with 4 1/2-gallon Euro tanks, low cafe handlebars, and rubber fork gaiters, were shipped to the United States as a marketing experiment. The tanks, handlebars, and control cables were really the only distinction and all could be ordered separately by Americans wanting the U.K. look. Designations and engine prefixes for the two models offered by the Meriden cooperative were ·T140V (Bonneville) and TR7RV (Tiger 750).

1977 Models

The Triumph factory workers began assembling the 1977 models in June of the previous year, but they were virtually identical to

Timing side view of the 1977 TR7RV. The 750 Bonnevilles were identical except for tank color and an extra carburetor. American models were fitted with smaller fuel tanks and larger handlebars. (Unrestored) *Gaylin*

In any color, the U.S. Triumph fuel tank was a classic. The 1977 Tiger-750s were available in either Sea Jade (dark green) or Signal Red (orange.) The white scallops on the green tank were pinstriped in gold while the orange version (seen here) was lined in black. (Unrestored) *Gaylin*

the 750cc twins they had been putting together in July! So similar were the two motorcycles that many 1977 machines in the United States were delivered with 1976 owners manuals, and when a 1977 spare parts manual was finally issued it listed both model years together on the cover.

1977 Frame and Cycle Parts

However, a trained eye could notice a couple subtle markers. Perhaps to save a few shillings, the aluminum taillight housing was no longer polished and was instead painted in textured black. On the front end of the machine,

Triumph's trademark tank scallops continued to adorn new vertical twins until 1983. The pinstripes were applied by hand and no two were ever a perfect match. Tanks with striping mistakes weren't uncommon and sometimes got by factory inspectors. (Unrestored) *Gaylin*

the upper fender braces were eliminated and replaced by a flat bridge that supported the guard from beneath. A single tongue extended forward to steady the front section and a lonely chrome Phillips-head screw held it in place from the top. This arrangement was much tidier but incidences of fender cracking resurfaced until the exterior braces returned in later years. A detail change that came only to U.K.-market twins was the switch to metal enshrouded resistor spark plug caps. But these gained a reputation for moisture retention and were often replaced by the owner.

For the first time, the Triumph factory offered a choice of tank colors on the Bonneville and Tiger. The Cherokee-red and white from the previous season was joined by Polychrome-blue and white (Pacific-blue in the U.S. #83-6212.) In America, the blue option was very much in the minority as unsold stocks of 1976 (maroon) T140Vs ruined Meriden projections. However, the orangish Signal-red and white (#83-6213) option for the TR7RV was a different story. This finish was only offered on U.S.-spec Tiger 750s and was a bit more common than the Jade-green TR7 option during 1977.

In Britain, Tigers were given optional tank graphics similar to the 1972 scheme. The solid green Euro-tank was given parallel white strips on the lower portion of the sides (approximately 2 1/2 inches wide). But the broad white center stripe on the tank top was divided in two by a smaller green partition. All borders were defined in gold pinstriping.

Bonneville Silver Jubilee

Late in the 1977 production run, a limited edition Bonneville was created to commemorate the twenty-fifth year (Silver Jubilee) of Queen Elizabeth's II reign. The machine's drivetrain specifications were standard T140V and all the model's special features were purely aesthetic. The silver finish used on the tank and fenders was an obvious choice.

Royal accents in red, white, and blue were used to embellish existing tank graphics. The winged scallops on both U.K. and American versions were in blue and then bordered in white and red lining, in that order.

There was a special plastic badge over the tank mounting hollow in silver with a blue Triumph trademark. It was ringed with the words "Silver Jubilee" (above) and "1977" (below), also in blue. But a few early machines might have escaped with standard (gold-and-white) emblems.

The steel fenders were painted silver, given a blue center stripe and lined in the same manner as the tanks. Recalling a feature from the 1950s, the wheel rim centers were painted in blue and trimmed in white and red. Even the silver-painted chain guard received the royal treatment and was accented in the three colors.

The instrument cluster of an unrestored 1976–1977 Twin. The Smiths gauges are completely housed within rubber cups and the speedometer still wears its trip odometer warning sticker. The headlight shell incorporates warning lights for oil pressure, turn signals, and high beam. The three-position toggle switch activated lights with or without ignition key. The steering lock's recessed location between the gauges and well below the handlebars made its use difficult. (Unrestored) *Gaylin*

By the time the unit-construction 650 twin was introduced in 1963, Triumph had rationalized its many patent plates into a simple printed tag without etching or embossing. A machine's age can generally be determined by this plate — the more numbers present, the newer the machine. The first prewar plates had only three patent numbers! (Unrestored) *Gaylin*

In 1969 Triumph made it more difficult to alter an engine's serial number by stamping the figures on top of raised pads that carried a tight grouping of the marque's logos. Beginning in the late 1950s, Triumph made a single stamp of the engine prefix and then applied the model variant code and numbers afterward. It is for this reason the prefix is usually very neat and not impressed as deep into the case, while the numbers are much deeper and often very uneven. (Unrestored machine) *Gaylin*

The tidy front wheel of a 1977 Tiger-750. From 1973 to 1976, the chromed front fender was supported with the traditional braces top and bottom. In 1977 the top braces were supplanted by a cleaner but more "sneaky" arrangement that supported the fender from beneath. Attractive chromed cover hides the hydraulic Lockheed brake caliper. (Unrestored) *Gaylin*

A larger version of Triumph's classic polished aluminum taillight housing reappeared in 1973. During the 1977 model year, the housing's finish was changed to a textured black enamel in order to save a few shillings. A sticker in black, gold, and white advertising Triumph's five-speed transmission was moved to the rear fender in 1972. The useful rear grab rails were now completely chrome-plated. (Unrestored) *Gaylin*

The T140J, as it was designated, also previewed several features that appeared on 1978 models. The seat cover was a new design upholstered in blue vinyl and red piping that drooped down the sides in the forward seating area to provide more comfort. The top panel was not aerated. Instead, the quilted section was cross-ribbed and narrowed in width. This pattern was confined to the center of the seat and did not pursue the piping down on the sides. A silver Triumph logo was still stenciled on the rear panel, underscored with the model's name "Silver Jubilee."

New decorative outer side covers were fitted that were eventually used on standard Bonnevilles as well. These boxy-looking plastic veneers were finished in matching silver and covered the existing side panels. A single chrome-plated screw was used to hold them in place with the aid of a tension spring that hooked into reinforced metal eyelets and crossed between the covers above the carburetors. Each side cover was adorned with a special left- or right-hand plastic badge that read "Bonneville 750" above a British Union Jack. Below the flag were the words "Silver Jubilee 1977—One of a Thousand." There were actually 1,000 T140Js produced for each of the U.K. and American markets, an additional 400 for general export (for a total of 2,400), so the lower inscription was later changed to "Silver Jubilee Limited Edition."

Also debuting on the Silver Jubilee were inverted Girling gas-filled suspension units (#70056007) with the load adjuster cam at the top. Mercifully these were spared the red-white-and-blue treatment. Not to worry — more glitter

Factory publicity photo of the 1977 (U.S. edition) Bonneville Silver Jubilee — a standard T140V with specially finished gingerbread. Chrome-plated engine covers and taillight added dazzle. Circus-colors are harmless in a black-and-white photo! *Author Collection*

Drive side of Tim Savin's unrestored 1977 U.S.-spec Bonneville Silver Jubilee. By this time the safety standards sticker had moved to the left side of the steering head. The T140J had specially finished parts everywhere — even the chain guard got the business. Blue twinseat was very . . . um . . . blue! New style seat cover would be used for the 1978 models (in black or brown). *Gaylin*

"One of a Thousand!" There were actually 1,000 examples produced for both America and the United Kingdom. The additional 400 Jubilees made for general export brought the total to 2,400. Meriden would strike the one of a thousand claim on later side panel emblems and replace it with "Limited Edition." Today, only low (or no) mileage examples have value beyond a standard T140V. (Unrestored) *Gaylin*

came with the use of extra chrome-plating on aluminum components that when polished, were shiny enough. These included the three outer engine covers and taillight housing. Some restored Jubilees have been seen with chrome lower front fork legs, but there is no evidence to support that this was part of the original finish.

The model was also fitted with special Dunlop K91 tires with red side lining (and directional arrows). When paired with the painted rims, the combination made a wheel that was very striking. Tire sizes were 4.10x19-inch on the front, 4.10x18-inch rear.

Though the official model designation was T140J, all engine numbers began with a T140V prefix. The letter J was added after the serial number and in many cases, the stamp completely missed the number pad and landed directly on

Silver Jubilee.

This close-up engine view of an unrestored American Silver Jubilee model shows the deep chrome-plating applied to the engine covers. However, in time some owners experienced peeling and flaking. Choke lever would remain on the left carburetor until the introduction of the Amal MkIIs in 1978. Close examination of the serial number reveals the model designation letter J in the engine case, just behind the number pad. *Gaylin*

the crankcase around the corner.

Original purchasers of each Jubilee were issued a prestigious certificate of ownership. The certificates produced in America were lavishly embossed and differed altogether from the U.K. documents. The serial number and owner's name had to be recorded prior to issuance and certificates were sometimes very long in coming. So long, in fact, that some machines actually changed hands a second time before the presentation was sent. These circumstances caused many papers to become separated from their assigned machines, and as a result the value of surviving Silver Jubilees are enhanced when accompanied by an appropriate document.

Sales of standard Bonnevilles weren't setting any records in 1977. When the Silver Jubilee model was introduced, many American motorcyclists couldn't identify with its remote theme or it $200 price premium. And the

Front wheel details of a U.S. 1977 Silver Jubilee model with double lined fender stripe and painted wheel rims. Rim décor didn't fare well with use. The T140J was given special Dunlop K91 tires with a (thin) red-wall on each side. A directional arrow was also in red. (Unrestored) *Gaylin*

model's circus looks were thought to be too much, even in America. Many Jubilees sat in U.S. showrooms collecting dust well into the 1980s. A major portion of Silver Jubilee sales were to individuals who squirreled them away for investment and today there are many carrying little or no miles. Indeed, unassembled examples still in their shipping crate are not unheard of. Because of this, ridden (and restored) Jubilees, even with only a few thousand miles, have barely more intrinsic value than a standard 1977 T140.

1978 Models

Because Meriden's fortunes had become hopelessly tied to the American market,

Triumph had little choice but to conform their product to U.S. federal regulations. Perhaps no other model year reflected this condition more vividly that 1978, which actually began with the manufacture of the Bonneville Silver Jubilee.

Engine revisions were slight at first. The solid copper head gasket was finally retired for a replacement made of metal and a composite material. The new Klinger gasket had to be positioned with the metal side facing the cylinder head. A gasket between the outer and inner gearbox covers was also now specified. The compression ratio became 7.9:1 on 750s in all markets, including America — helpful in improving reliability and reducing oil leaks, but another step backwards in performance. Other minor engine mods included a serrated lock washer under the crankshaft rotor nut, new dot-and-dash timing marks on the cam wheels, and at engine number 02690, UNF threads for the rockers and adjuster screws.

To comply with U.S. Environmental Protection Agency (EPA) directives mandating vapor and propellant integrity of vehicles made after January 1, 1978, Meriden introduced a new carburetor, cylinder head, and engine breathing arrangement for the Bonneville model. The marque's hallowed splayed-port head, introduced 20 years earlier on the 500cc twins, was replaced by one with perfectly parallel inlet tracts. The combustion chamber was slightly reshaped, and there were redesigned iron valve guides and new valve spring cups, but the cylinder barrels remained unchanged. Detachable intake manifolds were replaced by integrally cast stubs on which all new carburetors were connected with rubber collars.

The squared-bodied mixing chambers had a decidedly Oriental appearance but were made by Amal. The layout and function of the Concentric Mk II, as it was designated, was not much different from the earlier Concentric version. The cylindrical slides were PTFE (Teflon)-coated and the fuel tickler was eliminated. The button was replaced by a fuel enriching jet and plunger operated by a small control lever mounted on the left carb body. Because of the

TRIUMPH

Certificate of Ownership

This certifies that

is the original and proud owner of

The Bonneville Silver Jubilee Limited Edition

honoring the Silver Jubilee of Her Majesty

Queen Elizabeth II

This Date of June 2, 1977

Certificate Number 0001
Serial Number 432182

Triumph Motorcycles of America

Each purchaser of a new Bonneville Silver Jubilee was supposed to receive a prestigious certificate of ownership. U.K. document differed from the embossed items issued in the United States (pictured). In America, the presentation scheme was protracted and some were sent after the machine had already changed hands a second time. And leftover Jubilees were still being sold in the 1980s when the certificate program had been forgotten by many. Accompanying documents today are rare and add to the value of a surviving machine. *Author Collection*

new carbs' close proximity to one another, a single lever manipulated both instruments by use of a flat linking bar.

The engine breather elbow behind the clutch housing was now piped straight into the airbox, to achieve contained crankcase venting. This obviated the D-pipe mounting holes on the rear fender and the 1977 part number. To complete vapor suppression, the frame's oil chamber vent was connected to the exhaust rocker box. Although not specified at the time, it was learned later that Champion N-5 spark plugs worked better with the Mark II carbs especially at prolonged low speeds.

The new Bonneville's designation was T140E (the letter E indicated EPA). Most, if not all of these 1978 1/2 models, were exported to the United States beginning in March of that year. Because there was insufficient clearance between the cylinder head's detachable manifold and airbox housing to admit a (larger) single Amal Mark II carburetor, there was no TR7 version of the T140E Bonneville during that year. The trifles of Tiger TR7RV models shipped to America in early 1978 were the last to come over.

An unrestored 1978 1/2 T140E Bonneville owned by Bob Leppan. Midyear model debuted new Amal MkII carbs. New one-piece styling panels were attached over existing arrangement and twinseat cover borrowed from the Jubilee. Still not a bad looker! *Lindsay Brooke*

1978 Frame and Cycle Parts

To accommodate the Mark II carbs and their newly merged positions, the airbox housing was redesigned and new connecting rubbers used. One-piece outer side panels similar to the Silver Jubilee's were adopted but with a second fixing spring crossing over below the carburetors. The new covers projected out sideways beyond the nose of the seat. Besides adding inches to the Triumph's traditional waspish waistline, the wider panels also made the machine more difficult to straddle for smaller riders.

The panels retained their chrome bezelled nameplate and embossed sticker with gold lettering on a black background. To distinquish the T140E models, the decals were switched to black letters on silver. These were also changed (to black and silver) on the balance of Tiger 750s for that year. The decal ID number for the T140E Bonnevilles was 60-7054, and for the TR7RV Tigers, 60-7055. No other decal changes were recorded in 1978.

Of course, most of the changes incorporated within the running gear were implemented at the start of the model year and applied to both T140E and the earlier 1978 twins. Gas-filled inverted Girling rear suspension units as fitted to the Silver Jubilee were specified for all Triumphs after engine number BX05107. The front suspension was improved with better fork seals at the top of the sliders. These could also be retrofitted as a "fix kit" for forks back to 1971, and many were. The chrome upper fork covers used on the U.S. bikes were now fitted to machines in all markets.

Sealed wheel bearings became standard for the front. The rear wheel received heavier 9-gauge spokes and a modified rim to stop the rash of spoke failures caused by a more demanding disc brake. On U.S. models, Dunlop K81 tires became original equipment. The tire sizes were now 4.10x19 inches on the front and 4.10x18 for the rear. Home market machines (and U.S.-style bikes remaining in Britain)

Instrument close-up of an unrestored 1978 T140E Bonneville. Veglia gauges with Meriden logos on the face — others had the Veglia insignia instead. Tacky switch and warning lamp labeling usually wore rapidly. *Gaylin*

stayed with the K70 patterns for one more year.

When the supply of Smiths instruments was sporadically interrupted during 1978, French-made Veglia gauges were substituted. Some of these contained the Meriden logo on the face, some did not. For further clarification of these, please refer to the specifications Appendix.

In the electrical department, Lucas quartz halogen headlight units specified for the chrome 7-inch shell also meant a new reflector and harness plug. A louder Lucas 6H hooter was listed and the taillight housing was polished again and clear-coated afterward. Partway through 1978 production, Yuasa batteries (12N9-4B-1) replaced the increasingly expensive Lucas (PUZ5A) component. By this time Meriden had become the only (major) customer for Lucas motorcycle goods and the limited quantities they were ordering were a fraction of their past contracts. Even with

expanded prices, bike components had become an unprofitable nuisance for Lucas.

The twinseat upholstery that debuted on the Silver Jubilee model was used across the range in 1978. The piping slid down on the flanks of the forward section, but the ribbed pattern on top was broadened and followed the beading down. The saddle was available in wide or narrow (nose) versions to complement the rectangular U.K. and slimline U.S.-style fuel tanks. The seat color was solid black with a printed Triumph logo on the after panel, but an all-brown seat was created to complement the optional Chocolate tank finish noted below. The chrome-and-rubber trimming at the seat's lower edge was continued on all versions.

The 1977 fuel tank graphics and emblems were kept on both U.K. and American models. In the United States there were now three color options available on the T140s. The most common variant was a black tank with Crimson scallops bordered in a single gold pinstripe. There was also a version in Astral-blue with a silver scallop lined in gold. The least appreciated of the three (in America anyway) was a Chocolate-brown Bonneville with gold scallops. This tank accent was given double pinstriping, first in black and then in white. The Chocolate models were also coupled with distinctive seats covered in brown vinyl and side panels to match the tank. Black side enclosures were specified for all other U.S. versions, including the final Tiger 750. The color scheme for the American single-carb model was Crimson and silver. The scallops on these tanks were bordered in double lines of black and gold.

Two color options were available for each of the U.K. 750 twins. Bonnevilles were offered in Tawny-brown (Chocolate in the United States) with gold comma-shaped accents. These were double-striped in the same manner and colors as on American-spec slimline tanks. The second condition was Aquamarine with silver panels and double striped in black and gold. Color choices for the home market Tigers included a Candy Apple red (Crimson in the United States) option with silver accents surrounded

A 1978 T140E fuel tank with top scallops only. The dimensions of these were laid down in 1973 as a compromise between the 1970 and 1971 tank accents. Central tank fixing, borrowed from BSA, was a step forward from the underside screws. (Unrestored) *Lindsay Brooke*

by black-and-gold lining. The alternative was Burnished-gold with silver panels - the accents bordered first in baby blue and then black.

The side panels on all U.K. models were finished in the machine's main color, and the lower and back edges were trimmed in the second color forming the shape of a hockey stick. These accents were then bordered in matching pinstripes.

Chrome fenders still protected U.S.-spec twins, but mudguards on British models were now painted in the machine's main color. The front guard was given a chevron (apex toward the front) positioned midway on the forward section. The rear fender was accented in the same manner with a slightly wider stripe (curved away from the machine) in the exposed area between the fender support rail and taillight housing. The painted accents were then finished off in correlating double pinstripes to match the tank. Nylon washers were used at all attachment points to protect the painted surfaces on U.K. fenders.

Brown Bonnevilles with their dramatic pinstriping and matching seats were distinctive, but perhaps too much so for the 1978 motorcycle consumer. So scorned were the brown T140s

in America that 500 complete machines were shipped back to the United Kingdom, where they weren't any more popular. They have become fairly rare among surviving 1978 examples and are now considered by many collectors to be the most desirable color option for that year.

Model designations (and engine prefixes) were T140V for Concentric Mk1-carbed Bonnevilles and T140E for machines with Amal MK2s. The Tiger 750 kept its TR7RV code.

1979 Models

The new model year saw the T140E Bonneville's cylinder head, Mark II carburetors, and vapor containment system also become standard on the U.K. models as well. There were only a few other engine revisions, including a gasket between the timing cover and crankcase. All outer covers were now secured with Allen-head cap screws instead of the traditional Phillips-head screws.

Inside the transmission, the camplate was modified to improve selection and given a deeper neutral recess. A neutral indicator switch was also installed in the form of a protruding button on the gear-change camplate. But these were often unreliable, sending a neutral signal when still in gear — and vice-versa.

1979 Frame and Cycle Parts

The big story for 1979 was in the 750's electrical department. At engine number HA11001, Meriden joined the twentieth century and reversed the electrical polarity on their machines to negative ground. This allowed another big move, to electronic ignition. The solid state nerve center of the new Lucas Rita system was the AB11 amplifier module located behind the right-hand side panel. It took its signals from a reluctor and pulse sensor that were housed in the points cavity on the timing chest — the mechanical contact breakers having now been completely replaced. To retard or advance the spark, all that was necessary was to slacken the

pillar bolts and rotate the pickup plate. To enclose the electronic sensor, an attractive horizontally finned alloy cover replaced the chrome cap.

The alternator was upgraded to a three-phase Lucas RM24 unit that produced a level electrical output at all rpm, permitting day-long city use of the headlight, signals, and stop lights without depleting the battery. The new system required a Lucas 3DS rectifier and new Zener diode to dissipate the unwanted wattage.

The Lucas handlebar switch consoles were redesigned and much improved. The internals were actually the same, yet the button layout was easier to use and the black housings were better labeled. The consoles were also extended to incorporate pivot bases for the new alloy clutch and brake levers, and master cylinder attachment on the right. The warning lamps

The tank scallops on the 1978 Chocolate-brown-and-gold Bonnevilles were double lined, first in black and then in white. The effect was striking — but not striking enough. Five hundred units finished in brown were returned to Britain at a considerable loss for the struggling factory. (Unrestored) *Gaylin*

The tank flashes on the 1979 T140E models were defined with double lining and lengthened to reach the seat's nose. Pictured on this brand new machine is the red (tank) and black (scallop) option striped in gold. Spacing between the lines was the tank's main color — in this case red. *Gaylin*

Two engine views of Britech's brand-new 1979 750 Bonneville. Outwardly, not much change since 1963. Timing side shows Allen-head cover screws and a finned points cover. From the left side details of the tank badge and Japanese-like Amal MkIIs are easy to see. While the pair of side cover retention springs and safety standards decal are not as obvious. *Gaylin*

were moved and, along with the ignition switch, were consolidated within a T160 Trident-style dashboard between the gauges.

The idiot-light console was actually a complete housing that fastened to the upper fork yoke, which meant revisions to the top lug as well as the steering head lock plate on the frame. A fourth warning lamp (another in green) was added to the array as a neutral indicator light. The instruments were moved closer together and given new enclosures. They were still encapsulated in rubber but the solid base carriers were screwed to the central console box. Veglia speedometers and tachs now permanently replaced Smiths as original equipment.

Changes in the Triumph's seating area included a lockable (with a key!) twinseat. The

lock housing was welded to the upper frame rail and two helmet hooks were also provided to offer secure stowage. An attractive chromed luggage rack was incorporated into the rear fender support/grab rail that begged to be used. But its capacity was restricted to 15 pounds (or the weight of a small beer cooler) and a sticker (#60-7206) declaring such was fixed to the back end. All dual seats were skinned in black. The remaining brown saddles from the previous season, however, were paired with a special beige-and-gold color option on U.K. Bonnevilles that was quite satisfactory in appearance.

The rear fender engine breather pipe was now eliminated on the U.K. models and chrome fenders became standard again. At the front there was a stronger underside fender bridge fitted to cure the cracking problem. The alloy front wheel hub was polished and lacquered to match the spool at the rear, and the Dunlop K81s (TT100s) that were fitted to U.S. machines were now specified for the home market bikes. Tires sizes were 4.10x19 inches (front) and 4.10x18 (rear) on both the Bonneville T140E and U.K. Tiger 750.

Further modifications to the chassis included new squared-off footpeg rubbers that were given traction ribs on the top surface and a chamfered tip underneath for extra clearance when using the sides of the tires. Meriden was now powder-coating the frames in black before assembly, but their first attempts at the process were less than satisfactory. Many machines from this period suffered from cracking and peeling. The outer side panels were slightly reshaped and had revised recesses to allow new tiered plastic emblems. The top line carried the model name in italicized capital letters and extended past the lower "750" on both ends.

The factory expanded the color options with a vengeance in 1979. Beginning with the U.S. Bonnevilles there were three choices. The first was in Candy Apple red with black scallops and matching red side covers. There was also a blue version with a silver tank flash and corresponding blue side panels. American-spec Bonnevilles in both of these color schemes were also for sale in the home market, but a third color option was reserved only for America. The gas tanks on these were painted in black and scalloped in silver, and when bordered in double gold pinstriping (applied to all slimline tanks), yielded perhaps the most attractive finish of the three. A classic look was reinforced with jet black side enclosures.

The plastic emblems were screwed to the panels and lettered in chrome over black backgrounds. However, the emblems on the blue Bonnies were given a special silver setting.

For 1979, the 4-gallon fuel tanks on the British models were finished in new graphics. The kneegrips were eliminated and the painted side panels were extended into the rear section. The comma-shaped accent was swapped for a narrower strip that ran parallel with the tank.

Tail section of a brand-new 1979 T140E. Last year for the bottom-mounted brake calipers. Sensible taillight with attractive housing and a tasteful luggage rack that invited use, as long as parcels were kept below 15 pounds. License plate brackets appear unused. *Gaylin*

The ends were cut on diagonals and the overall effect was that of a stretched "zig-zag." Available in two color schemes, the prevailing option for the U.K. T140s was black with Candy-red accents. Parallel gold pinstriping was used to emphasize the tank panels and the side covers were finished in black.

Six-hundred of the "European style" Bonnevilles (as they were known) finished in these colors were sent to the U.S. in 1979. In addition to the metal spark plug caps (mandated in the United Kingdom) and low cafe handlebars, they also retained the rubber fork gaiters that had been absent on American models for almost ten years.

The second T140 color choice in the United Kingdom was beige with burnished gold tank flashes. These were given dual pinstriping, first in black and then in white. The machine's side covers were finished in beige with black plastic emblems lettered in gold. These machines were fitted with the remaining Tawny-brown twinseats from 1978, and it is highly likely that the beige color scheme was created just for that purpose. The Tiger 750 was still made available in all markets except the United States. The British-style version was painted in blue with silver tank flashes and double-lined in gold. The side enclosures were in matching blue and given special plastic "Tiger 750" emblems lettered in black on a silver background. And there were still U.S.-spec Tigers with high handlebars and slimline tanks produced (not for America) but using the remaining 1978 fuel tanks in red and silver.

Bonneville Special

In March 1979, a limited edition variant of the T140E was introduced and christened the Bonneville Special. The designated T140D model was Meriden's response to Yamaha's wildly popular range of 650cc twin-cylinder "factory customs" that were actually inspired by earlier Triumphs! As in the case of the Silver Jubilee, the differences between the Bonneville Special and the existing product were in the cycle parts, many of which would be incorporated into future 750 models.

American-style slimline gas tanks were used on the T140D exclusively, but with the simpler U.K. Triumph tank badge. The tank was painted black and outlines of scallop forms were applied in gold pinstriping above and below both Triumph emblems. There were matching black side covers with two horizontal lines immediately below a newly created tiered emblem. (Bonneville

Tim Savin's unrestored 1979 Bonneville Special with gold outline finish on black, American Lester mag wheels, and chrome fenders. New-generation twinseat would later be used across the range. Not an unattractive package! *Gaylin*

Front three-quarter view of Savin's 1979 T140D model shows TT-type exhaust system and cross-hatched stepped saddle. *Gaylin*

remained in italicized capitals but over the word "Special" in red script.)

A new stepped twinseat was created with a taller profile and a new cross-hatched pattern for the top panel. It was covered in black vinyl and showed the same extruded chrome and rubber trim around the lower edge. A Triumph trademark printed in gold remained on the saddle's posterior. The underside pan was unchanged and permitted retrofitting. There was also a new rear fender support rail fashioned in chrome, with a squared-off grab handle behind the seat.

The T140D's elevated seat height was compensated by a nearly 2-inch rise in the footpegs. Along with a redesigned centerstand the higher pegs gave more ground clearance when leaned over; however, the new right-hand exhaust system easily bottomed. The frame was also upgraded at the rear with thicker-section swingarm tubes. The rear brake caliper was repositioned to the top of the disc and bolted to a new mounting plate and torque arm. This change greatly simplified wheel removal and was soon adopted across the range.

The Bonneville Special was also the first Triumph to roll on anything other than spoked wheels. U.S.-made Lester seven-spoke mags lent a custom appearance (and further emulated

For 1979 the 750 twins adopted a light and instrument console similar to the T160 Tridents. Clock carriers were screwed to the central housing which incorporated warning lamps and ignition switch. Also visible are tank top details including a black badge over the mounting cavity. *Gaylin*

Back end of an unrestored 1979 Bonneville Special. Lockheed caliper's new position at the top of the disc meant a longer and enshrouded brake line. Annular discharge muffler is reminiscent of the late Tridents and inverted Girling suspension units were now being fitted to all models. *Gaylin*

the Yamaha models). The outer rims of the cast-aluminum wheels were unpainted and polished to a high luster, while the recessed areas of the spokes as well as the raised wheel centers were painted black. Dunlop TT100s (K81s) were fitted front and rear — a 4.10x19-inch in front, and a fatter 4.25x18 in the rear, so necessary for the "cruiser" look. These covers were switched to 4.10x18 inches on later T140s when Meriden discovered there was insufficient fender clearance (and subsequent tire punctures) when riding double-up. Both fenders were chrome-plated, but the front guard was abbreviated in length (bobbed) and supported only by the underside brace.

Bonneville Special Engine and Drivetrain

There were no significant variations in the Bonneville Special's engine specification (from the standard T140E) other than the reappearance of threaded exhaust ports in the cylinder head to allow positive attachment of the pipes. In an arrangement similar to Triumph's 1948–50 Grand Prix racing models, the exhaust pipe ends were flanged and sat within the head. Threaded rings with short cooling fins followed them in and held the pipes in place.

The T140D was given an attractive new chrome-plated exhaust system with its head pipes bent to resemble the U.S. TT Specials of

The Bonneville Special was the first U.S. model to wear the simplified Triumph tank emblem. Squatty scallop outlines were copied from Yamaha (who copied theirs from Triumph!) Finned points cover on the T140D was inlaid in black for effect. Exhaust pipe details can also be seen. (Unrestored) *Gaylin*

the mid-1960s. The tubes made a level exit from the splayed ports, turned and aimed directly for the bottom of the downtubes. The crossover balance tube was eliminated and steadying tabs were welded halfway down and connected to the front of the motor with angled flat straps. Instead of spreading again (as on the TTs), the head pipes merged into a junction pipe that fed a single muffler on the right-hand side.

A compromise location was necessary to allow the centerstand to remain, at the expense of the machine's cornering clearance. And the muffler body was a new two-stage megaphone with an end cap similar to the T160 Trident's annular discharge muffler.

A final feature specific to the D model was a "points" cover finished in black with the raised fins left bare to emphasize their presence. There were no known decal changes or additions recorded for any of the 1979 750 twins. Engine prefixes were either T140E, T140D, or TR7RV (United Kingdom only), depending on the model.

Chapter Ten

Final 750 Twins (1980–1983)

At the end of the 1979 model year, Triumph's U.S. warehouses were filled with unsold T140E Bonnevilles. This situation, caused by overzealous sales forecasts and severe currency swings, forced Meriden to delay the American introduction of the 1980 models with new features, such as electric starting and color-coordinated fairings. These bikes would have to wait until the U.S. logjam was reduced.

Therefore, many of the new features examined here for 1980 were available only on U.K. and export models. It should also be pointed out that Triumph production was reduced by almost 75 percent from 1979 levels and that the factory's focus returned to the British and European markets. Triumph's annual motorcycle imports to America were now measured in the hundreds, and very few genuine 1980 models were imported.

American sales of the T140D Bonneville Special during 1979 did not live up to Meriden's expectations, and as a result the Special became available in the United Kingdom. These were offered with either the dual exhaust system of the T140E, or the original two-into-one arrangement.

A new four-valve oil pump was introduced in 1980, with secondary ball-checks in both the feed and scavenge side to ensure against wet-sumping. The pump's brass body was now angled (and splayed) at the bottom and given two additional access caps, but the unit could be retrofitted with a suitably modified timing cover. The primary chain tensioner was also revised to allow adjustments without dumping the chain case oil.

Beginning at engine number CB29901, batches of 750cc models were produced with redesigned crankcases to accept an electric starter. The motor used was the Lucas M3, a 12-volt unit previously seen on the British Reliant three-wheeler. The starter was located behind the cylinders, in the old pre-unit magneto position.

New timing cover and inner crankcase casting extended rearward to house the starter drive, recalling the pre-unit Triumph appearance. Unlike the T160 Trident starter, which engaged a geared clutch hub, the T140ES arrangement spun the engine to life through the timing gears. The system employed a Borg-Warner sprag-type clutch and a strengthened intermediate gear, solidly bushed on both the crankcase face and the more substantial polished timing cover.

Sadly, Triumph's hallmark patent plate was not attached to the newly shaped cover due to the depth of the mounting rivets and the new bearing seat. The cover featured a detachable rear section to allow access to the starter motor's mounting bolts. And unlike the lazy 15:1 reduction ratio used on the Norton Commando's troublesome electric foot, the Triumph's was a more aggressive 20:1. The designation for the electric start 750 model was T140ES.

1980 Frame and Cycle Parts

The starter solenoid was mounted on a bracket in the void under the right-hand side cover and airbox. The T140ES (and eventually the U.K.-only TR7VS electric-start Tiger) required a mightier Yuasa 14 1/2-amp-hour battery. A bigger battery meant a new battery carrier and a recess in the underside of the seat pan to jump over the taller storage cell. Other changes necessitated by the electric starter included a higher wattage Lucas RM24 alternator and a triple pack of Zener diodes (one for each phase of the alternator) mounted in the airbox for cooling. A higher output sensor was included in the Lucas Rita electronic ignition

T140E Bonneville American

With a mountain of unsold machines in U.S. warehouses, Meriden found little need to send over new machines during the 1980 model year. The T140E (and later T140ES) Bonneville American models were assembled from the U.S.-spec components piling up at the factory and then put on sale in the home market. Features differing from actual U.S.-bound models included fork gaiters, naked trademark tank emblem, and of course the rear number board. (Publicity photo) *Author collection*

system to supply a stronger spark at low rpm.

Besides the electric-start frame changes, there were many other revisions to the running gear on all 1980 machines. The home market Tiger 750s adopted the T140E engine breathing arrangement and the chrome rear fender without the D-Pipe mounting holes. All models came with the raised foot rests and redesigned center-stand from the Bonneville Specials. The centerstand mounting was also reinforced with additional braces to the main frame tube, while the mufflers (and passenger peg mounts) were pulled up at the rear for better cornering. Even the brake pedal forging was strengthened.

The rear swinging arm had the shape of its tubes rationalized, to simplify fabrication, and tube diameter was increased from 32 to 38 millimeters. The rear brake caliper was moved to the top of the disc, per the T140D. This meant a new shrouded brake line had to travel past the end of the swingarm and then up to a banjo fitting behind the Lockheed caliper.

The fluid reservoir for the rear brake was moved down on top of the master cylinder, and the rear section of the right-hand inner side cover given an access window. The front hydraulic fluid bowl was also changed to a white opaque plastic so that visual checks could be made without removing the cap. The speedometer drive takeoff was moved to the left side of the rear axle, requiring a new rear hub, root sprocket, and shorter disc bolts.

Additional changes to the 1980 cycle parts included rubber-mounted turn signals to combat the vertical twin's filament-fracturing, stem-loosening vibration. There was a larger tool tray in the battery compartment, and B.A.P. fuel taps were specified to stop the leaks once and

Later in the 1980 season Meriden introduced a touring version Bonneville designated the Executive, with matching luggage and handlebar fairing in smoked Ruby-red. The first electric-start models sent to the United States were Bonneville Executives. The example pictured is a 1981 U.K. edition with new-generation Euro fuel tank and optional straight bench seat. Bing carburetors with redesigned side panels were standard. (Factory photo) *Author Collection*

for all. Avon Roadrunners replaced the Dunlop tires as original equipment on all Triumph models. Front tire size was 4.10x19-inches; rear was 4.25x18. Meriden's miscalculation on 1979 sales, and the subsequent decision to restrict U.S. shipments in 1980, left Triumph awash in U.S.-spec components. In Britain, a variant of the T140E, designated the Bonneville American, was pushed alongside the standard versions.

The American was fitted with the high-rise handlebars and peanut-shaped fuel tanks of the U.S.-spec bikes, but differed in a couple of other ways. Rubber fork gaiters concealed the upper stanchions (U.S.-bound examples continued with the dust scrapers) and the larger "naked" Triumph tank emblem was used, but in chrome with only the letter centers inlaid with black. The fuel tanks were given scallops top and bottom in the squatty dimensions of the Bonneville Specials, and level twinseats from the 1979 T140E models were fitted as standard. However, Bonnevilles sent Stateside that year had the T140D-type stepped saddle.

There were at least three color options for the 1980 American-style Bonnevilles. The most prevalent was black with Candy-red tank scallops, surrounded with a single gold stripe. Less common was the combination of Olympic Flame and black scallops bordered in gold. Sales literature shows another option as Steel-gray with red flashes and black lining, but parts manuals (in all markets) describe a tank with black wings lined in gold, and some of these are known to have landed in the U.S. The colors of the T140D remained unchanged for 1980, in black with gold pinstriping.

The standard U.K. Triumphs continued with the "zig-zag" tank graphics from 1979 and were offered in only two color schemes. The first was Steel-gray with Candy-red accents, double bordered in black. The second choice was an all-black tank, with the shape of the accents described in double white pinstriping, the inside line broader than the outside to achieve a classic look. The single color option listed for the Tiger 750 was Astral-blue, with black zig-zags surrounded in double lines of gold. Although none were exported to America, there was a U.S.-spec TR7 with slimline tank and high bars. These were also finished in blue and black, but with a single gold line bordering T140D-style scallops. Black side covers were fitted to the Triumph 750s in all color options, their plastic emblems also in black.

Model designations for 1980 were T140E, T140ES, TR7RV, TR7VS (electric-start Tiger), and T140D. Late in the season a sport-touring edition of the Bonneville was introduced. At first the Bonneville Executive, as it was called, was without an electric starter. Later versions had the electric foot, but in both cases there was no distinct engine prefix code — all were stamped T140E or T140ES. But for all intents, these were early 1981 models. None were seen in America until well into that season.

1981 Models

When Bonneville Executives finally landed in the United States, they carried electric starting. In fact, the first T140ES models to arrive were Executives. Announced in February 1980, the original U.K. versions were identical in engine specification to the T140E (without self-starting), but by the end of June, T140ES Executives were ready to go.

The obvious difference from the standard Bonneville was the Executive's striking color-matched fairing and rear travel luggage. Made by Brealey-Smith, Ltd., in Britain, the attractive fork-mounted quarter-fairing had a business-like BMW appearance. The cockpit side was finished in leather-grained ABS plastic, and the instruments remained separately mounted to the central fork top console. Early windshields were clear while later (and all U.S.) versions were slightly smoke-tinted and protected at the upper edge by black trim.

Twin round safety mirrors in black sprouted from the upper wings of the fairing, and the turn signals were relocated to the lower edge at the fork tubes. The first Executive models wore chrome Lucas blinkers, but these were soon changed to the rectangular BMW-type items fitted across the Triumph range. The handlebars were originally police-type pull-backs, but Executive parts book supplements from both 1980 and 1981 do not indicate a special bar.

Another feature found on the initial British market Executives was the larger 4.8-gallon Euro fuel tank. By the time the U.S. models arrived, most were fitted with a new Italian-made tank destined for other Triumph models the following season. This tank had softer curves and was certainly more modern in appearance, but didn't seem as appropriate when fitted on the touring model. Capacity remained the same 4 1/2 gallons, and there was a hinged, lockable Monza-type filler cap. The rear of the Executive included a tubular carrier (in black) for a pair of Sigma hard suitcases. These panniers were quickly detachable and were dead ringers for the Krauser bags fitted to BMWs. A large matching top box was carried on the upper portion of the rack. Its upper lid contained a bright reflectorized warning triangle that faced oncoming traffic when opened. There was also a first-aid kit hidden under a false floor.

All three containers were color coordinated, with the fuel tank, side covers, and fenders in smoked-red darkening to black. The degree of the burnt finish varied widely among examples but generally the darkened areas were to the rear and bottom, and progressively lightened toward the front. (This was characteristic of the other smoked finishes in the range.) Technical literature likewise describes a smoked-blue version of the Executive, but it is unclear if any of these were sent to the United States. In any market, Bonneville Executives in smoke-blue are rare.

The forward and lower edges of the tank, side covers, and pannier doors were pinstriped in an L-shaped gold accent. Simplified British-style cast Triumph emblems in chrome were used for the fuel tank and early edition saddlebags. Later luggage insignias were changed to a plain circular badge in plastic with a smaller Triumph logo. A "king-and-queen" type seat was designed with deeper stepped portions for each rider (not to be confused with a king-and-queen accessory seat offered in the United States

during 1979.) The saddle's cover was sewn with wider cross-hatched stitching, and there was a hand strap midway for the passenger's piece of mind. The plastic trim used at the lower edge was completely in black. For those not wanting a seat with dedicated sections, the standard 1979-type T140 seats could be ordered but with a hand strap.

U.S.-spec T140ES Bonneville Electros were finally offered for sale in America in 1981 and incorporated many improvements. The engine featured the T140D-type cylinder head with threaded exhaust ports. But unlike the Bonnie Specials, stubs were screwed in and the exhaust pipe was expanded to fit over in the traditional manner. Finned exhaust clamps were returned to practical duty and the balance tube remained to keep the engine in harmony. Another modification came to the inlet valve guides, which were given separate oil seals to slow oil consumption and wear.

Early U.S. T140ES models came with Amal MkII carburetors with bigger needle jets and a handlebar-mounted choke lever. But due to stiffening American emission regulations, these were later replaced with German-made Bing Type-94 constant-velocity carbs. Choke assemblies on these were not linked, obviating the separate handlebar lever. The side covers were redesigned and extended forward to protect the Bings' vulnerable side-mounted linkages from loose-fitting Levis. The protruding panels added even more width in the leg area and were not generally admired.

Within the engine, the timing side main bearing was beefed to a four-lip roller. Pressured oil feed to the tappets was eliminated altogether, and both inlet and exhaust cam followers were commonized for interchangeability. The position of the starter motor had completely obstructed access to the TDC plug. The plug was moved to the front of the crankcase and the flywheel notch changed accordingly.

Clutch action was lightened by fitting weaker T120 springs and deleting a drive plate (to six total). And the cable was given a nylon lining which also helped stop premature failures.

The 1981 U.S.-spec Bonneville now with electric-starter and Bing carburetors. Notice the stepped twinseat left over from T140D models. The tank emblem was entirely in chrome with only the letter-centers painted in black. Factory press photo

Another change involved the remaining T140D models still stockpiled in the United States. A shorter, straight-sided megaphone became optional. This muffler was slash cut at the end and did not extend past the rear disc brake. It had a slightly ruder voice and generally improved the looks of the model. There is no record of this option in the United Kingdom.

1981 Frame and Cycle Parts

Britain's once dominant motorcycle industry was all but gone in 1981, and it is little wonder that support for the manufacture of bikes had also disappeared. Traditional component suppliers such as Smiths, Lucas, and Girling had completely abandoned their motorcycle trade, or were planning to.

Even the Triumph factory discontinued in-house production of some key components. For example, 1981 was the last year for Meriden-made fuel tanks with removable filler caps and the "small eyebrow" emblem. When stocks were exhausted, these were replaced by Italian-made versions of both the U.S.-style peanut tanks and Euro-tanks, with all-new contours. Monza filler caps and a more modern form made these tanks attractive when the edges were highlighted in gold pinstriping.

Four different twinseats were listed for 1981, but most road-going 750s came with a form of the Bonneville Special's stepped dual seat

(#83-7391) still trimmed at the lower edge in a chrome-and-black motif. However, the earlier T140E (#83-7272) saddles, in black, continued to make an irregular appearance. The chrome-plated fenders on the early models gave way to polished stainless steel guards.

Although sizes and dimensions of the Avon Roadrunner tires remained the same, the wheels and brakes were slightly revised. On U.K. models, two teeth were dropped from the rear wheel sprocket (45-tooth) to give taller gearing and slow the engine speed on the highway. Dual front AP Lockheed disc brakes were also made an option, initially on the Executive models. Halfway through the model year, the single discs reverted to an unplated condition, to allow the more abrasive Dunlopad brake pads. And toward the end of 1981, the U.S.-made Lester cast wheels were replaced with less -flashy Morris cast wheels. These also featured seven-spokes and were finished in black, with polished outer rims. The new wheels were available on any Triumph model.

Other running gear upgrades included a circlip retention groove at the top of the fork sliders to secure the oil seals. When the supply of Lucas turns signals dried up midway in the season, German-made replacements were installed. These square-bodied blinkers and their mounting stalks were painted black. Round, black, safety mirrors (also German-made) became standard on all, including U.S. models. The headlamp was changed to a 60/45-watt sealed beam, and the support arms on the fork were modified to better isolate the light unit from vibration.

The smaller batches and shorter production runs at Meriden permitted factory customizing and mix-or-match specifications, including the laced or cast wheel option already mentioned. You could now order a Triumph in one of six color schemes, in U.S. or British trim. However, the Bonnevilles actually shipped to the United States came in only two finishes. The first was in smoked Astral-blue with gracefully sweeping silver scallops above the tank emblem and bordered with a single gold pinstripe. The

alternative was smoked Olympic Flame with white accents lined in gold.

Both U.S. color options came with color-coordinated side panels. In both cases the smoked portion was to the rear of the tank (or side cover) and the color progressively lightened to either Astral-blue or Olympic-orange at the front. On the early examples with Amal MkII carburetors, the side enclosures carried no accents other than the black and chrome plastic emblems. Later models with Bing CV carbs had enlarged covers that extended forward to protect the German instruments. These were given a stylish two-toned finish and split diagonally with a single gold pinstripe — the bright color laying over the burnt — although the black sometimes tended to bleed over the boundary line. Electric-start models in all markets now carried a special "Electro" decal (#60-7386) in the lower front corner of both side covers. The transfers were gold, with the final letter harpooned by a small lightning bolt. U.S.-bound Bonnevilles also kept their "small eyebrow" tank emblems that were now completely chrome-plated, with only the trademark's letter centers painted in black.

These emblems differed from the simplified cast logo fitted on the "Bonneville Americans" for sale in the United Kingdom and the rest of Europe. Stubby scalloped wings in the T140D form arched back from the emblems top and bottom. For these there were four color schemes: black with Candy-red wings; Steel-gray with black wings; pale silver-blue with black wings; and finally, all black with the ghost scallops employed on the Bonneville Specials. Gold pinstriping was used to define the accents on all four tank finishes, but to simplify assembly the side panels remained in black.

There were six reciprocal color choices for the standard home market models as well. The first two were in smoked blue or smoked orange, but without the flanking zig-zag displays to break the effect. Instead, a simple L-shaped pinstripe in gold was applied to the lower front corners. These were accompanied by matching side panels in the smoked finish — sometimes

To capture some of the dual-purpose market raging on the European continent, Meriden created the TR7T Tiger-Trail for 1981. A single-carbed 750 twin in bright yellow and a pregnant snake for a muffler. Ground clearance was slightly increased by larger wheels and losing the centerstand. Not many were produced and none went to America. Factory photo. *Author collection*

with corresponding (gold) L-shaped lines at the front corners, other times without.

The remaining four 1981 tank options carried the normal zig-zag war paint. The first two finishes were black with Candy-red or Steel-gray with red. Both were bordered in double gold lines. Option number three was a strange, pale silver-blue skirted in black with surrounding parallel pinstripes, first in gold, then in black. The final tank color was all black, with only the shape of the accent double outlined in gold. In this case only the widths of the lining varied with the broader pinstripe on the inside.

In April 1981, Meriden introduced a mutant Tiger 750 that was squarely aimed at the Europeon market (particularly France) where

the trend for dual-purpose bikes was in high gear. Although never available in America, the TR7T Tiger Trail deserves a brief description as a TR7 variant. The drivetrain was standard TR7 fare, with an Amal MkI Concentric carburetor but a softer 7.5:1 compression ratio. A special two-into-one exhaust system was painted black and exited on the left-hand side. There it connected with a convoluted, pregnant black snake of a muffler that crawled up alongside the rear subframe, finally leveling off to terminate in front of new Marzocchi suspension units.

The Tiger Trail's front fork was finished entirely in black and equipped with rubber gaiters between the sliders and bottom lug. There were new headlight support arms between the yokes and a smaller 6-inch lamp fitted with a pebble guard. Only a speedometer was specified, the tachometer cup used to house the warning lamps and ignition switch, their relocation forced by the new headlight.

The pseudo-off-roader's wheel hubs were laced to Italian made stainless steel rims and these were shod with trials-pattern Avon Mudplugger tires — 3.00x21-inch front and 4.00x18-inch rear. The front brake was a 10-inch Lockheed disc and a retro-style 7.5-inch single-leading shoe drum came on the rear.

The Tiger Trail's fuel tank was the U.S. peanut type, but without kneegrips or a cast badge. Instead there was a five-piece sticker with a split-T motif, broken in the center by a smaller Triumph logo. Reportedly these could easily be loosened, intentionally or not. The paint color was a bright safety yellow for the tank, side covers, and elevated plastic fenders. A special "Trail" transfer was applied to the lower front corner of the side panels.

Other details included a shortened three-quarter-version seat, black filler cap, a token skid plate, and no center stand. With changes, this model was catalogued until 1983, but in all, less than 250 were delivered.

Including the TR7T Tiger Trail and T140AV Police bike, Triumph's U.K. range consisted of nine models. The other designations were T140E (standard or American), T140ES (standard or American), T140ES Executive, TR7RV, and TR7VS. The U.S. line-up comprised only three variants: T140ES Bonneville,

1982 Bonneville Electro with (optional) American-made Morris mag wheels and Spanish-made Amal MkII carburetors. Other non-British components included the fuel tank, gauges, turn signals, mirrors, and handlebar controls. Factory photo. *Author collection*

Front half of Britech's brand-new 1982 Bonneville Electro. Model year markers are the black headlight bucket and fork sliders, as well as naked Lockheed calipers. Not many were exported to the United States during 1982-83. *Gaylin*

Brand new T140ES showing the manufacturer's origin and serial number plate just above the amber safety reflector on the steering head. Turn signals could have been ripped off a BMW and iron front disc was no longer chrome-plated. *Gaylin*

T140ES Executive, and leftover T140D Bonneville Specials.

1982 Models

In July 1981, the Triumph factory announced another limited edition Bonneville, the Royal (T140LE), commemorating the wedding of Prince Charles to Lady Diana Spencer. Continuing the Silver Jubilee theme, each Bonneville Royal purchaser was issued a prestigious certificate of ownership. But because many of the model's specially-finished components, such as fuel tanks, seats, wheels, and so on, could be mixed-matched, some confusion has arisen over how these models actually appeared in their respective markets.

In the home and general export markets, there were two variants of the Bonneville

Royal each with discernible levels of vulgarity. Standard trim for the T140LE was only slightly less ornate than the deluxe edition. Liberal use of black paint included the front fork lowers, headlight shell, support arms, and most notably the entire 750 powerplant. The engine components were painted before assembly, leaving most of the unpainted fasteners to stand out. Additional drama was created by polishing the outer edges of the finning on the cylinder, head, rocker boxes, and "points" cover.

The frame and centerstand on this version of the Royal were finished in silver-gray, with matching gray Marzocchi shock springs but inexplicably, the brake pedal was chrome-plated. A pair of Bing CV carburetors were fitted, and the black extended side covers were divided diagonally (descending to the front) by

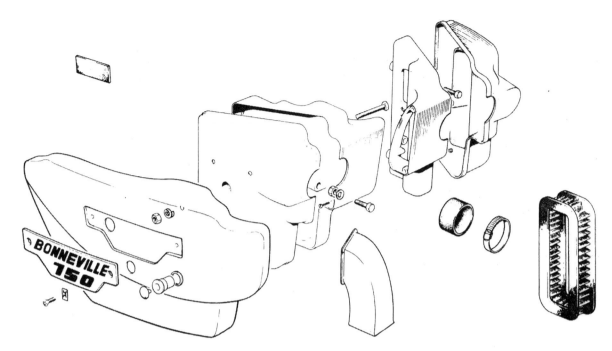

Later air cleaner and styling panel arrangement of the Bing-carbureted models.

a single gold line. There were special emblems in black, with the word "Royal" and a small crown insignia in chrome on the lower tier beneath "Bonneville." The limited edition transfer (#60-7364) from the Executive model was adopted and placed at the lower rear corner of each panel.

The T140LE was equipped with an all-new twinseat, in black vinyl, with a softer transition between levels and a wider quilted top surface. The trim at the lower edge changed back and forth during the year, from all-black to chrome. Standard Avon Roadrunners were used and black Morris mag wheels made the scenery change. These also came with Triumph's new-generation soft contour fuel tanks, but they were entirely plated in chrome. Short black scallops (lined in gold) of new dimensions were squeezed in above and below the plain cast Triumph emblem. A special "Royal Wedding" plastic badge covered the mounting cavity.

The second level of finish was even more ostentatious and was probably intended for the American market. However, there is no evidence suggesting that any Royals finished in this manner were ever exported to the States. The motor didn't have a trace of black

on it anywhere (the cylinders were also painted silver) and all outer covers including the rocker boxes were polished to high brilliance. Even the spark plug caps were chrome! There was lavish use of chrome everywhere, including the headlight bucket, support arms, instrument cups, turn signals stems (only), brake pedal, and kickstand. (Oddly the frame, centerstand, and shock springs remained black.) In addition, the U.S.-spec peanut-shaped fuel tank was completely chromed and fitted with the "small eyebrow" emblem. A single scallop for each side in smoked-blue (bordered in gold) began below the emblem and passed straight through it, sweeping rearward once above. The "Royal Wedding" emblem was again used to dress the mounting bolt well.

The shorter side panels in smoked-blue were given a single L-shaped gold pinstripe on the darkened front and lower edges. And the special edition plastic emblems were changed to blue and chrome (Royal and crown insignia) lettering on a silver background.

But the most appalling feature of this version of the Bonneville Royal (if one could be singled out) was the hideous disco-style

The reshaped timing cover of the electric-start Bonnevilles awakened memories of the pre-unit engines. Detachable back corner allowed access to starter mounting bolts. Side panel's protective valance extends over the Bing carburetor on this unrestored 1982 Executive. *Lindsay Brooke*

twinseat. A king-and-queen saddle from the Executive model was given a two-toned effect by changing the top seating sections to a light gray, while the flanks and a top partitioning strip remained in black. The seat looked its best when covered by operator and passenger — in winter gear!

Mercifully, the rim centers on the spoked wheels were left unpainted. Other details included polished fork lowers, single-disc front brake, and the earlier 8-inch "ape hanger" handlebars. The only things missing were fat megaphones and an even fatter 16-inch rear tire. As it happened, they were on the way!

Very few (less than 50) Bonneville Royals were sent to America. Apparently, Meriden had learned its lesson with the Jubilee. The T140LE models actually exported to the United States

Top view of the 1982 Britech Bonneville Electro. Italian-made Euro-tank still centrally mounted but now with locking Monza-type filler cap. The 33 miles recorded on the Veglia odometer ensures the machine's value as long as no more are added to it! *Gaylin*

Rear clip of a new 1982 Bonneville T140ES still with taillight and polished aluminum housing first seen ten years earlier. Squared-off grab rail was introduced on the Bonnie Special and inverted gas-filled shocks from the Jubilee. Printed trademark is still used on one of the final twinseat forms. *Gaylin*

were the most conservatively finished of all three versions and perhaps the most desirable. On these, only the top of the T140ES engine was finished in black. The crankcase was left unpainted and the outer covers polished in the traditional manner. Bing carburetors were mandated on all U.S.-bound machines, which meant extended side covers for protection. These panels were black and diagonally accented by a single gold line. The special Bonneville Royal emblem was in black, highlighted by chrome lettering. And the "Limited Edition" decal sometimes shared the panel with an "Electro" sticker at opposite lower corners.

The U.S. market Royal featured the new-generation Euro-tank, painted solid black (no scallops), and its flanking contours circumscribed with a dual gold pinstripe. No documentation of chrome-tanked U.S. T140LE models has surfaced. Aside from perhaps a special order or an introductory machine, the gas tanks assigned to these few U.S. models were black.

There was a choice of either laced wheels or Morris 7-spoke "mags." The latter option looked quite appropriate when paired with the new-generation tank, twin Lockheed front disc brakes, and the low Euro bars also specified for U.S. Royals. Combined with the new style dual seat in black, the overall impression was unpretentious and very classic.

The details of the Royal's remaining cycle parts were as found on the standard 1982 U.S.

Bonnevilles, including black-painted frame, centerstand, headlight bucket, turn signals, instrument cases, fork sliders, and shock absorber springs.

1982 Frame and Cycle Parts

Revisions to the remaining 1982 Triumphs models were directed only at the cycle parts. Engine specs stayed unchanged from the previous season. Both of the Meriden-made fuel tank designs were completely phased out early in the year and replaced by the new 4.0-gallon (Imperial) version. This meant a farewell to the old-style removable filler cap, and the "small eyebrow" tank emblem first seen in 1969. The simple cast Triumph trademark and Monza filler cap were rationalized for economy.

There were still four seat options for the range. The Executive was available with a king/ queen tandem seat or the T140E-style bench, while the Bonneville Electros could be ordered with anything on the shelf. Seat choices for the Royals have already been detailed. The extended styling panels fitted to the Bing-carbed bikes were secured by a single Allen screw on each side and the front crossover springs eliminated. The shorter side panels that accompanied the U.K and Euro-spec Amal MkII carburetor models went unchanged. Polished stainless steel fenders were fitted on all except the touring model, which were still painted, and the plastic-fendered Tiger Trail.

The suspension parts received a few tweaks in 1982. The right front fork slider was modified at the base to accept a second Lockheed alloy brake caliper when dual discs were required. This feature was first seen only on U.K examples, but by season's end it was on all new Triumphs. At the top of the forks, the rubber-sleeved headlight support arms became standard across all ranges, as did Marzocchi rear shocks and a 45-tooth rear sprocket.

An unrestored 1982 Bonneville Executive with king/queen seat, German turn signals and gaiterless front forks. Notice the circular insignias on the travel bags. This example belongs to Triumph speed legend Bob Leppan. *Lindsay Brooke*

Alternative version of the 1982 Bonneville Executive with glass work from the AV model. It is unclear if or how many of these were actually produced. Factory photo. *Author collection*

Bonneville Electros sent to America had handlebars with new bends and a lower 6 1/2-inch rise, while U.S. Royal and Executive models were standard with low Euro bars. In Britain, U.S.-style Bonnevilles were now identified as "Electro-USA" and unhappily wore the hand-me-down 8 1/2-inch "ape-hangers." But lower handlebars were specified for all other home market 750 twins except the Tiger Trail, which used specially braced motocross-type handles. U.K models were also the first to received the alloy Magura "dog-leg" control levers.

Color choices in the United States continued from 1982, albeit with different style tanks. The T140ES Electros were offered in smoked-blue or Misty-red (the new name for smoked-Flame). The tanks were not scalloped but trimmed in a single gold pinstripe around the outer contours on each side. The Executive model carried over its smoked Candy-Apple-red scheme. The Bonneville Royal conveyed the only variety with an all-black finish and twin gold coach lining.

The U.K. color options also remained relatively fixed. There were smoked-blue (silver scalloped) and smoked-Flame (off-white scalloped) versions of the U.S.-style Bonnevilles, as well as the European-style T140ES models (without scallops). All came with matching side covers and for the Euro editions, a single

The 1982 TR65 Thunderbird shared the T140ES cycle parts. It was also available with American-style tank and handlebars although none were exported to the United States. Note the two-into-one exhaust, Dunlop K70 tires and the T140E seat. Factory photo. *Author collection*

gold line tank accent. Black made a third choice for the "Electro-Euro" models as they were now cataloged. In addition, two more choices lingered from 1981 on the peanut-tanked Electro-USA models. The most popular tank was black with red wings, while pale-blue with black wings was the rarer condition. These were scalloped above and below the small Triumph emblem, in the form of the T140D. The side panels were in black.

Triumph's 1982 American range consisted of only three models: T140ES Bonneville Electro, T140LE Bonneville Royal, and T140EX Executive. In all cases the engine prefix was stamped as T140ES. By now all U.S. models came with a factory spec plate riveted vertically to the left-hand steering head. These were also impressed with the machine's serial number. On the Bonneville Royals, the plates also carried a

limited edition number and the inscription "In celebration of the wedding of Prince Charles and Lady Diana Spencer."

In the United Kingdom and other European markets, nine different 750 twins were available when adding a kickstart version to the mix. Engine prefix codes were either T140E, T140ES, or TR7T.

1983 Models

Triumph's lack of capital and dwindling credit were strangling production, and batch runs were much smaller. Regarding machine details for that year and faithful adherence to catalog specifications, factory service veteran John Nelson explained that as the end drew near, the practice of mix-matching components to get a machine out the door for cash was widespread — "It was anything goes!"

Meriden took its last few shillings to produce two new models for 1983, in the hope of finding a winner — and an investor! The first Bonneville variant was a legitimate project and perhaps with more time, and money, things might have turned out differently. The TSS model featured a factory derivative of the Weslake eight-valve kit, available to Triumph owners on the aftermarket since the late 1960s.

The TSS (T140W) used a standard electric-start T140 crankcase and gearbox, but its crankshaft was anything but standard. The one-piece forging was completely reworked. The big-end journals were increased in diameter but narrowed, allowing beefier lateral webbing. Careful machining of the outboard cheeks created a lighter and much stiffer shaft that reportedly permitted reliable crank speeds in excess of 10,000 rpm. The existing roller bearing on each side remained adequate and thus produced no change in the crankcase (set) part numbers.

There was an all-new connecting rod shape with redesigned big ends and caps. The small ends were also changed but for a different purpose: The bores of the new cylinder block were spaced 1/2 inch farther apart, and to spread the pistons the con-rods' small ends were offset by 3-millimeters.

The TSS's barrels were squarish in form, cast in aluminum with pressed in steel liners. The barrels' closer-pitched finning permitted more cooling plates to be attached. For continuity, the contour and fin spacing of the new alloy head matched the cylinder below. The ten-stud T140 head arrangement was maintained, but the forward and rear through-bolts (four in all) reached clear down to the crankcase. Separate Cooper sealing rings replaced the head gasket and were seated in the head's squish bands around the steel liner.

The rocker boxes were cast integrally with the cylinder head, and a single detachable finned cover (over each side) was held down by eight Allen-head cap screws. The pushrods and tubes were only slightly modified from T140 use, but each rocker grew another arm to depress a pair

of valves over each port. New camshafts were also specified for the TSS that had a softer inlet profile but a more aggressive exhaust form.

Smaller, symmetrically placed valves ran in bronze guides at a steeper 30-degrees, and Y-shaped inlet tracts serviced shallow combustion chambers. Flat-topped pistons with relief cuts for four valves were fitted as were centrally placed 12-millimeter spark plugs. With a 10:1 compression ratio, the eight-valve Triumph made more power and better use of its fuel, especially with the 34-millimeter Amal MkIIs fitted to U.K. and Euro versions. American TSS owners had to be satisfied with the wimpier Bing CV carburetors. A hint of mystery was supplied by the engine's all-black finish-only the outer covers were polished.

The TSS Bonneville's cycle parts were the same as those on the 1982 T140ES models. Laced steel wheels or Morris mags could be ordered, but all the eight-valve models came with dual front disc brakes. On the back wheel there was a 43-tooth drive sprocket and Brembo twin-piston disc brakes were interchanged with the Lockheed component.

Only Euro-style fuel tanks were installed on the TSS and these were finished in two ways. The first and most commonly seen option was black with Candy-red scallops above and below the Triumph badge. These tank accents were in the manner of the U.K. Royal models with the large wing on the bottom and a thinner one squeezed in between the emblem and upper contour line. These were bordered with a single gold pinstripe. The second finish was solid black with twin gold lining applied around the perimeter of the sides - the same scheme used on the 1982 U.S. Bonneville Royals.

The machine's side covers were finished in mat and gloss black, the sections divided diagonally by a single gold line. The covers carried a special plastic TSS badge with extended letter-tops on the ends. The emblems were at first screwed in place in the normal manner, while later examples had self-adhesive backs. Final TSS versions (perhaps intended for 1984) were shown with stylish angled side covers to permit a shorter leg path to the ground. A gold pinstripe defined the change in direction and a block-letter emblem was applied on the upper taper. These were also accompanied by a new seat design with an integral tailpiece and grab rail. How many in this trim were produced, if at all, is unclear.

Whereas the TSS model saw all of its development around the engine and little change in the running gear, the T140 TSX Custom was a product only of new cycle parts. This factory custom was powered by the same basic T140ES motor, with no departure in specification other than the exhaust system. Separate, unlinked 1 3/4-inch pipes exited the splayed head and took familiar turns to feed a pair of shortened chrome megaphones, with substantial innards to pass U.S. noise restrictions.

For additional support, the exhaust pipes were anchored to the front of the engine with flat chrome stays that screwed to welded tabs midway down the front bends. The mufflers were inconspicuously linked by a crossover tube passing under the frame and drive chain. Other items of interest were the engine's black finish, polished outer covers, and the twin 32-millimeter Bing constant velocity carburetors that went unprotected by the shortened side panels.

Black American-made Morris mags were standard on the TSX. They were skinned with

British Only's unrestored 1983 TSS Bonneville. All came with dual front discs, tailored exhaust system, and black-painted eight-valve engine. American versions were standard with low handlebars, Bing carburetors, and Euro-fuel tank with narrow scallops. Morris mag wheels were optional. Triumph's best? Because of early teething problems many would argue the opposite — but with more time and money, who knows? *Lindsay Brooke*

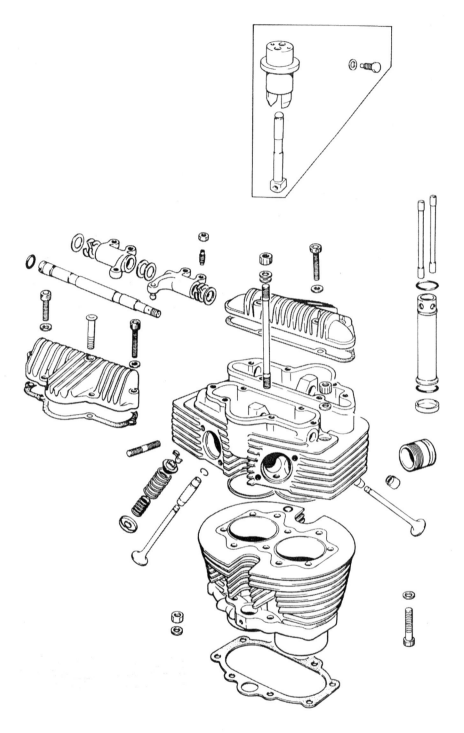

Exploded view of TSS top end.

Avon Roadrunners with raised white sidewall lettering. The front 3.25x19-inch tire was narrower than usual, but the rear Avon was an obese 5.10x16-incher! To accommodate this, the rear swinging arm was widened and the chain guard butchered on the inside

valance. The latter was also chrome-plated.

Chunkier Paioli rear shocks with chrome springs added to the cruiser look. A single disc brake was screwed to each mag wheel, the rear caliper a Brembo twin-piston item. The sprocket was increased to 47 teeth and the change in the

The TSS model was developed from the Weslake eight-valve kit, a longtime performance add-on. Crankcase was a standard T140ES item but the crankshaft was all-new. Engine covers were spared the black finish. Other details seen here include the straight-through shifter rubber, unpainted number pad, and riveted spec plate above the reflector. Nylon wraps were now used to secure cables, instead of the aluminum straps. *Lindsay Brooke*

rear wheel diameter also necessitated a new speedometer drive with a revised ratio.

The TSX's forks were ungaitered and the lower members polished. To complete the "West Coast" look, the fork's upper covers and headlight were chrome-plated. The 1970s-type Lucas turn signals were resurrected and mounted (at the front) behind the upper fork shrouds. Another item from the past was the bent-wire headlight mounting bracket; however, unlike the 1971–72 setup, the new version was one-piece and fastened to the faces of both fork lugs.

A factory photo showing the left side details of a Gypsy-red Triumph TSX. Uncoupled 1-3/4-inch exhaust pipes fed thoroughly baffled megaphones. Side panels angled at the top allowed a shorter leg path to the ground but left the Bing carburetors exposed. Low-rider seat was only a deception and rainbow graphics were not for everyone. *Author collection*

TSX riders sat on (or in) a huge new twinseat designed especially for the model. Covered in black vinyl, the stepped saddle projected a lower than normal seat height—the illusion created by the nose riding up on the back of the fuel tank. The tail section was squared-off, and a new chrome grab rail/fender support was created to follow its shape. The top panel was cross-ribbed and the trim on the lower edge was in black.

Other TSX features included newly shaped, shorter fenders, front and rear. There were 8-inch high-rise handlebars with Magura "dog leg" clutch and brake levers. And Italian-made 2 1/2-gallon peanut-shaped fuel tanks were standard with removable (lockable) filler caps and a single petcock.

The most outrageous feature of the TSX was its gas tank graphics. A painfully brilliant rainbow decal in red, orange, and yellow began at the lower edge beneath the small emblem. It then swept up and back without interruption to the nose of the seat. Against this sunburst effect, the hand-lined gold pinstriping (doubled on the forward edge) used to completely surround the decal was hardly noticeable.

The motorcycle's bikini side panels were reshaped and tapered in at the top, but the lower section was given a matching three-color transfer and bordered in sweeping gold lines.

An Avon Speed master tire was used on the front of the 1983 TSX and a fat 16-inch Roadrunner on the rear — both with raised white letters. To allow this the swinging fork had to be widened and new Brembo master cylinder repositioned. Brake line now traveled above the caliper. Note the chubby Paioli suspension unit. Factory photo. *Author collection*

The cover's top curve carried a special TSX cast emblem in block letter outlines.

Four base colors were intended for the model: Burgundy (Gypsy-red in the United States), Midnight-black, Midnight-blue, and finally, solid black with only the outline of the rainbow in gold pinstriping. In each case the side panels were accented to match. In addition, the fenders were painted to correspond and lined in gold at the outer edges.

1983, Remaining Range

Although sales literature from the final year of Coventry manufacture promised much in the way of new model features, not all of it was actually delivered. There were minimal modifications to the 1983 drivetrain. A sturdier intermediate gear was fitted to the electric start models, and at engine number DEA33133, the gearbox main shaft thread were changed to 9/16, requiring a new lock washer and self-locking nut. On the Tiger Trail, a more squarish muffler can was fitted that tucked into the rear upright and given a long perforated heatshield.

That was it! Any resources Meriden had for engineering improvements were now going to buy components to get a few more bikes out the door. This generally applied to the cycle parts as well. Their specifications were as in 1982, although the peanut-shaped tanks reappeared, made by Triumph's Italian supplier. These kept the same shape but had a hinged alloy filler cap and single fuel tap with a crossover pipe from the far side. On the TSX tanks, the filler cap was removable but had a lower profile than standard. Seating options were per 1982, including leftover 1979 T140E saddles. The only new chair listed was the low-slung TSX item.

The only new T140 color scheme announced for 1983 was a solid burgundy, trimmed in parallel gold lines, but it is unknown how many of these were actually produced. Most standard model Bonneville tanks for that year were finished in black with Candy-red wings. On the U.S.-spec peanut tanks, the scallops took the form of the T140D accents, while the Eurotanks were painted in the manner of the TSS and Royal models. Solid black was also listed for the Bonnevilles, pinstriped in double gold lines around the tank contours.

All T140 side panels were black except on the TSX and Executive models. Other than this, it is likely that some 1983 Triumphs were sent out in colors from the previous year, as many stocks still remained. The smaller cast tank badges were generally chrome-plated, with only the background setting finished in black. On the Executives and black tank bikes (those trimmed in gold), the logo was also inlaid with gold. This was switched for black on some TSX models.

The 1983 U.S. range for the final year consisted of only four models: T140-TSX, T140W-TSS, T140ES Bonneville, and T140EX Executive. They were all electric-start models and despite their designations, all carried T140ES engine prefix codes. In the United Kingdom there were still kickstart versions of all available, and with the TR7 Tiger Trail and Police T140ES AV variants, the Triumph range numbered ten. But only three engine prefixes were needed — T140E, T140ES, and TR7.

The last (production) motorcycle to be assembled at the Meriden factory was on January 21, 1983 and contained engine number AEA32213. However, there were a batch of machines built for the home market prior to January 21 that carried higher serial numbers of which the last was AEA34389. In addition, there is documentation of at least one motorcycle being built on June 27, 1983 with serial number 034392. Triumph Motorcycles (Meriden), Ltd., went into voluntary liquidation on August 26, 1983. The end was not unexpected and many people snapped up examples from the final production year only for their investment value. As a result, the survival rate among 1983 Triumphs is very high and potential restorers of the 750cc twins should consider this before beginning their project.

The company was broken up under the auctioneer's hammer in December 1983, with much of the tooling, remaining parts stocks, and a five-year license to continue Bonneville manufacture secured by L. F. Harris (Rushden), Ltd., of Newton Abbot, England. But difficulties in finding component suppliers delayed production for more than a year. When manufacture did begin, Harris was unable to export any motorcycles to the United States, due to the exorbitant cost of product liability insurance. Of the 1,200 or so of the hand-built Harris Bonnevilles actually assembled, none officially landed in America.

Appendix A

Specifications and Technical Data

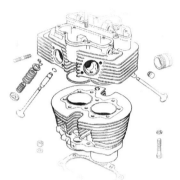

Engine and Frame Numbers

By the time the TR6's arrived in 1956, engine and frame serial numbers were corresponding and would remain so until the end of production in 1983. Any surviving Bonneville or Trophy 650 models with conflicting numbers did not get them at Meriden and acquisitions of motorcycles in this condition should be considered carefully. Unfortunately, altered identification numbers that have been falsified to complement a motor or frame aren't uncommon and are harder to discover.

Meriden engine builders would assemble a motor to a certain model specification prior to frame assignment. When the engine build was completed, the model's prefix code (e.g., T120) would be stamped into the engine case without any other numbers. To speed production, the prefix was a single stamp. The characters were usually very even and not impressed as deeply as the individual numbers that followed.

Many times, application of the variant suffix (e.g., C or R) would also be delayed until the engine was paired with its running gear. This often resulted in a suffix letter of different size and style to the prefix (e.g., T120 c). The individual numbers that followed the prefix code were usually uneven, often a different size, and stamped deeper into the crankcase. So perfect looking numbers are good ones to suspect! As a rule these guidelines can also be applied to the frame number.

Restorers and buyers should always use the engine number to determine the model year (and machine features), not the ownership certificate. In the United States, the practice of registering a machine in the year it was sold was widespread until the federal government cracked down on it in 1970. Until then, leftover models (in many cases more than a year old) were often titled as current ones. Add to this the problem of typographical errors made by indifferent bureaucrats and using a log book or certificate of title as the sole verification for the date of manufacture becomes a bad idea.

Bonneville/TR6 Engine and Frame Numbers

Model Year	Beginning Eng. Nos.	Ending Eng. Nos.
1955	56700	70929
1956	70930	82797
(then)	0101	0944
1957	0945	011165
1958	011166	020075
1959	020076	029633
1960	029634	030424
(Duplex)	D10l	D7726
1961	D7727	D15788
1962	D15789	D20308
1963	DU101	DU5824
1964	DU5825	DU13374
1965	DU13375	DU24874
1966	DU24875	DU44393
1967	DU44394	DU66245
1968	DU66246	DU85903
1969	DU85904	DU90282
(then)	NC00100	HC24346
1970	JD24848	ND60540
1971	NE01436	FUE30869
1972	HG30870	JGXXXXX
1973	JH15101	GH36466
1974	GJ55101	NJ60061
1975	DK61000	GK62248
1976	HN62501	GN72283
1977	GP73000	JP84931
1978	HX00100	HX10747
1979	HA11001	KA24999
(then)	XB24609*	XB24790*
1980	PB25001	KB27500
1981	KDA28001	DDA29427
1982	EDA3000I	BDA3 1693
1983	BEA33001	AEA34389

Engines were pre-assembled away from the final assembly line and were imprinted only with their particular prefix which was a single stamp. After being mated with a frame the motor was then struck with a serial number. Valid numbers usually have perfectly straight prefixes that are not pushed in as deep as the digits that follow, which are often uneven. The untidiness of these 1967 numbers gives NO reason for suspicion. *Gaylin*

* 182 1979 models marked in error with B letter code

Engine Number Prefixes

In 1969, Triumph added a two-letter prefix to the actual engine number in order to indicate the month and model year (not actual year) of manufacture. In 1981, when the coding system would have repeated, a third letter (A) was added to distinguish the number from earlier years.

First letter indicates MONTH of manufacture:		Second letter indicates the MODEL YEAR of manufacture:	
A	January	C	1969
B	February	D	1970
C	March	E	1971
D	April	G	1972
E	May	H	1973
G	June	J	1974
H	July	K	1975
J	August	N	1976
K	September	P	1977
N	October	X	1978
P	November	A	1979
X	December	B	1980
--	--	DA	1981
--	--	DA	1982
--	--	EA	1983

Example	Model	Month	Year	Number
	TR7RV	P	P	78083

The example number above depicts a 1977 Tiger 750 that was actually manufactured in November 1976.

Engine Number Modification List 1966–1969

1965 B-Range — commencing engine number DU13375

DU22682	Alloy exhaust adaptors
DU22590	Wide chain tensioner blade

1966 B-Range — commencing engine number DU24875

DU25497	Longer kickstart crank
DU26143	Solid layshaft, undrilled speedometer drive gear location
DU26I43	New cylinder base and tappet block gasket
DU27007 approx.	Improved rectifier mounting bracket
DU27375	Oil metering dowel shortened to 1 3/8 inch

1966 B-Range — commencing engine number DU24875 (continued)

DU27672 approx.	Increased steering lock (#H1999 middle lug fitted to T120R, T120TT, TR6C)
DU27893	Oil bleed hole (behind clutch) closed
DU28068	C-range inlet tappet block adopted
DU28248	Oil hole deleted from E3606 con-rod
DU28491	Thicker washers under contact breaker pillar nuts
DU28904	New flywheel casting
DU29248 approx.	Copper washer (#E2441) fitted at tappet block
DU29306	Timing cover modification to allow screen filter
DU29738 approx.	1 3/16-inch carburetors replaces 1 1/8-inch (T120R)
	New cylinder head with 1 3/16 inlet ports (T120R)
DU30179	Exhaust valve material changed to 214NS
DU30600	Ground terminal relocated rear of heat sink.
DU30800 approx.	Brighter aluminum Zener diode heat sink #F7237
DU31119 approx.	Fork damper sleeve changed from aluminum to high-density plastic
DU31119 approx.	3134-form racing cam introduced (T120R, T120TT)
DU31168 approx.	Larger clutch pressure plate adjuster screw allows extraction of clutch rod without disturbing cover
DU31565 approx.	High-beam warning light fitted
DU32898	Right-angled heat sink for diode
DU32994	Lucas PUZ5A battery becomes standard
DU34086	New battery carrier (#6891)
DU34086	#4 throttle slides (T120R, T120TT)
DU39464	Return to steel exhaust adaptors (T120R, T120TT)
DU41005	Return to steel exhaust adaptors (TR6)
DU42399	Cylinder barrel to crankcase oil feed dowel

1967 B-Range — commencing engine number DU44394

DU44394	Hepolite pistons fitted as OEM N3 Champion spark plugs replace N4
DU47006	Stronger connecting rods (#E3606T) fitted
DU49539	Encapsulated stator on AC ignition models
DU51771	160-degree contact breaker cam
DU52096	O-ring groove machined into fork slider nut
DU52578	240 main jets fitted (T120)
DU53772	Scavenge feed to rockers taken from oil tank base
DU54659	Blanking disc over parking lock screw
DU55278	240 main jets fitted (T120R)
DU58565	Encapsulated coil ignition stator (TR6R)
DU59320	Amal Concentric carburetors replace Monoblocs

1967 B-Range — commencing engine number DU44394 (continued)

DU59320	High tensile studs, self-lock nuts at carburetor
DU59320	Mazda bulbs fitted (T120R)
DU59320	Flexible handlebar mounts
DU63043	Timed tappet lubrication; trembler eliminated
DU63241	O-rings fitted at tappet block to cylinder joint. Inlet block changed approximately 300 machines prior
DU63344- DU63443	Plus 0.002-inch Hepolite pistons fitted to standard bore
DU64758- DU64858	Mainshaft second gear alternate dogging deleted
DU64772	Hydroseal at gearbox sprocket
DU65100	Adjustable gas taps with Dowty and thin steel washer

1968 B-Range — commencing engine number DU66246

DU66246	UNF threads on front forks (all but T120R)
DU68363	UNF threads on front forks (T120R)
DU68368	Heavier rear swingarm fork bracket
DU70083	Split pin in front brake cable abutment
DU70164	Girling AHV and AIV (exposed spring) forks fitted
DU70164	Iron front fork bushings changed to sintered bronze
DU74052	Ignition timing slot moved to 38 degrees BTDC
DU74058	Production models stroboscopically timed
	Holes and grooves eliminated from oil pump
DU75430- DU75449	Heavy-gauge tube used on front frame section 12-point nuts at cylinder base
DU75452	Oil pump holes and grooves eliminated (final cond.)
	Exhaust camshaft taper modified for Lucas NR unit
DU75452	Front tires changed to Dunlop K70s (eastern U.S.)
	Redesigned muffler baffles
DU75452 approx.	Rear grab rail fitted to twinseat (western U.S.)
DU76690	Modified seat pans with 112-inch clearance
DU76900 approx.	1 1/16-inch hole added to swingarm oil seal cover
DU77018 approx.	Rear grab rail fitted to twinseat (eastern U.S.)
DU77670	Front tank mounts changed to studs and self-lock nuts
	O-ring impregnated washer fitted above gas taps
DU78400	Rocker ball pin turned 180 degrees to cut off oil supply
DU78900	Steel gauze at oil tank and crankcase filter
DU79965	Undrilled rocker arm and ball pin (final condition)
DU79975	Piston modification — under crown bar eliminated and thicker ring grooves

1968 B-Range — commencing engine number DU66246 (continued)

DU81196	Thicker section tubing for swinging fork
DU81709	Front fender lengthened (not stainless guards)
	Throttle cable lengthened 3 inches (TR6R, TR6C)
DU82000	Carburetor changed from 930/23 to 930/B/23 (TR6R)
DU82146	Felt lube wicks added to 6CA points assembly
DU82574	H-pipe exhaust coupling added to TR6C models
DU82920	Battery overflow tube cemented in place
DU83021	Timing pointer fixed in crankcase
DU84433	Ultrasonic cleaning of crankcase parts (not polished items)

1969 B-Range — commencing engine number DU85904

DU85904	Increased capacity oil pump. New pistons with domed crowns.
	Hexagonal cam plate plunger nut
DU86965	Tamper-resistant (raised) engine number pad with impressed Triumph motifs
DU87105	Nitride-hardened camshafts
DU88383	Balance clutch housing. Cast pockets eliminated
DU88625	New pattern control levers. Tank styling strip secured with threaded J-hook
DU88630	Modified gearbox cam plate
DU88714	Shortened oil scavenge pipe
DU89530	Reinforced bracket for wind-tone horns. (T120R, T120UK)
DU90282	Last machine with DU series engine number
NC02256	Heavy flywheels fitted; balance factor unchanged
NC02600	Modification to U.S. handlebar mounts
AC10464	Internal fork stanchion modification
CC14783	Louder wind-tone horns (T120 United Kingdom)
CC15546	Gearbox shafts manufactured to full drawing size
HC23445	Con-rod nuts torqued to 22 pounds per foot
JD24961	Modification to rocker box Thackery washers
JD24996	Modified tachometer drive at camshaft
JD25768	New sealing material at top of pushrod tube
JD25965	Revised timing marks on cam wheels
JD26313	Modified gear change quadrant
JD26355	Polished ends on clutch pushrod
KD27287	Loctite plastic jointing compound used on engine

Carburetors —
Bonneville, TR6, and TR7

Year	T120/T140: Right	T120/T140: Left	TR6/TR7
1956	n/a	n/a	376/40
1957	n/a	n/a	376/40
1958	n/a	n/a	376/40
1959	376/204 (bowl-14/363)	376/204	376/40
1960	376/233 (bowl-14/624)	376/233	376/40
1961	376/257 (@ D11193)	376/257 (@D11193)	376/40
1962	376/257	376/257	376/40
1963	376/257	376/257	376/40
1964	389/203	389/203	389/97
1965	389/203	389/203	389/97
1966 (U.K)	389/203	389/203	389/97
1966 (U.S.)	389/95 (@DU29738)	389/95 (@DU29738)	389/97
1967 (U.K)	389/203	389/203	389/239
1967 (U.S.)	389/95	389/95	389/239
1967 (later)	930/9 (@DU59320)	930/10 (@DU59320)	930/23 (@DU50320)
1968	930/9	930/10	930/23
1969	930/9	930/10	930/23
1970	930/9	930/10	930/23
1971	R930/66	L930/67	930/60
1972	R930/66	L930/67	930/60
1973	R930/87 (T140)	L930/88 (T120)	930/89 (TR7)
1974	R930/92	L930/93	930/89
1975	R930/92	L930/93	930/89
1976	R930/92	L930/93	930/89
1977	R930/92	L930/93	R930/94
1978	R930/92	L930/93	R930/94
1978 (later)	R2930/1 (T140E)	L2930/2 (T140E)	R930/94
1979	R2930/1	L2930/2	R930/94
1980	R2930/1	L2930/2	R930/94
1981	R930/8	L930/9	R930/108 (TR7T)
1982	R930/8	L930/9	R930/108 (TR7T)
1982 (U.S.)	60-7419 (Bing)	60-7418 (Bing)	n/a
1983	R2934/7	L2934/8	R930/108 (TR7T)
1983 (U.S.)	60-7419	60-7418 (all T140s)	n/a
1983 (later)	60-7726	60-7725 (TSX)	n/a
1985–88	R930/111	RT930/112	n/a

Carburetors —
TT Specials/Trophy Specials

Year	T120TT: Right	T120TT: Left	Trophy Specials
1963	389/203	389/203	376/40
1964	389/95	389/95	389/97
1965	389/95	389/95	389/97
1966	389/95	389/95	389/97
1967	389/95	389/95	389/239

Magnetos and Alternators

Magnetos

Year	T120/T140	TR6/TR7	Options/Others
1956	n/a	42298 (K2FC)	42324A (K2FR)
1957	n/a	42298	42324A
1958	n/a	42298	42324
1959	42298	42298	42344 (K2F Auto)
	n/a	n/a	42350 (K2FC Man.)
	n/a	n/a	42368 (K2FC Auto.)
	n/a	n/a	43234
1960	42344 (47134 Stator)	42298 (47134 Stator)	n/a
1961	42344 (47178 Stator)	42298 (47134 Stator)	n/a
1962	42344 (47183 Stator)	42298 (47183 Stator)	47162 (U.K.)

Alternators

Year	T120/T140	TR6/TR7	Options/Others
1963	47164 (Stator)	47164 (Stator)	n/a
1964	47162	47162	47164 (U.K.)
	n/a	n/a	47188 (TT, TR6SC)
1965	47162	47162	47188 (TT, TR6SC)
1966	47162	47162	47188 (TT, TR6C)
1967	47162	47162	47188 (TT, TR6C)
1968	47204 (Encapsulated)	47204 (Encapsulated)	47205 (U.K.)
1969	47204	47204	47205 (U.K.)
1970	47204	47204	47205 (U.K.)
1971	47205	47205	n/a
1972	47205	47205	n/a
1973	47205	47205	n/a
1974	47205	47205	n/a
1975	47205	47205	n/a

Alternators (continued)

1976	47205	47205	n/a
1977	47205	47205	n/a
1978	47205	47205	n/a
1979	47252	47252	n/a
1980	47252	47252	n/a
1981	47244	47244	n/a
1982	47244	47244	n/a
1983	47244	47244	n/a

Alternator Supersessions

Superseding No.	Original No.
47171	47134, 47178
47181	47164
47197	47173, 47188
47204	47162, 47205

Wiring Harnesses — Bonneville, TR6, and TR7

Year	Part Number	Model
1956	831200	TR6
1957	831200	TR6
1958	831200	TR6
1959	836381	T120
	831200	TR6
1960	54944995	Both
1961	54944995	Both
1962	54930000	Both
1963	54933182	Both
1964	54933182	Not TT, TR6SC
1965	54936415	Not TT, TR6SC
1966	54938941	Not TT, TR6SC
1967	54950449	Not TT, TR6C
1968	54953443	Not TR6C
1969	54955257	Not TR6C
1970	54957095	Not TR6C
1971	54959629	Both
1972	54959629	Both
1973	54961593	Both
1974	54961593	Both

Wiring Harnesses — Bonneville, TR6, and TR7 (continued)

Year	Part Number	Model
1975	54961593	Both
1976	54961593	Both
1977	54962258A	Both
1978	54962258A	Both
1979	54965505	All
1980	54965505	All
1981	54965505	All
1982	60-7465	All
	60-7458	TR7T
1983	60-7465	All
	60-7458	TR7T

Wiring Harnesses — TT Specials/Trophy TR6C

Year	Part Number	Model
1963	54933229	Both
1964	54934830	Both
1965	54937097	Both
1966	54937097	Both
1967	54937097	Both
1968	54953440	TR6C
1969	54955719	TR6C
1970	54957096	TR6C

Lighting — Bonneville, TR6, and TR7

Year	Bonneville Headlights	TR6/TR7 Headlights	Taillights
1956	n/a	51892A	53432A (Type 564)
1957	n/a	51892A	53432A
1958	n/a	51892A	53432A
1959	51860A (Nacelle)	51892A	53432B
1960	58556	58556	53432
1961	58556	58556	53432
1962	58934	58934	53432
1963	58934	58934	53432
1964	58934	58934	53432
1965	58934	58934	53972 (Type 679)
			53432 (Euro)

Year	Bonneville Headlights	TR6/TR7 Headlights	Taillights
1966	59579	59579	53973
	n/a	58395 (TR6SC)	53454 (Euro)
1967	59734	59734	53973
	n/a	59699 (TR6C)	53454
1968	59883	59883	53973
	n/a	59882 (TR6C)	53454
1969	59883	59883	53973
	n/a	60037 (TR6C)	53454
1970	59969	59969	53973
	n/a	59965 (TR6C)	53454
1971	60260	60260	53973
	n/a	60262 (TR6C)	n/a
1972	60260	60260	53973
	n/a	60262 (TR6C)	n/a
1973	60512	60512	56513 (Type 917)
1974	60512	60512	56513
1975	60512	60512	56513
1976	60512	60512	56513
1977	60512	60512	56513
	60513 (Euro)	60513 (Euro)	56515 (Euro)
1978	60513	60513	56513
	n/a	n/a	56515
1979	61387	61387	56513
	61386 (Euro)	61386 (Euro)	56513
1980	61387	61387	56513
	61386	61386	56515
1981	61387	61387	56513
	61386	61386	56515
1982	60-7461	60-7453 (TR7T)	56513
	60-7460 (Euro)	n/a	56515
1983	60-7461	60-7453 (TR7T)	56513
	60-7460	n/a	56515
	60-7461 (TSS)	n/a	n/a
	60-7331 (TSX)	n/a	n/a

Rear Suspension Units — Bonneville, TR6, and TR7

Year	Bonneville	TR6/TR7	Options
1956	n/a	S/MDA4/104	n/a
1957	n/a	SB4/259	SB4/275 (sidecar)
1958	n/a	SB4/259	SB4/275
1959	SB4/259	SB4/259	SA193/57
1960	64054164	64054164	SB4/275
1961	64054164	64054164	SB4/275
1962	64054164	64054164	SB4/275
1963	64054164	64054164	n/a
1963 (U.K.)	64054506	n/a	SB4/275
1964	64054164	64054164	n/a
1964 (U.K.)	64054506	n/a	SB4/275
1965	64054164	64054164	n/a
1965 (U.K.)	64054506	64054506	SB4/275
1966	64054164	64054164	n/a
1966 (U.K.)	64054506	64054506	SB4/275
1967	64054164	64054164	n/a
1967 (U.K)	64054506	64054506	SB4/275
1968	64054164	64054164	n/a
1968 (later)	64052017	65052017	n/a
1968 (U.K.)	65054506	64054506	SB4/275
1969	64052017	65052017	n/a
1969 (U.K.)	64052106	64052106	n/a
1970	64052107	64052107	n/a
1970 (U.K.)	64052106	64052106	n/a
1971	64052341	64053241	n/a
1972	64052341	64053241	n/a
1972 (later)	64052564	64052564	n/a
1973	64052564	64052564	n/a
1974	64052564	64052564	n/a
1975	64052564	64052564	n/a
1976	64052564	64052564	n/a
1977	64052564	64052564	70056007 (T140J)
1978	70056007	70056007	n/a
1978 (U.K.)	64052564	64052564	70056007 (T140J)
1979	70056007	70056007	n/a
1980	70056007	70056007	n/a
1981	70056007	70056007	n/a

Rear Suspension Units — Bonneville, TR6, and TR7 (continued)

Year	Bonneville	TR6/TR7	Options
1982	60-7549 Marzocchi	60-7449 (TR7T)	60-7540 Marz. (Royal)
	n/a	n/a	60-7540 (Executive)
1982 (U.K.)			
	˙60-7037	n/a	n/a
1983	60-7549	60-7449 (TR7T)	60-7540 (TSS, Exec.)
	n/a	n/a	60-7644 Pailoi (TSX)

Speedometer — Bonneville, TR6, and TR7

Year	Bonneville	TR6/TR7	Options
1956	n/a	S433/3 (120 mph)	S433/7/L (180 kph)
1957	n/a	S433/3	S433/7/L
1958	n/a	S433/3	S433/7/L
1959	S467/107/L	S433/3	S433/7/L-TR6
	n/a	n/a	SC3304/07 (240 kph) T120
	n/a	n/a	S467/47/L (180 kph) T120
	n/a	n/a	S467/91/L (120 kph) T120
1960	SC5301/09 (125 mph)	SC5301/09	SC5301/18 (240 kph) T120
	n/a	n/a	SC5301/16 (190 kph) TR6
1961	SC5301/26 (140 mph)	SC5301/09	Options as per 1960
1962	SC5301/26	SC5301/09	Options as per 1960
1963	SC5301/23	SC5301/03	SC5301/28 (kph) T120
	n/a	n/a	SC5301/12 (kph) TR6
1964	SSM5001/00	SSM5001/00	SSM5001/01 (kph) T120, TR6
1965	SSM5001/00	SSM5001/00	SSM5001/01
1966	SSM5001/00	SSM5001/00	SSM5001/01
	n/a	n/a	CD430 (VDO) TR6C U.S.
1967	SSM5001/06	SSM5001/06	Options as per 1966
1968	SSM5001/06	SSM5001/06	Options as per 1966
1969	SSM5001/06	SSM5001/06	SSM5001/01
1970	SSM5001/06	SSM5001/06	SSM5001/12
1970 (later)	SSM5007/00	SSM5007/00	SSM5007/02 (120 mph) U.K.
1971	SSM5007/00	SSM5007/00	SSM5007/02
	n/a	n/a	SSM5007/01 (kph)
1972	SSM5007/00	SSM5007/00	SSM5007/02
	n/a	n/a	SSM5007/01

Speedometer — Bonneville, TR6, and TR7 (continued)

Year	Bonneville	TR6/TR7	Options
1973	SSM5007/00	SSM5007/00	SSM5007/01
1974	SSM5007/00	SSM5007/00	SSM5007/01
1975	SSM5007/00	SSM5007/00	SSM5007/01
1976	SSM5007/00	SSM5007/00	SSM5007/01
1977	SSM4003/00	SSM4003/00	SSM4003/01 9 (kph)
1978	SSM4003/00	SSM4003/00	SSM4003/01
1979	SSM4003/02	SSM4003/02	SSM4003/01
1979 (later)	9190929901 (Veglia)	9190929901 (Veglia)	99-7100 (Veglia kph)

Vendor Identification Numbers No Longer Used

Year	Bonneville	TR6/TR7	Options
1980	60-7222 (Veglia)	60-7222 (Veglia)	60-7272 (85 mph) U.K.
	n/a	n/a	60-7270 (kph)
1981	60-7222	60-7222	Options as per 1980
1982	60-7222	60-7222	Options as per 1980
1983	60-7222	60-7222	Options as per 1980
TSS	60-7222	n/a	n/a
TSX	60-7222	n/a	n/a

Tachometers — Bonnevilles, TR6, and TR7

Year	Bonneville	TR6/TR7
1956	n/a	RC109
1957	n/a	RC109
1958	n/a	RC109
1959	n/a	RC109
1960	RC109	RC109
1961	RC1307/00	RC1307/00
1962	RC1307/00	RC1307/00
1963	RC 1307/01	RC1307/01
1964	RSM3001/02	RSM3001/02
1965	RSM3001/02	RSM3001/02
1966	RSM3003/01	RSM3003/01
1967	RSM3003/01	RSM3003/01
1968	RSM3003/01	RSM3003/01
1969	RSM3003/01	RSM3003/01
1970	RSM3003/0l	RSM3003/0l
1970 (later)	RSM3003/13	RSM3003/13
1971	RSM3003/13	RSM3003/13
1972	RSM3003/13	RSM3003/13

Tachometers — Bonnevilles, TR6, and TR7 (continued)

Year	Bonneville	TR6/TR7
1973	RSM3003/13	RSM3003/13
1974	RSM3003/13	RSM3003/13
1975	RSM3003/13	RSM3003/13
1976	RSM3003/13	RSM3003/13
1977	RSM3006/00	RSM3006/00
1978	RSM3006/00	RSM3006/00
1979	RSM3003/23	RSM3003/23
1979 (later)	9200929900 (Veglia)	9200929900 (Veglia)

Vendor Identification Numbers No Longer Used

1980	60-7223 (Veglia)	60-7223 (Veglia)
1981	60-7223	60-7223
1982	60-7223	60-7223
1983	60-7223	60-7223

TT Specials/Trophy Specials

1963	RC1307/02
1965	RSM3001/02
1965	RSM3001/02
1966	RSM3003/01
1967	RSM3003/01

Fuel Tank and Fender Finishes — Bonneville, TR6, and TR7

This chart is arranged with U.S. models appearing first and U.K. finishes following beneath. Where there is no separate U.K. listing, the finishes were the same in both markets. In all cases the fuel tank's upper or predominant color is the one shown first in the column.

Year	Bonneville Tanks	Bonneville Fenders	TR6/TR7 Tanks	TR6/TR7 Fenders
1956	n/a	n/a	Shell-blue	Blue/black stripe
1957	n/a	n/a	Ivory/Aztec-red	Ivory/red stripe
1958	n/a	n/a	Aztec-red/ivory	Ivory/red stripe
1959	Gray/Tangerine	Gray/org. stripe	Ivory/Aztec-red	Ivory/red stripe
(Later U.K.)	Gray/Azure-blue	Gray/blue stripe	n/a	n/a
1960	Gray/Azure-blue	Gray/blue stripe	Ivory/Aztec-red	Ivory/red stripe
1961	Sky-blue/silver	Silver/blue stripe	Ruby/silver	Silver/ruby stripe
1962	Flame/silver	Silver/flame stripe	Burgundy/silver	Silver/burgundy stripe
1963	Alaskan-white	White/gold stripe	Purple/silver	Silver/purple stripe

Year	Bonneville Tanks	Bonneville Fenders	TR6/TR7 Tanks	TR6/TR7 Fenders
1964	Gold/white	White/gold stripe	Scarlet/silver	Silver/scarlet stripe
1965	Pacific-blue/silver	Silver/blue stripe	Gold/white	White/gold stripe
1966	White/red strips	Stainless	Pacific-blue/white	White/blue stripe
(U.K.)	Grenad-red/white	White/red stripe	n/a	n/a
1967	Aubergine/gold	Stainless	Mist-green/white	Green/no stripe
(Later)	Aubergine/white	Stainless	n/a	n/a
(TR6C)	n/a	n/a	n/a	Stainless steel
1968	Scarlet/silver	Stainless	Riviera-blue/silver	Blue/silver stripe
(TR6C)	n/a	n/a	n/a	Stainless steel
(U.K.)	Scarlet/silver	Silver/scar strip	n/a	n/a
1969	Olympic/silver	Silver/red strip	Trophy-red	Red/white stripe
(TR6C)	n/a	n/a	n/a	Stainless steel
(U.K.)	n/a	n/a	Trophy-red/silver	Silver/red stripe
1970	Astral-red/silver	Red/silver stripe	Spring-gold/black	Gold/black stripe
(TR6C)	n/a	n/a	n/a	Stainless steel
1971	Tiger-gold/black	Gold/black stripe	Pacific-blue/white	Blue/white stripe
(TR6C)	n/a	n/a	n/a	Chrome
1972	Tiger-gold/white	Gold/white stripe	Pacific-blue/white	Blue/white stripe
(TR6C)	n/a	n/a	n/a	Chrome
1973	Vermilion/gold	Chrome	Astral-blue/white	Chrome
(U.K. 650s)	Tiger-gold/white	Gold/white stripe	Pacific-blue/white	Blue/white stripe
(Can. 650s)	Astral-red/silver	Chrome	Spring-gold/black	Chrome
1974	Cherokee/white	Chrome	Sea Jade/white	Chrome
(T120)	Purple/white	Chrome	n/a	n/a
1975	As per 1974	As per 1974	As per 1974	As per 1974
1976	As per 1974	As per 1974	As per 1974	As per 1974
(or in U.K.)	Pacific-blue/white	Chrome	n/a	n/a
1977	As per 1974	As per 1974	As per 1974	As per 1974
(or)	Pacific-blue/white	Chrome	Signal red-white	Chrome
(T140J)	Pale-blue/Royal	Pale-blue/royal	n/a	n/a
1978	Black/crimson	Chrome	Crimson/silver	Chrome
(or)	Blue/silver	Chrome	n/a	n/a
(or)	Brown/gold	Chrome (U.S.)	n/a	n/a
(or in U.K.)	Brown/gold	Brown/gold	Crimson/silver	Crimson/silver
(or in U.K.)	Aquamarine/silver	Aquamarine/silver	Gold/silver	Gold/silver

Year	Bonneville Tanks	Bonneville Fenders	TR6/TR7 Tanks	TR6/TR7 Fenders
1979	Black/silver	Chrome	n/a	n/a
(or)	Blue/silver	Chrome	n/a	n/a
(or)	Red/black	Chrome	n/a	n/a
(T140D)	Black/gold lines	Chrome	n/a	n/a
(or in U.K.)	Black/red	Chrome	Blue/silver	Chrome
(or in U.K.)	Beige/gold	Chrome	Red/silver	Chrome
1980	Black/red	Chrome	n/a	n/a
(or)	Steel-gray/black	Chrome	n/a	n/a
(T140D)	Black/gold lines	Chrome	n/a	n/a
(or in U.K.)	As per U.S.	As per U.S.	Astral-blue/black	Chrome
(or in U.K.)	Olympic/black	Chrome	n/a	n/a
(or in U.K.)	Steel Gray/Red	Chrome	n/a	n/a
(or in U.K.)	Black/white lines	Chrome	n/a	n/a
1981	Smoke-blue/silver	Chrome	n/a	n/a
(or)	Smoke-flame/white	Chrome	n/a	n/a
(or in U.K.)	As per U.S.	As per U.S.	Black/gold lines	Chrome
(or in U.K.)	Black/red	Chrome	Smoked-flame	Chrome
(or in U.K.)	Steel-gray/black	Chrome	Smoked-blue	Chrome
(or in U.K.)	Silver-blue/black	Chrome	Yellow (TR7T)	Yellow (TR7T)
(or in U.K.)	Black/gold lines	Chrome	n/a	n/a
1982	Sm-Flame/ivory	Stainless steel	n/a	n/a
(or)	Smoke-blue/silver	Stainless steel	n/a	n/a
(T140EX)	Smoked-red	Smoked-red	n/a	n/a
(Royal U.S.)	Black/gold lines	Stainless steel	n/a	n/a
(or in U.K.)	As per U.S.	As per U.S.	n/a	n/a
(or in U.K.)	Black/gold lines	Stainless steel	Yellow (TR7T)	Yellow (TR7T)
(or in U.K.)	Black/red	Stainless steel	n/a	n/a
(or in U.K.)	Pale-blue/black	Stainless steel	n/a	n/a
(Royal U.K.)	Chrome/blue	Stainless steel	n/a	n/a
1983	Black/red	Stainless steel	Yellow (TR7T)	Yellow (TR7T)
(or)	Black/gold lines	Stainless steel	n/a	n/a
(T140EX)	Smoked-red	Smoked-red	n/a	n/a
(T140EX)	Smoked-blue	Smoked-blue	n/a	n/a
(TSS)	Black/red	Stainless steel	n/a	n/a
(or TSS)	Black/gold lines	Stainless steel	n/a	n/a
(TSX)	Gypsy-red	Gypsy-red	n/a	n/a
(TSX)	Midnight-black	Midnight-black	n/a	n/a

Decal Identification Guide

Users of this list of transfers should be reminded that it was created to cover only the Bonneville, TR6, and TR7 models. Some decals used on Triumph singles, 500 twins, and Tridents will not be shown

Part No.	Description	Location
A3	Minimum oil level	Oil tank (to 1970)
A40	Drain and refill	Oil tank (to 1970)
A44	Recommended lubricants	Oil tank (to 1970)
A51	Valve clearances	Front engine plate
A52	Positive earth	Battery area
A53	Valve clearances	Front engine plate, seat pan
A56	World Speed Record Holder	Tank top, LH front fork cover
A56A	Transfer A56 in black	Tank top (1963–66)
A57	Bonneville 120 (1959–67)	LH side panel, (Nacelle top 1959)
A57A	Transfer A57 in black	Side panel (1960-63)
A61	Made in England (Boxed)	Tank top (Nacelle top 1959)
A61A	Transfer A61 in black	Tank Top (1963–66)
AD7 (pair)	Trophy Bird (U.S.)	Front number plate
AD17 (pair)	Leaping Tiger — TR7 (U.S.)	Front number plate
D68	Triumph trademark (gold)	Rear number plate (1956–65)
D676	Tiger Competition	Tank top, side panel (1968)
D678	Trophy Sports	Tank top, side panel (1968)
D679	Trophy Special	Tank top, side panel (1968)
D680	Bonneville script	Tank top, side panel (1968)
D681	Bonneville TT Special	Side panel (not before 1968)
D1816	Combined A40, A44, A61	Oil tank (to 1970)
D1918	Tiger 650	Tank top, side panel (1968)
D1920	Trophy 650	Tank top, side panel (1968)
D2025	Tiger 650 (small)	Tank top (1969–71)
D2026	Bonneville (small)	Tank top (1969–71)
D2027	Trophy 650 (small)	Tank top (1969–71)
D2102	Tiger 650 (large)	Side panels (1969–71)
D2103	Bonneville (large)	Side panels (1969–71)
D2104	Trophy 650 (large)	Side panels (1969–71)
D2138	Point gap instructions	Inside points cover (1969–78)
D2452	Safety Standards	Frame steering head
D3361	Made in England (script)	RH front down tube (1971–83)
D3722	Bonneville (T120R)	Side panels (1972–73)
D3723	Tiger 650 (TR6R)	Side panels (1972–73)

Decal Identification Guide (continued)

Part No.	Description	Location
D3724	Trophy 650 (TR6C)	Side panels (1972–73)
D3748	Five-speed (gold/black)	Taillight, rear fender (1972–78)
D3750	Bonneville (T120RV)	Side panels (1972–73)
D3752	Tiger 650 (TR6RV)	Side panels (1972–73)
D3953	Trophy 650 (TR6CV)	Side panels (1972–73)
60-4145	Thunderbolt 650 (T65)	Side panels (1973)
60-4148	Bonneville 750 (T140V)	Side panels (1973–74)
60-4156	Trademark Sticker	Caliper cover (1973–83)
60-4169	Tiger 750 (TR7RV)	Side panels (1973–74)
60-4385	Bonneville 750 (T140V)	Side panels (1974–78)
60-4384	Tiger 750 (TR7RV)	Side panels (1974–78)
60-4672	Labeled face	Warning light console (1979–1983)
60-7003	Ignition switch label	LH front fork cover (1976–79)
60-7004	Warning lamp label	Headlight bucket (1976–79)
60-7005	Lighting switch label	Headlight bucket (1976–79)
60-7071	Data label	Seat pan (1980–83)
60-7054	Bonneville 750 (TR7RV)	Side panels (1978)
60-7055	Tiger 750 (TR7RV)	Side panels (1978)
60-7159	Negative earth	Seat pan (1979–83)
60-7168	Radio suppression	Frame (1980–83)
60-7206	15 pound weight restriction	Grab rail (1979–81)
60-7226	Data Label (T140D)	Seat pan (1979–80)
60-7235	Tire specifications	Under seats (T140D 1979–80)
60-7364	Limited Edition (Royal, EX)	Side panels (1980–83)
60-7386	Electro (ES models)	Side panels (1979–83)
60-7442/46	Five-piece tank emblem	TR7T fuel tanks (1980–83)

Magazine Road Tests

In addition to a machine's overall specifications and performance, magazine road tests offer the restorer a wealth of useful information such as fuel tank graphics, decal placement, cable routing, and more. Unlike factory sales literature, these articles usually include period photographs of the model that have not been retouched by Triumph's advertising department. Some issues have the added bonus of a color cover shot of the model and make a nice presentation when showing the bike.

This record of Bonneville and TR6/TR7 tests cannot be considered complete and includes only what was readily at hand. Intentionally not listed, however, are retrospective road tests found in enthusiast publications which almost always feature a restored machine and as such cannot be used for reference.

Although many Triumph motorcycles were tested during the years 1957–1960, not much ink was given to the 650 sport models on either side of the Atlantic. To help the restorer somewhat with machines from this period, some magazines carrying model range descriptions were included.

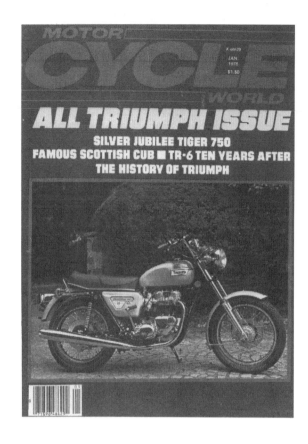

Year	Subject	Magazine Issue
1956	TR6, U.S.	*Cycle*, July 1956
1956	Range decription	*Motor Cycling*, October 27, 1955
1956	Range description	*Cycle*, December 1955
1957	Range description	*Motor Cycling*, October 25, 1956
1957	Range description	*Motorcyclist*, December 1956
1957	Range description	*Cycle*, December 1956
1958	Range description	*Motor Cycling*, October 24, 1957
1958	Range description	*Cycle*, January 1958
1958	Range description	*Motorcyclist*, January 1958
1959	Range description	*Motor Cycling*, October 23, 1958
1959	TR6, U.K.	*Motor Cycling*, January 29, 1959
1959	TR6B, U.S.	*Hot Rod*, April 1959
1959	Range description	*Cycle*, December 1958
1960	Range description	*Motor Cycle*, October 15, 1959
1960	Range description	*Motorcyclist*, January 1960

Magazine Road Tests (continued)

Year	Subject	Magazine Issue
1960	Range description	*Cycle*, January 1960
1960	TR7A, U.S.	*Cycle*, September 1960 (cover shot)
1961	Range description	*Motor Cycle*, October 6, 1960
1961	T120, U.K.	*Motor Cycle*, December 1, 1960
1961	T120, U.K.	*Motor Cycling*, June 1, 1961
1961	TR6, U.K.	*Motor Cycle*, June 15, 1961
1961	T120, U.K.	*Motor Cycling*, August 24, 1961
1962	T120R, U.S.	*Cycle World*, January 1962
1963	T120R, U.S.	*Hot Rod*, June 1963
1963	T120, U.K.	*Motor Cycle*, November 1, 1962
1963	T120C TT Special	*Cycle World*, May 1963
1964	T120, U.K.	*Motor Cycle*, May 21, 1964
1964	T120, U.K.	*Motorcycle Mechanics* (GB), May 1964
1965	T120R, U.S.	*Motorcyclist*, April 1965
1965	T120, U.K.	*Motor Cycle*, May 27, 1965
1965	TR6SR, U.S.	*Cycle World*, May 1965
1965	TR6SC, Special	*Cycle World*, October 1965
1965	TR6SR, U.K.	*Motor Cycle*, December 9, 1965 (with sidecar)
1965	Range description	*Cycle*, February 1965 (cover shot of TR6SR, U.S.)
1966	T120R, U.S.	*Cycle World*, January 1966
1966	T120R, U.S.	*Motorcyclist*, February 1966 (cover shot)
1966	TR6, U.K.	*Motorcycle Mechanics*, August 1966
1966	T120R, U.S.	*Cycle*, September 1966
1966	T120R, U.S.	*Modern Cycle*, December 1966
1967	T120R, U.S.	*Cycle Guide*, August, 1967
1967	T120R, U.S.	*Motorcycle World*, September 1967
1967	T120, U.K.	*Motor Cycle*, February 2, 1967
1967	T120, U.K.	*Motorcycle Mechanics* (GB), December 1966
1967	TR6, U.K.	*Motor Cycle*, April 6, 1967
1967	TR6P, U.S.	*Cycle World*, November 1967 (cover shot of T120R)
1968	T120, U.K.	*Motor Cycle*, February 7, 1968
1968	T120R, U.S.	*Triumph Sport Cycle*, summer issue
1968	T120, U.K.	*Motorcycle Mechanics* (GB), May 1968
1968	TR6R, U.S.	*Cycle*, February 1968 (cover shot)
1968	TR6R, U.S.	*Modern Cycle*, February 1968
1968	TR6R, U.S.	*Triumph Sport Cycle*, summer issue
1968	TR6C, U.S.	*Triumph Sport Cycle*, summer issue
1968	TR6C, U.S.	*Cyclesport* (*Supercycle*), September, 1968

Magazine Road Tests (continued)

Year	Subject	Magazine Issue
1969	T120, U.K.	*Motorcycle Mechanics*, January 1969
1969	T120R, U.S.	*Cycle*, March 1969
1969	T120R, U.S.	*Cyclesport*, December 1969
1969	T120R, U.S.	*Modern Cycle*, March, 1969 (color image)
1969	TR6C, U.S.	*Motorcyclist*, June 1969
1969	TR6R, U.S.	*Cycle World*, March 1969
1969	TR6R, U.S.	*Motorcycle World*, October 1969
1970	T120R, U.S.	*Cycle Guide*, February 1970 (cover shot)
1970	TR6R, U.S.	*Cycle*, August 1970
1970	T120R, U.S.	*Motorcycle Sport Quarterly*, Fall 1970
1971	T120R, U.S	*Cycle World*, May 1971 (cover shot)
1971	TR6R, U.S.	*Motorcyclist*, May 1971
1971	T120R, U.K.	*Motorcycle Sport*, June 1971
1971	TR6R, U.S.	*Supercycle*, October 1971
1971	T120R, U.S.	*Modern Cycle*, November 1971
1972	T120RV, U.S.	*Cycle World*, June 1972 (cover shot)
1972	T120R, U.S.	*Cycle Guide*, January 1972
1972	T120R, U.S.	*Cycle*, May 1972
1972	T120R, U.S.	*Big Bike*, May 1972
1972	T120R, U.S.	*Cycle Illustrated*, June 1972
1972	T120R, U.S.	*Popular Cycling*, March 1972
1972	TR6C, U.S.	*Popular Cycling*, June 1972
1972	T120R, U.S.	*Supercycle*, June 1972 (compared to BSA A65, cover)
1972	TR6C, U.S.	*Motorcyclist*, February 1972 (cover shot)
1972	TR6C, U.S.	*Supercycle*, December 1972
1973	T140V, U.K.	*Motorcycle Mechanics*, March 1973 (cover image)
1973	T140V, U.S.	*Cycle World*, May 1973 (cover shot)
1973	TR7RV, U.S.	*Cycle*, April 1973
1973	T140V, U.K.	*Motorcyclist Illustrated*, July 1973
1973	T140V, U.S.	*Motorcyclist*, July 1973
1973	T140V, U.S.	*Modern Cycle*, October 1973
1973	T140V, U.K.	*Motor Cycle World*, February 1974
1973	T65 (BSA), U.K.	*Classic Bike*, July 1986
1975	T140V, U.K.	*Bike*, November 1975 (color image)
1976	T140V, U.S.	*Rider*, June 1976
1976	T140V, U.S.	*Cycle Guide*, September 1976 (cover shot)
1976	T140V, U.S.	*Cycle Illustrated*, March 1976 (cover shot)
1977	TR7RV, U.K.	*Motorcycling Monthly*, January 1977

Magazine Road Tests (continued)

Year	Subject	Magazine Issue
1977	TR7RV, U.K.	*Motorcycle Mechanics*, February 1977
1977	T14OJ, U.S.	*Motorcycle World*, January 1978 (cover shot)
1977	TR7RV, U.S.	*Motorcycle World*, January 1978
1978	T140V, U.S.	*Cycle World*, April 1978
1978	T140E, U.S.	*Motorcyclist*, August 1978 (compared to Harley-Davidson XL)
1978	T140E, U.S.	*Cycle*, November 1978
1978	T140E, U.S.	*Cycle Guide*, December 1978
1978	T140E, U.K.	*Rider*, February 1979
1979	T140, U.K.	*Bike*, January 1979
1979	T140D, U.S.	*Cycle Guide*, July 1979
1979	T140D, U.S.	*Motorcyclist*, August 1979
1979	T140D, U.K.	*Bike*, September 1979
1980	T140, U.K.	*Superbike*, January 1980
1980	T140EX, U.K.	*The Biker*, August 1980
1981	T140ES, U.K.	*Bike*, May 1981
1981	T140ES, U.S.	*Motorcyclist*, July 1981
1981	T140ES, U.K.	*Classic Bike*, April/May 1981
1981	T140ES, U.S.	*Cycle World*, November 1981
1981	T140EX, U.S.	*Rider*, February 1981
1981	TR7T, U.K.	*Super Bike* (GB), October 1981
1981	TR7T, U.K.	*Bike*, December 1981
1982	T140ES, U.K.	*Motor Cycling*, September 1981 (color image)
1982	TR7T, U.K.	*Motor Cycling*, September 1981 (color image)
1982	T140EX, U.S.	*Rider*, January 1982 (compared to others)
1982	T140W, U.K.	*Classic Bike*, July 1982
1982	TR65, U.K.	*Classic Bike*, November 1981
1982	TR7T, U.K.	*Bike*, December 1981 (color image)
1982	T140W, U.K.	*Motorcycle Mechanics*, March/April 1982
1982	T140W, U.K.	*Bike*, August 1982
1983	T140W, U.S.	*Rider*, February 1983 (cover shot)
1983	T140/TSX, U.S.	*Hot Bike*, September 1983
1986	Harris T140, U.S.	*Classic Bike*, March 1986
1986	Harris T140, U.K.	*Classic Bike*, May 1986

Triumph Resource Directory

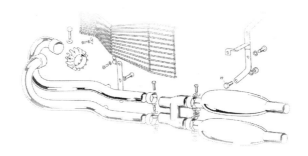

Parts Sources, United States

Baxter Cycle
311 4th Street
Marne, IA 51552
(712) 781-2351
www.baxtercycle.com

British Cycle Supply
146 Porter Street
Hackensack, NJ 07601
(902) 542-7478
www.britcycle.com

British Only Motorcycles
And Parts, Inc
32451 Park Lane
Garden City, Michigan 48135
1(800) BRT-ONLY
www.britishonly.com

Brittwins
Al Hartman
New, used & NOS parts
(610) 683-9313
email: brittwins@entermail.net

Collins Cycle
129 1st Avenue
Sutersville, PA 15083
(724) 872-8475
www.collinscycle.com

Countryside Cycle Shop
2326 Amelia Circle
Tallahassee, FL 32304
(850) 575-6889
www.countrysidecycle.com

D & D Cycles
2400 Fernwood Avenue
Pensacola, FL 32505
(850) 456-0354
www.danddcycles.com

Deer Park Cycle
105 Competitive Goals Drive
Eldersburg, MD 21784
(410) 795-7800
www.deerparkcycle.com

Donelson Cycles
9851 Saint Charles
Rock Road
St Ann, MO 63074
(314) 427-1204
www.donelsoncycles.com

Georgia Cycle Depot
666 Pucket Drive
Mableton, Georgia 30126
(770) 948-4688
www.georgiacycledepot.com

Hermy's Tire & Cycle Inc
Route 61, Box 65
Port Clinton, PA 19549
(610) 562-7303
www.hermys.com

Job Cycle
86 Boston Turnpike
Willington, CT 06279
(860) 848-0607
www.jobcycle.com

Klempf's British Parts
61589 210 Avenue
Dodge Center, MN. 5592
(507) 374-2222
klempfsbritishparts.com

Map Cycle
7165 30th Avenue N
St Petersburg, FL 33710
1(800) 875-BRIT
www.mapcycle.com

Raber's Parts Mart Inc
1984 Stone Avenue
San Jose, CA 95125
(408) 998-4495
www.rabers.com

RMB Motorcycle
Restoration
118 Avondale Avenue
Stratford, ON N5A 6M8
CANADA
1(519) 271-9575
www2.cyg.net/~trirmb

Tiger Spares USA
Pre-unit Triumph Parts
(651) 338-5943
www.triumphpartsusa.com

Walridge Motors LTD
33988 Denfield Road RR. 2
Lucan, ON N0M 2J0
CANADA
(519) 227-4923
www.walridge.com

Wolf Cycles
5413 East Drive
Arbutus MD 21227
(410) 247-7420
www.wolfcycles.tripod.com

Parts Sources, United Kingdom

Ace Classics London
101-103 St Mildreds Rd
London SE12 0RL
020 8698-4273
www.aceclassics.co.uk

Armours LTD
(Exhaust Systems)
784 Wimborne Road
Bournemouth Dorset
BH0 2MS
01202-519409
www.armoursltd.co.uk

Burton's Bike Bits
PO Box 7691
Ashby de la Zouch
LE65 2YZ
44 (0)1530-564362
www.burtonbikebits.net

Carl Rosner Triumph
Station Approach, Off
Sanderstead Road
Sanderstead, South
Croydon, Surrey CR2 0PL
020 86570121
www.carlrosner.co.uk

L. P. Williams
Unit 3 South Barn,
Low West End
Claughton, LANCASTER
LA2 9JX
44 1524-770956
www.triumph-spares.co.uk

TMS
92-94 Carlton Road,
Nottingham NG3 2AS
Tel: +44 (0)115 9503447
www.tms-motorcycles.co.uk

Tony Hayward
28 Kelsterton Road
Connahs' Quay, Deeside,
Flintshire CH5 4BJ
01244-830776
No current website

Tri-Cor England LTD
The Old Hop Kiln,
Whitwick Manor Estate,
Lower Eggleton, Ledbury,
Hereford HR8 2UE
01432 820 752
www.tri-corengland.com

Tri-Supply
Meriden House
Gittisham, Honiton, Devon
EX14 3AW
44 01404-47001
www.trisupply.co.uk

Reg Allen
39 Grosvenor Road
Hanwell, London W7 1HP
020 8579-1248
www.reg-allen-london.co.uk

R. K. Leighton (seats)
Unit 2, Partridge Court,
Price Street
Birmingham B4 6JZ
44 0121-359 0514
www.rk-leighton.co.uk

SRM Engineering
Unit 22, Glanyrafon
Enterprise Park
Aberystwyth, Ceredigion
SY23 3JQ
44 01970-627771
www.srmclassicbikes.com

Supreme Motorcycles
1 High Street
Earl Shilton, Leicestershire
LE9 7DH
44 01455-841133
www.supreme
motorcycles.co.uk

Wilemans Motors
99 Siddals Road
Derby DERBYSHIRE
DE1 2PZ
01332 342813
Email: sales@wilemans.
wanadoo.co.uk

Paint Sources, U.S. & U.K.

The Finishing Touch
26 East Hanningfield Road
Rettendon, Chelmsford,
Essex CM3 8EQ UK
01245-400918
No current website

Don Hutchinson
116 Foundry Street
Wakefield, MA 01880 USA
(781) 245 - 9663
www.triumphman.com

Lewis Templeton
34 Potton Close
Barn End, Coventry CV3
3EA UK
(Coventry) 024-76305884
lewistempleton@yahoo.co.uk

Mike's Restorations
1455 Blue Mountain Drive
Danielsville, PA 18038 USA
(610) 760-2187
email: mkwambold@aol.com

M. S. Motorcycles
Mr John Chrichlow
No mailing address found
(UK)
07773-296826
www.msmotorcyclesuk.com

Precision Motorcycle
Painting
51751 Emmons Rd.
South Bend, IN 46637 USA
(574) 298-2199
www.precisionmotorcycle
painting.com

RS Motorbike Paint LTD
Unit 5, Alpha Business Park
Travellers Close, Welham
Green, Herts AL9 7NT UK
01707-273219
www.rsbikepaint.co.uk

Decal Sources, U.S. & U.K.

British Cycle Supply
146 Porter Street
Hackensack, NJ 07601
(902) 542-7478
www.britcycle.com

British Only Motorcycles
And Parts, Inc
32451 Park Lane
Garden City, Michigan
48135 USA
1(800) BRT-ONLY
www.britishonly.com

Classic Transfers UK
PO Box 17
Wotton-Under-Edge, Glos
GL12 8YX UK
44 01454-260596
www.classictransfers.co.uk

The Vintage Motor Cycle
Club Limited
Allen House, Wetmore Road
Burton Upon Trent,
Staffordshire DE14 1TR UK
44 01283-495107
www.vmccshop.com

Literature Sources, U.S. & Canada

Amazon
www.Amazon.com

British Cycle Supply
146 Porter Street
Hackensack, NJ 07601
(902) 542-7478
www.britcycle.com

British Only Motorcycles
And Parts, Inc
32451 Park Lane
Garden City, Michigan
48135 USA
1(800) BRT-ONLY
www.britishonly.com

Ebay
www.Ebay.com

Don Hutchinson
116 Foundry Street
Wakefield, MA 01880 USA
(781) 245 - 9663
www.triumphman.com

GT Motors
816 E Howe Ave
Lansing, MI 48906-3343
(517) 485-6815
No website found

Walter Miller
Automobile Literature
6710 Brooklawn Parkway
Syracuse, New York 13211
(315) 432-8282
www.autolit.com

Motorbooks (Quayside
Publishing Group)
400 First Avenue North,
Suite 300
Minneapolis, MN 5540
(800) 826-6600
www.motorbooks.com

Motorsport Publications
7164 County Road N,
Suite 441
Bancroft, WI 54921
(715) 572-4595
www.classicbikebooks.com

Walridge Motors LTD
33988 Denfield Road RR. 2
Lucan, ON N0M 2J0
CANADA
(519) 227-4923
www.walridge.com

Literature Sources, United Kingdom

Andover Norton
International LTD
3 Old Farm Buildings,
Standen Manor Estate
Hungerford, Berks RG17
0RB UK
44 01488-686816
www.andover-norton.co.uk

Bruce Main-Smith LTD.
5 Lincoln Drive
Wigston, Leicestershire
LE18 4XU
44 01162-777669
www.brucemainsmith.com

Merlin Books
P.O. Box 153
Horsham, West Sussex
RH12 2JG
01403-257626
www.merlinbooks.com

Pooks Motor Books
Unit 4, Victoria Mills,
Fowke Street
Rothley, Leicestershire, LE7
7PJ UK
0116 237-6222
www.pooksmotorbooks.co.uk

Clubs, U.S & U.K.

Antique M/C Club of
America (US)
P.O. Box 1715
Maple Grove, MN 55311
www.antiquemotorcycle.org

Triumph International
Owners (US)
P.O. Box 158
Plympton, MA 02367
www.tioc.org

Triumph Owners M/C Club
(UK)
6 Bramley Walk
Horley RH6 9GB
www.tomcc.org

Vintage Motor Cycle Club
(UK)
Allen House, Wetmore Road
Burton Upon Trent,
Staffordshire DE14 1TR,
UK
www.vmcc.net

U.S. Rallies/ Fleamarkets

Battle of the Brits
Detroit, Michigan
www.metrotriumphriders.com
Second Sunday in September

British in the Blue Ridge
Hiawassee, Georgia
www.gabma.us
Third (full) weekend
in August

British & European
Motorcycle Day
Germantown, Maryland
www.classicmotorcycle
day.org
Third Sunday in May (usually)

British Motorcycle Meet
(oldest in US)
Auburn, Massachusetts
britishmotorcyclemeet.com
First Sunday in June

Barber Vintage Festival
Birmingham, Alabama
www.barbervintage
festival.org
Second or third weekend
in October

El Camino Classic
Motorcycle Show
Torrance, California
www.classiccycleevents.com
Third Saturday in September

Hanford Vintage
Motorcycle Show
Hanford, California
www.classiccycleevents.com
Third Saturday in May

Triumph Come Home Rally
Jefferson, Pennsylvania
www.triumphcome
home.com
Second or third (full)
weekend in June

AMA Vintage
Motorcycle Days
Lexington, Ohio
(Mid-Ohio race course)
www.amavintage
motorcycledays.com
Second (full) weekend in
July (usually)

Virginia British Motorcycle
Club Rallye
Manassass, Virgina
www.virginiabritish
motorcycleclub.org
First Sunday in October

U.K Rallies/Jumbles
Beaulieu Autojumble
Beaulieu, Hampshire
www.beaulieu.co.uk
Second full weekend in
September

Classic Motorcycle
Mechanics Show
Stafford Show Grds. Stafford
www.classicbikeshows.com
Third weekend in october

Festival of 1000 Bikes
Mallory Park Racing Circuit
www.vmcc.net
Second weekend in July

International Classic
MotorCycle show
Stafford Show Grds. Stafford
www.classicbikeshows.com
Third or fourth weekend
in April

Ace Cafe Reunion
London, England
Second weekend in
September
www.ace-cafe-london.com

Index

AMA (American Motorcyclist Association)
  race rules, 139, 142
Bettmann, Siegfried, 10, 11, 13
Britech, 160, 162,212, 227, 230
BSA, 84, 86, 90, 93, 96, 98, 132, 167
Guild, Cliff, 18
Harry Ricardo Company, 12
Hathaway, Charles, 11
L F. Harris, Ltd., 240
Page, Val, 7, 10
Routt, Sonny, 72
Sangster, Jack, 13
Shulte, Mauritz, 10
TriCor, 142
Triumph Company, Ltd., 13
Triumph Engineering Company, Ltd., 13
Turner, Edward, 13-18
World War II, 16, 17

1956-1959 TR6 Trophy, 21-37
  Brakes, 21,30, 35, 37
  Carburetors, 24, 28, 35
  Colors, 23, 24, 25, 26, 28, 29, 35, 37
  Drive chain, 22, 30
  Engines, 21, 24, 28, 34, 35, 36
  Exhaust systems, 24, 25, 26, 37

Fenders, 23, 29, 37
Frames, 21, 23, 24, 29, 36, 31, 35, 36, 37
Fuel tanks, 23, 26, 28, 29, 31, 37
Gearboxes, 25, 32, 33
Generators/dynamos, 21, 31, 32, 34
Handlebar control, 22, 35, 36
Handlebars, 22, 30
Headlamps, 21, 31
Instruments, 21, 22, 25, 26, 28
Magnetos, 24
Model designations, 25, 26, 32
Oil tanks, 24, 29, 31,33, 37
Rims, 21, 22
Seats, 23, 25,36, 37
Stripes, 23, 24, 28, 29
Suspension, 21, 27, 30
Tires, 21, 26, 35
Transfers and decals, 29, 31, 32, 33, 36
Wheels, 21, 22, 26

1959 Bonneville, 38-51
  Brakes, 45
  Carburetors, 38, 39, 43, 44, 45, 46, 48, 51
  Colors, 40, 44, 47, 48, 49, 50, 51
  Drivetrains, 38-41
  Electrical components, 40, 41, 42, 50

Engines, 38, 39, 40, 41
Exhaust systems, 40, 42
Fenders, 47, 48
Frames, 41, 48
Fuel tanks, 41, 44, 45, 47, 49
Gearboxes, 40
Generators/dynamos, 41
Handlebar controls, 42, 50
Handlebars, 41
Headlamps, 42
Instruments, 42, 50
Patent plates, 40
Rims, 43
Seats, 44, 45, 46
Suspension, 44
Tires, 44
Transfers and decals, 48, 50, 51
Wheels, 42, 43, 44

1960-1962 Duplex Twins, 52-69
Alternators, 59, 64, 69
Carburetors, 54, 55, 59, 67
Colors, 57, 58, 65, 66, 69
Drivetrains, 58, 59, 64
Electrical components, 57, 59, 64, 65, 69
Engines, 54, 58, 59, 63, 64, 67
Exhaust systems, 62, 67, 69
Fenders, 57, 58, 65, 69
Frames, 52, 54, 55, 62
Fuel tanks, 52, 55, 57, 62, 66, 69
Gearboxes, 64
Handlebar control, 57
Handlebars, 55, 57, 66
Headlamps, 57
Instruments, 57, 63, 64, 66
Model designations, 53, 57, 62, 66, 69
Oil tanks, 58, 65, 69
Seats, 58, 59, 67, 69
Suspension, 54, 63, 65
Tires, 56, 57
Transfers and decals, 58, 60
Wheel, 56, 57, 61

1963-1965 Unit-construction Twins, 70-96
Carburetors, 73, 74, 88
Colors, 78, 87, 88, 96
Decals and transfers, 88, 96

Electrical systems, 72, 79, 80, 94
Engines, 70, 71, 72, 73, 74 76, 88, 90
Exhaust systems, 74, 76, 88, 91
Fenders, 78, 83, 85, 87, 96
Frames, 74, 75, 77, 85, 94
Fuel tanks, 72, 77, 78, 81, 82, 96
Gearboxes, 71, 89, 90
Handlebar controls, 76
Handlebars, 75
Headlamps, 80
Instruments, 76, 85, 96
Model designations, 74, 81
Oil tanks, 74, 78, 79, 85
Rims, 77
Seats, 79, 85, 87, 94
Suspension, 75, 82, 83, 91
Tires, 77, 85, 94
Wheels, 76, 77, 85, 91

1966-1970 Unit-construction Twins, 97-142
Brakes, 117, 118, 129, 130
Carburetors, 97, 99, 105, 106, 116, 124, 135
Colors, 104, 105, 110, 111, 112, 122, 123, 130, 131, 138
Decals and transfers, 105, 112, 123, 132
Electrical systems, 101, 102, 110, 116, 121, 122, 130, 138
Engines, 97, 98, 105, 106, 114, 116, 124, 125, 132, 134
Exhaust systems, 99, 100, 106, 116, 127, 136
Fenders, 103, 105, 112, 130, 132, 138, 139
Frames, 100, 108, 116, 117, 118, 120, 121, 127, 135
Fuel tanks, 100, 103, 104, 110, 111, 112, 122, 123, 130, 131, 138, 139
Gearboxes, 98, 106, 116, 126, 127, 134
Handlebar controls, 102, 108, 120, 121
Handlebars, 100
Headlamps, 101, 102, 121
Instruments, 98, 99, 103, 110, 137
Model designations, 105, 113, 123, 139
Oil tanks, 103, 121
Seats, 105, 108, 112, 113, 123
Suspension, 117, 119, 130, 137
Tires, 100, 110, 121, 127, 137, 138

T120RT, 139-142
Wheels, 110, 121, 130
1963-1967 TT Specials, 143-166
  Carburetors, 144, 145, 146, 155, 164
  Colors, 144, 146, 154, 161, 166
  Decals and transfers, 162, 166
  Engines, 143, 145, 147, 155, 164
  Exhaust systems, 144, 147, 148, 154, 155
  Fenders, 145, 146, 154, 161, 166
  Frames, 144, 164
  Fuel tanks, 144, 146, 154, 160, 161, 166
  Gearboxes, 146, 155
  Handlebars, 146, 160, 166
  Instruments, 145, 146, 154, 155, 160, 166
  Model designations, 145, 154, 162, 166
  Seats, 144, 146, 161, 162, 166
  Suspension, 146, 154
  Tires, 144, 146, 164
  Wheels, 144, 146, 164

1971-1975 Umberslade Twins, 167-195
  Brakes, 170, 172, 188, 189, 193
  Carburetors, 180, 181, 185
  Colors, 179, 182, 183, 194, 195
  Decals and transfers, 179, 183, 192
  Electrical systems, 172, 173, 192
  Engines, 179, 180, 185
  Exhaust systems, 172, 180, 187
  Fenders, 169, 170, 194, 195
  Frames, 167, 168, 177, 181, 182, 187
  Fuel tanks, 178, 179, 182, 183, 193, 194, 195
  Gearboxes, 180, 185, 195
  Handlebar controls, 174, 176, 181, 182, 191
  Handlebars, 191
  Headlamps, 173, 192
  Instruments, 169, 182
  Model designations, 185
  Seats, 177, 178, 191, 192
  Suspension, 168, 181, 182, 184, 189
  Tires, 172, 193
  Wheels, 172, 193

1976-1979 Meriden Co-op 750 Twins, 196-217
  Bonneville Silver Jubilee, 200-207
  Bonneville Special, 214-217
  Brakes, 196, 215
  Carburetors, 196, 206, 207, 210
  Colors, 200, 209, 210, 213, 214
  Decals and transfers, 197, 208
  Electrical systems, 209
  Electronic ignition, 211
  Engines, 206
  Exhaust systems, 216, 217
  Fenders, 197, 199, 200, 210, 212, 216
  Frames, 196, 199, 207
  Fuel tanks, 198, 200, 209, 213, 214
  Handlebars, 198
  Handlebar controls, 211
  Headlamps, 209
  Instruments, 197, 209, 212
  Model designations, 198, 204, 207, 210, 217
  Seats, 197, 198, 209, 210, 212, 214, 215
  Suspension, 208
  Tires, 197, 204, 208, 212, 216
  Wheels, 208, 212, 215, 216

1980-1983 Final 750 Twins, 218-239
  Bonneville Electro, 218, 219, 222, 226, 232
  Bonneville Executive, 220-222, 229, 231, 232, 233
  Bonneville Royal, 227-231, 233
  Bonneville Special, 218, 221
  Brakes, 220, 224, 234, 236
  Carburetors, 222, 225, 227, 230, 231, 234, 235
  Colors, 221, 222, 224, 227, 230, 232, 233, 238-240
  Decals and transfers, 224, 226, 228, 230
  Engines, 222, 234
  Exhaust systems, 223, 235
  Fenders, 238
  Frames, 220, 231
  Fuel tanks, 221, 222, 233, 225, 230, 231, 233, 234, 238-240
  Handlebars, 221, 222, 229, 232
  Headlamps, 226
  Model designations, 221, 226, 227, 233, 240
  Seats, 221-224, 229, 231, 238
  Suspension, 225, 231, 236
  Tiger Trail TR7T, 225-226
  Tires, 221, 226, 228, 236, 239
  TSS, 234-237
  TSX, 235-239
  Wheels, 221, 224, 226, 230, 235, 236, 239

About David Gaylin

Growing up in Baltimore, Maryland and near the U.S. Triumph motorcycle distributor, David's first bike (a 1970 Bonneville) had to be one of these British-built machines. After The Triumph Corporation closed in 1975, he was able to acquire much of their internal documents and memos along with truckloads of brochures, manuals and service bulletins. This vast archive would become the foundation for two books: *Triumph Motorcycles in America*, coauthored with Lindsay Brooke, and *Triumph Motorcycle Restoration Guide*. His feature articles have appeared in *Vintage Bike* and *Classic Bike* magazines, and he is currently gathering material for an illustrated history of the Wall of Death.

If you enjoyed this book, spread the word.

- Go to the book's page on Amazon.com and write a review.
- Like our Facebook page (facebook.com/octanepress).
- Follow us at twitter.com/octanepress.
- Email info@octanepress.com and suggest books you'd like to read.
- And don't forget to check out octanepress.com for our latest books!

About Octane Press

Octane Press is an independent publishing company, created and owned by long-time editor and author Lee Klancher. Our team of authors, editors, designers, salespeople, and more are independent-minded book professionals with more than 100 years of experience making books, and even more restoring, modifying, and enjoying enthusiast motorcycles, cars and tractors. We believe that vehicle enthusiasts deserve high-quality publications, and ensure that our books are accurate, attractive, and relevant. We exist thanks to hard work and new technology, and our books are available in electronic forms and strongly supported by our Web site.

We encourage your suggestions, ideas, and corrections. Your input helps us improve our publications and make better ones in the future.

Please send any feedback to: info@octanepress.com

octanepress.com